Austrian Yearbook
on
International Arbitration 2025

The Editors

Christian Klausegger, Peter Klein, Florian Kremslehner, Alexander Petsche, Nikolaus Pitkowitz, Irene Welser, Gerold Zeiler

The Authors

Michael Barnert, Antje Baumann, Maria Bejan, Ondrej Cech, Philippa Charles, Daniel Dibon, Marija Dobrić, Gerard Doolin, Samuel Farokhnia-Mimnagh, Brian Gabriel-Oiwoh, Nata Ghibradze, Anne-Karin Grill, Amelie Huber-Starlinger, Ilma Kasumagić, Johanna Kathan-Spath, Katherine Khan, David Kirnbauer, Marios Kourtis, Sofia Kovačević, Niamh Leinwather, Torsten Lörcher, Arnela Maglić, Kamalia Mehtiyeva, Alice Meissner, Maximilian Menz, Ludmila Meszarosova, Isabelle Michou, Nazli Morali, Nina Pichler, Nikolaus Pitkowitz, Jessica Puhr, Peter Rižnik, Violeta Saranciuc, Milica Savić, Friederike Schäfer, Nicol Schneider, Alfred Siwy, Marina Stanisavljević, Caroline Strohmeier, Irene Welser

Wien 2025

MANZ'sche Verlags- und Universitätsbuchhandlung

Verlag C.H. Beck, München

Stämpfli Verlag, Bern

To be cited as:

Author [first and last name], *Title of Work*, in AUSTRIAN YEARBOOK ON INTERNATIONAL ARBITRATION 2025 [first page on which work appears, pincite] (Klausegger, Klein, Kremslehner, Petsche, Pitkowitz, Welser & Zeiler eds., 2025)

ISBN 978-3-214-26064-4 (Manz)
ISBN 978-3-406-83612-1 (Beck)
ISBN 978-3-7272-0231-5 (Stämpfli)

Kohlmarkt 16, 1010 Vienna
Austria
Telephone: +43 1 531 61-0
E-Mail: verlag@manz.at
World Wide Web: www.manz.at

Data Conversion and Type Setting: EXAKTA GmbH, Wien, www.exakta.at
Printed by: FINIDR, s. r. o., Český Těšín

Introduction

It is with great pleasure that we present the 2025 edition of the *Austrian Yearbook on International Arbitration*, now in its 19th edition. Since its first publication in 2007 this Yearbook has served as a trusted resource for arbitration practitioners, scholars, and students and established itself as a respected platform for discussing developments, challenges, and innovations in international arbitration.

Authored by experienced arbitration practitioners, the contributions in this edition cover a range of current and highly relevant topics. From procedural innovations to emerging challenges in arbitral practice, this Yearbook offers valuable perspectives that will assist readers in addressing and resolving issues in their daily work.

The Yearbook is closely linked to the *Vienna Arbitration Days*, which in 2025 will be held for the 19th time. As Austria's leading arbitration conference, the *Vienna Arbitration Days* continue to bring together experts, practitioners, and scholars from around the world to exchange insights and shape the future of arbitration. The Yearbook reflects this dynamic discourse by offering high-quality contributions from leading voices in the field.

The past year has once again demonstrated the crucial role of arbitration in resolving complex international disputes efficiently and fairly. As the global landscape evolves, so too must arbitration, adapting to new technologies, regulatory changes, and shifting geopolitical realities. This Yearbook seeks to capture these transformations, providing a comprehensive overview of key trends and developments.

We extend our sincere gratitude to all authors, contributors, and supporters who have made this edition possible. Your expertise and dedication continue to enrich the discourse on international arbitration.

We hope this Yearbook serves as an insightful and valuable resource for practitioners, academics, and all those engaged in arbitration. We look forward to another year of stimulating discussions – both within these pages and at the *Vienna Arbitration Days 2025*.

Vienna, May 2025

Peter Klein
on behalf of the Editors

Overview

Table of Contents

The Editors and Authors

© Photo Simonis

Michael Barnert is a partner of Barnert Egermann Illigasch Rechtsanwälte GmbH in Vienna and heads its Corporate/M&A and Arbitration practice groups.

Michael Barnert acts as party representative in arbitral proceedings under various rules and in ad hoc arbitrations. He also represents parties before Austrian courts in matters relating to arbitration (including the challenge and enforcement of arbitral awards).

Michael Barnert studied Law at the University of Vienna. In 1995/96 he obtained his Master of Laws degree at the College of Europe in Bruges. He holds a Doctor of Laws degree from the University of Vienna (2000). Michael Barnert was admitted to the Vienna Bar in 2000.

Contact: Barnert Egermann Illigasch Rechtsanwälte GmbH
Rosenbursenstrasse 2
1010 Vienna, Austria
T: +43 1 513 80 08
E: barnert@beira.at
www.beira.at

Antje Baumann is an arbitration practitioner with over 22 years of experience. She advises clients in complex and large economic disputes. Antje is founding partner of BAUMANN Resolving Disputes, a boutique law firm based in Hamburg, Germany. She regularly acts as an arbitrator in international arbitration proceedings and is praised (*e.g.*, by WWL) as "one of the best arbitrators in the country", with one peer adding, "she excels in large-scale disputes" and receives plaudits for her work on high-profile cases.

Antje holds a Master of Laws (LL.M.) degree from the University of California at Berkeley and is admitted to the German and New York Bar. She is honorary professor at the University of Osnabruck where she teaches negotiations and mediations skills as well as international arbitration. She is a frequent speaker and regularly publishes on international arbitration (*e.g.*, Co-editor of the Practitioner's Handbook on International Commercial Arbitration published by Oxford University Press, and author of the commentary on the ICC Rules). Furthermore, she is a member of the ICC Court of Arbitration.

Contact: Prof. Dr. Antje Baumann
Alsterarkaden 12
20354 Hamburg, Germany
T: +49 40 226 5943-10
F: +49 40 226 5943-12
E. antje.baumann@baumann-disputes.de
https://baumann-disputes.de/

Maria Bejan has been a partner at SAXINGER in Vienna since October 2023. She previously worked as an attorney at law in a renowned Viennese business law firm. She is a member of the international dispute resolution team, with extensive experience in representing clients in both national and international arbitration proceedings (in particular VIAC, ICC, DIS, ad hoc) as well as in litigation.

After completing her law studies at the University of Vienna (Mag. iur. 2012), Maria Bejan completed a master's program at Boston University (LL.M. 2015) with a focus on international business law. Maria Bejan then worked as a law clerk at the Federal Supreme Court for the State of Massachusetts in the USA. During this time, Maria Bejan completed training in mediation and conflict resolution at Harvard Law School and passed the New York State Bar Exam (2016). From 2017, Maria Bejan worked as an associate and lawyer in various international business law firms in Vienna.

In 2021, Maria Bejan completed the MIDS program (LL.M. 2021) at the Graduate Institute of International and Development Studies in Geneva and later joined a renowned law firm specializing in dispute resolution in Geneva.

A particular focus of Maria Bejan's practice is arbitration proceedings involving complex corporate issues. She often represents international companies in post-M&A disputes.

Contact: SAXINGER Rechtsanwalts GmbH
Wächtergasse 1
1010 Vienna, Austria
E: m.bejan@saxinger.com
https://at.schindhelm.com/rechtsanwalt-graz-linz-wels-wien-oesterreich

Ondrej Cech is a Senior Associate and attorney at ZEILER and focuses on international dispute resolution, with a strong focus on commercial and investment arbitration. He also has significant experience representing aggrieved parties and creditors in criminal and bankruptcy proceedings. Ondrej's clients include sovereign and corporate parties, particularly in the energy and construction sectors. Ondrej is fully licensed as an attorney in the Czech Republic.

Ondrej is listed as an arbitrator at the Czech Arbitration Court. He also acts as a tribunal secretary in proceedings before the LCIA, PCA and ICC.

Ondrej is also active in the academic field as a teacher of several courses at Charles University. As one of the co-founders of the Young Czech Arbitration Professionals, Ondrej acts as the spokesperson of the initiative for implementation of the UNCITRAL Model Law on International Commercial Arbitration in the Czech Republic.

He is a graduate of Charles University in Prague and Columbia University in New York. For his academic achievements, Ondrej was awarded Josef Hlavka's Prize for the Best Graduate, Randa's Foundation Prize for an Exceptional Master Thesis in Commercial Law and Harlan Fiske Stone Scholarship.

Contact: Zeiler Rechtsanwälte GmbH
The ICON, Wiedner Gürtel 11
1100 Vienna, Austria
E: ondrej.cech@zeiler.eu
https://www.zeiler.eu/

Philippa Charles is a full-time arbitrator at Twenty Essex Chambers in London. She sits as sole arbitrator, party-nominee and presiding arbitrator, and has experience of sitting in cases under the Rules of the ICC, LCIA, SIAC, DIAC, SCC, FIA, AAA-ICDR, BVIIAC, CIMAC and in ad hoc proceedings under the UNCITRAL Rules. She has particular experience in disputes relating to energy, telecoms, crypto-currency and defense procurement, and of cases involving states and state-owned parties. She also sits as a Judicial Panel Member of the British Horseracing Authority and is on the legal panel of Sport Resolutions. She has been a member of the ICC Court, representing Ireland, since 2024. She is a faculty member of the Pepperdine University Caruso School of Law..

Contact: https://www.twentyessex.com/people/philippa-charles/

Daniel Dibon is an attorney at law and senior associate at CERHA HEMPEL, specializing in international commercial and corporate dispute resolution.

He has substantial experience representing clients as counsel and serving as secretary to arbitral tribunals under various institutional rules, including ICC, VIAC and Swiss Rules. His practice focuses on complex disputes across sectors such as construction, post-M&A, shareholder conflicts and trusts.

Daniel holds a law degree from the University of Vienna (Mag. iur., 2016) and regularly publishes on topics related to commercial and corporate law.

Contact: CERHA HEMPEL Rechtsanwälte GmbH
Parkring 2
1010 Vienna, Austria
T: +43 1 514 35 0
E: daniel.dibon@cerhahempel.com
www.cerhahempel.com

Marija Dobrić is an Attorney at Law in the Dispute Resolution Team of BINDER GRÖSSWANG. She focuses on commercial and investment arbitration, enforcement of arbitral awards and civil law disputes with an international background. She regularly acts as counsel in international arbitral proceedings and as tribunal secretary.

Marija Dobrić joined BINDER GRÖSSWANG in 2020 as an associate. Previously, she worked as a researcher and lecturer at the Section for International Law and International Human Rights Law at Bundeswehr University Munich. She holds a degree in law (Mag. iur. 2016) from the University of Vienna. After her judicial clerkship in Austria, she completed a postgraduate degree (LL.M.) at the University of Cambridge.

Marija Dobrić regularly publishes on arbitration-related issues and international law.

Contact: BINDER GRÖSSWANG Rechtsanwälte GmbH
Sterngasse 13,
1010 Vienna, Austria
T: +43 1 534 80
E: m.dobric@bindergroesswang.at
www.bindergroesswang.at

Gerard Doolin is a Vienna based New Zealand trained lawyer and an accredited CEDR Mediator (Software Project Disputes). He is a mediator on the New Zealand International Arbitration Centre (NZIAC) Mediators' Panel, and the Mediators' List of the Vienna International Arbitration Centre (VIAC).

He has worked internationally for over 25 years including for 2 global IT consultancy groups and also represented other global and SME providers, users, investors and early-stage companies in the ANZ, Asia-Pacific, North American, UK and European markets. He has engaged in and supported technology consulting, development, and implementation and outsourced services engagements. He has participated in and experienced the endless evolution of cloud software and services models. He has also undertaken complex renegotiations or remediations in relation to troubled software enterprise system projects in a number of markets.

Since 2016 he has also operated a specialized contractual services offering for the IT sector, Be Amorgos IT Contractual Services. Between 2019 and 2022, in collaboration with the NZIAC, he led an international research and design project with industry stakeholders to consider the causes of software project misalignment and emerging conflict and how conflict is resolved through dispute resolution methods. From this research Gerard and NZIAC designed adoptable contract modules focused on project governance and a sequence of conflict mitigation and dispute resolution processes that promote prompt and expedient resolution.

Gerard is an admitted solicitor of the High Court of New Zealand and Supreme Court of New South Wales, Australia. Gerard also completed a Master of Laws (Honors) in international trade law (with a thesis concerning an UNCITRAL convention) at the University of Auckland, New Zealand.

Contact: Gerard Doolin, Be Amorgos IT Contractual Services
T: +43 677 619 33033
E: Gerard.doolin@beamorgos.com
https://www.beamorgos.com

Samuel Farokhnia-Mimnagh, LL.M. is an Irish solicitor and European lawyer with extensive international experience. Sam specializes in international commercial and investment arbitration conducted in English and German.

Sam routinely acts as counsel in a variety of arbitrations arising predominantly out of contractual disputes in the energy, construction and technology sectors. Whether institutional arbitration pursuant to the Vienna, ICC, UNCITRAL, ICSID or LCIA rules, or ad hoc arbitration, Sam has advised clients through every facet of these procedures. Clients often recognize Sam for his diligence and client-centric approach to conducting arbitration.

In addition to his work as counsel, Sam has also acted as administrative secretary to a number of arbitral tribunals conducting arbitration proceedings in a variety of languages.

Sam holds law degrees from University College Dublin Ireland (LL.B. 2014) and the University of Vienna (LL.M. 2016) with a focus on international and EU law as well as international arbitration.

His working languages are English, Dutch and German.

Contact: CERHA HEMPEL Rechtsanwälte GmbH
Parkring 2
1010 Vienna, Austria
T: +43 1 514 35-135
E: samuel.mimnagh@cerhahempel.com
www.cerhahempel.com

Brian Gabriel-Oiwoh is a senior associate at PARAGON Advocacy, a dispute resolution boutique law firm in Vienna. He specializes in international dispute resolution, including international commercial and investment arbitration and mediation, and the legal structuring and negotiation of international project contracts. Brian has advised and represented clients in numerous complex and high-stakes arbitrations under major arbitration rules (including the Vienna, ICC, LCIA, ICAC, ICSID and UNCITRAL Rules). He has particular experience in disputes arising from M&A transactions and joint ventures, with a focus on the energy, commercial, telecommunications, and major projects sectors. He has also advised on arbitration-related issues in the drafting of articles of association and private foundation deeds.

Brian Gabriel-Oiwoh has published on a wide range of practical topics and areas of law, including controversial issues in arbitration, corporate law, and international law. He has also given workshops on arbitration law at various European universities.

Brian studied law in Austria (University of Graz) and the UK (University of Edinburgh). He is admitted to the Austrian Bar.

Contact: Paragon – Peters Ortner Partners Rechtsanwälte GmbH
Am Hof 13
1010 Vienna, Austria
E: office@paragon-advocacy.com
https://www.paragon-advocacy.com/

Nata Ghibradze is Counsel in the International Arbitration Group at Hogan Lovells International LLP in Munich.

Specialized in international arbitration, Nata acts as both counsel and arbitrator. She has extensive experience in advising clients and representing them in high-stakes arbitrations, both ad hoc and under the auspices of major arbitral institutions. Her practice spans a wide array of industries, including infrastructure (roads, bridges, tunnels, water, and sewage and wastewater systems), energy (oil and gas, offshore and onshore wind, hydroelectric power), aerospace and defence, and transportation (metro, railways). Nata's practice is notably focused on cases involving parties and projects from the Caucasus, Central and Eastern Europe, and Central Asia.

Nata is actively engaged in the international arbitration community, serving as an ICC Commission on Arbitration and ADR member, Community Ambassador to Georgia for VIAC, Arbitration Council member of GIAC and as Secretary of ArbitralWomen. She frequently speaks, lectures, and contributes to leading publications, promoting professional development.

Fluent in English, German, Russian, and Georgian, Nata leverages her multilingual skills to provide strategic, she leverages her multilingual and cross-cultural expertise to provide nuanced and strategic advice, ensuring effective representation for her clients on the global stage. Nata is recommended as "Future Leader" by Lexology Index (Former Who's Who Legal).

Contact: https://www.hoganlovells.com/de/ghibradze-nata

Anne-Karin Grill is an accomplished international arbitration lawyer and well-versed in other forms of alternative dispute resolution (ADR). In addition to her advocacy work before international tribunals, Anne-Karin serves as an arbitrator and acts as CEDR-accredited mediator in multi-jurisdictional commercial disputes. She also advises in litigation proceedings before the Austrian state courts, in particular in proceedings for the domestic enforcement or setting-aside of international arbitral awards, and serves as court-certified legal interpreter/translator (English).

Anne-Karin heads the Austrian Arbitration Association (Arb|Aut) and is a member of the Mediation Advisory Board of the Vienna International Arbitral Centre (VIAC). She is also a member of the Panel of Conciliators of the International Centre for Settlement of Investment Disputes (ICSID) and part of the European Commission's pool of arbitrators for appointment in bilateral disputes under EU trade agreements with third countries.

Contact: https://akg-advisory.at/team/anne-karin-grill/

Amelie Huber-Starlinger is a full-time independent mediator with accreditations in Austria, Singapore and England. Having worked for years as an attorney and arbitrator herself as well as mediator, she brings a wealth of experience in resolving national and international disputes under various institutional rules (*e.g.*, VIAC, ICC, LCIA, ICSID, and more).

She customizes the mediation process to suit the unique needs of the parties, their representatives, and the specific dispute at hand, integrating the most effective methods and techniques. Her expertise is built on both comprehensive training and years of practical experience.

Having lived in Austria, Germany, Sweden, and the USA, Amelie brings valuable intercultural insights to her practice. She further enhances her expertise through specialized training in intercultural communication.

Amelie is also a respected educator and speaker, regularly presenting at international dispute resolution conferences, including those focusing on mediation. She is the author of numerous publications on the subject. Amelie is fluent in both German and English.

Contact: https://tailored.solutions/

Ilma Kasumagić is an independent attorney at law from Sarajevo, Bosnia and Herzegovina and member of Wolf Theiss Regional Arbitration Team with over 12 years of experience. She has advised and represented clients in numerous largescale projects and commer-cial disputes in BiH, and was representing and advising clients in various international (commercial, construction and investment) arbitration matters under major international arbitration rules.

Ilma is a founder and cochair of Association of lawyers specia-lised in arbitration ArbBH. Ilma is also ambassador of Vienna International Arbitration Center for BiH. In cooperation with US Department of Commerce, she coordinated the implementation of the Willem C. Vis International Commercial Arbitration Moot pro-ject in BiH. She is one of the co-authors of the publications "Dis-pute Resolution in Central, Eastern & Southeastern Europe" (2018), "International Arbitration in Central, Eastern & Southeas-tern Europe" (2018) and "Balkan Yearbook of European and International Law" (2019).

Contact: Wolf Theiss Bosnia and Herzegovina, Sarajevo
T +387 33 953 - 458
E ilma.kasumagic@lawoffice-kasumagic.com

Johanna Kathan-Spath, LL.M. is an Associate and a certified Mediator in the Dispute Resolution Team of Pitkowitz & Partners. Johanna primarily focuses on Dispute Resolution with a distinct focus on international arbitration proceedings.

Prior to joining Pitkowitz & Partners, Johanna has worked for VIAC (Vienna International Arbitral Centre) as Legal Counsel, where she gained significant experience in institutional arbitration and case management services. Furthermore, Johanna has worked at reputable law firms in Vienna and gained work experience at UNCITRAL.

Johanna has completed the postgraduate LL.M. degree courses in International Law (with distinction) at the University of Vienna, and studied law at the University of Graz (Mag.iur.) and the University of Antwerp (Belgium).

Johanna is a member of the Young Austrian Arbitration Practitioners (YAAP) and the Austrian Federal Association of Mediators (OEBM).

Contact: Pitkowitz & Partners
Schwarzenbergplatz 3
1010 Vienna, Austria
T: +43 1 41301-0
E: j.kathan-spath@pitkowitz.com
www.pitkowitz.com

Katherine Khan is a principal associate at Freshfields in Vienna and a member of the firm's dispute resolution practice group.

Katherine specializes in international arbitration, with a particular focus on commercial and investment arbitration. She acts as counsel or co-counsel in cases under various arbitration rules, most often in the financial, corporate, commercial, construction or energy sectors.

Before joining Freshfields in 2015, Katherine gained experience working at the United Nations office in Vienna (UNOV) and an insurance defence/litigation firm in Florida. Katherine is admitted to practice and is a member of the bar in Florida (attorney at law). She speaks English, Italian, German and intermediate French.

Contact: Freshfields Rechtsanwälte PartG mbB
Peregringasse 4
1090 Vienna, Austria
T: +43 1 5151 5605
M: +43 6991 8910 605
https://www.freshfields.de/

David Kirnbauer is an Associate at Fieldfisher Austria, specializing in International Arbitration. With several years of experience in dispute resolution teams at well-known international law firms in Vienna, David has developed a robust expertise in advising clients in international commercial arbitration proceedings under the arbitration rules of the ICC and VIAC as well as national litigation proceedings.

These cases have involved complex disputes in sectors such as energy, construction, banking and post-M&A. Additionally, David Kirnbauer has significant experience in advising clients in investor-state arbitration proceedings under the UNCITRAL Arbitration Rules and ICSID Arbitration Rules.

David Kirnbauer holds both a bachelor's and a master's degree in business law from the Vienna University of Economics and Business, as well as a bachelor's degree in business administration from the same institution.

Contact: Fieldfisher Austria
Rotenturmstrasse 5–9
1010 Vienna, Austria
T: +43 1 928 163 40 05
David.Kirnbauer@fieldfisher.com
https://www.fieldfisher.com/en/locations/austria

Christian Klausegger is a partner of Binder Grösswang Rechtsanwälte since 1997 and heads Binder Grösswang's dispute resolution group.

He has more than 15 years experience as counsel in international arbitration proceedings, both in institutional proceedings under the VIAC, ICC and UNCITRAL rules and in ad-hoc-arbitration proceedings. Christian Klausegger regularly represents clients before Austrian courts in matters relating to arbitration, including the challenge and enforcement of arbitral awards. Christian Klausegger is a member of the Austrian exam board for judges and a member of the board of the Austrian Arbitration Association (ArbAut), which he chaired as President in 2016 and 2017. He publishes regularly on international litigation and arbitration.

He holds a doctorate in law (1987) and a degree in economics (1987), both from the University Vienna, and was admitted to the Austrian Bar in 1992.

Contact: Binder Grösswang Rechtsanwälte GmbH
Sterngasse 13
1010 Vienna, Austria
T: +43 (1) 534 80-320
E: klausegger@bindergroesswang.at
www.bindergroesswang.at

Peter Klein is partner of Petsch Frosch Klein Arturo Rechtsanwälte with offices in Vienna and Milan. He has considerable experience in the field of mergers & acquisitions transactions (including share and asset acquisitions), joint ventures, and civil and commercial law in general.

Peter Klein has been involved in many international and domestic arbitrations either as co-arbitrator, sole arbitrator, chairman of arbitral tribunals or party counsel including proceedings under various rules (such as Vienna Rules, ICC, UNCITRAL and Milan Chamber of Commerce arbitration rules). Many of his transactions are with Italian and Austrian companies and clients having business relations with Austria and Italy.

Peter Klein was admitted to the Vienna Bar in 1993 and holds a Doctor of Laws (Dr. iur.) degree from the University of Vienna (1985).

Contact: Petsch Frosch Klein Arturo Rechtsanwälte
Esslinggasse 5
1010 Vienna, Austria
T: +43 (1) 586 21 80

Corso di Porta Romana 46
20122 Milan, Italy
T: +39 2 58 32 82 62
E: peter.klein@pfka.eu
www.pfka.eu

Marios Kourtis is an associate of the dispute resolution boutique WACH UND MECKES in Munich.

Marios practice covers a broad spectrum of complex, and mainly international, commercial disputes resolved through litigation, arbitration and alternative dispute resolution.

His core areas of expertise are corporate and commercial disputes, capital markets disputes, mass proceedings, energy sector disputes, construction disputes and disputes arising from large-scale, cross-border business transactions.

Marios represents clients across a broad range of industry sectors including private equity, banks/financial institutions, investors, trade, machine engineering, energy, health science, and the automotive industry.

Marios is a member of the Athens Bar, Greece (2020) as well as the German bar (2021) and holds an LL.M. from the Ludwig-Maximilians-University, Munich (2019).

Contact: WACH UND MECKES und Partner
Rechtsanwälte PartGmbB
Karlstrasse 12
80333 Munich, Germany
T: +49 89 1222 464 0
E: marios.kourtis@wachundmeckes.com
https://wachundmeckes.com/de/why

Sofia Kovačević is an Energy Lawyer at Energy Community Secretariat, having joined the organization in 2025. Before the current role, she was working as a Senior Associate at Wolf Theiss Arbitration Team in Vienna, as well as in several prestigious law firms in Vienna and Serbia advising both international and local clients in litigation, arbitration and mediation matters. Her areas of expertise focus on international investment arbitration, commercial arbitration, and construction arbitration under the FIDIC rules. She has acted as counsel in several high-profile investment, construction and commercial arbitration proceedings under the ICC Rules, UNCITRAL Arbitration Rules, CEAC Rules.

Sofia obtained her law degree from the University of Belgrade, Faculty of Law where she also earned a degree in Master of International Law (MIL). In addition, she holds a Master of Laws (LL.M.) degree from the University of Cambridge and is currently a candidate for a PhD in Civil Law at the University of Belgrade.

She is admitted to the Serbian bar and is a licensed mediator registered in the Serbian Ministry of Justice. She is listed on VIAC's List of Practitioners in International Arbitration and is a member of the Young Austrian Arbitration Practitioners (YAAP), ICC Young Arbitrators Forum (YAF), Young International Council for Commercial Arbitration (Young ICCA), and ASA Below 40. She founded the Serbian Chapter and co-founded the Austrian Chapter of ENERAP (Energy Related Arbitration Practitioners).

Sofia's working languages are Serbian/Croatian/Bosnian, English, German, Spanish, and she is conversational in French.

Contact: Energy Community Secretariat
Am Hof 4
1010 Vienna, Austria
T: +43 (0)1 535 2222-0
M: +43 (0)664 881 455 86
E: sofia.kovacevic@energy-community.org
www.energy-community.org

Florian Kremslehner joined DORDA in 1988. He heads the Dispute Resolution group and deals with general litigation, arbitration, and white-collar crime. He advises in civil and criminal law matters as well as in transnational and international disputes. Florian has extensive experience as counsel and arbitrator under ICC, UNCITRAL, LCIA, Milano and Vienna Rules. He is fluent in German, English and Italian.

Florian chaired the IBA Litigation Committee and is a member of the International Law Association and the Austrian Arbitration Association.

In addition, he is one of the editors of the Austrian Yearbook on International Arbitration.

Florian studied law at the University of Vienna (Dr. iur. 1985).

Contact: DORDA Rechtsanwälte GmbH
Universitätsring 10
1010 Vienna, Austria
T: +43 (1) 533 47 95-18
E: florian.kremslehner@dorda.at
www.dorda.at

Niamh Leinwather is the Secretary General of the Vienna International Arbitral Centre ("VIAC"). She took over the lead of VIAC in January 2022. Niamh has both a common and civil law background (Bachelor of Civil Law, University College Dublin, Mag.iur., University of Vienna, Master of European Studies, University of Vienna). She was the first Irish woman to be admitted to the Austrian Bar in 2013.

Niamh has over a decade of experience in international dispute resolution at Freshfields in Vienna where she acted as both counsel and arbitrator. She has held the office of Secretary Treasurer of the International Federation of Commercial Arbitration Institutions (IFCAI) since February 2023. In July 2024 Niamh was appointed to the Board of Directors of Arbitral Women and chairs the Education Committee. In October 2024 Niamh was invited to her alma mater as an Adjunct Professor of the Sutherland School of Law (University College Dublin).

Contact: VIAC – Internationale Schiedsinstitution der Wirtschaftskammer Österreich
Wiedner Hauptstrasse 63
1045 Vienna, Austria
T: +43 (0)5 90 900-4398
F: +43 (0)5 90 900-216
E: niamh.leinwather@viac.eu
www.viac.eu

Torsten Lörcher has been a lawyer with CMS Hasche Sigle since 1999. He became a partner in 2007. Before joining CMS Hasche Sigle, he worked with Professor Böckstiegel at Cologne University and wrote his doctoral thesis on international dispute resolution.

His practice is focused on acting as counsel and arbitrator in arbitration proceedings under the arbitration regimes of various international institutions. He has acted as counsel in state court and arbitration proceedings in a large number of cases and his track record as arbitrator comprises more than 80 cases.

His practice is mainly focused on post-M&A, commercial and technology-related disputes and disputes from the energy and the pharmaceutical sector.

Torsten is a member of the International Advisory Board of the Vienna International Arbitration Center (VIAC), a Board Member of the German Institution for Arbitration (DIS) and an International Board Member of the Finish Arbitration Institute (FAI).

Contact: CMS Hasche Sigle
Kranhaus 1
Im Zollhafen 18
50678 Cologne, Germany
T: +49 221 7716 200
E: torsten.loercher@cms-hs.com

Arnela Maglić is an Associate at KNOETZL. Arnela holds a degree from University of Zenica School of Law and had obtained her LL.M. at University of Pittsburgh School of Law.

Arnela's work focuses on international arbitration with a particular focus on construction and energy disputes, as well as ESG, in the CEE region. Arnela is also a member at ARBITRI Association – a non-profit professional association focused on supporting the creating of a modern ADR system in BiH.

Arnela has authored an ISDS glossary for government officials of the Western Balkans countries published by GIZ, which provides for a practical layout of terms essential for understanding of ISDS.

Contact: https://knoetzl.com/team/arnela-maglic/

Kamalia Mehtiyeva is a Professor of Law at the University of Paris-Est Créteil (France) where she co-directs LLM in International Arbitration and International Economic Litigation. Her teaching and research fields focus on international arbitration law, civil procedure, mutual legal assistance in both civil and criminal matters, international sanctions, parallel proceedings as well as international enforcement.

Kamalia's doctoral dissertation (Sorbonne University) focused on "The Notion of Judicial Cooperation" (La notion de coopération judiciaire, LGDJ, t. 597, 2020). Her dissertation was awarded the International Law Prize of the French Branch of the International Law Association. She is also author of the annual digest on international mutual legal assistance ("La chronique de coopération judiciaire internationale") for the Journal du Droit international (Clunet). In her research, Kamalia focuses on parallel proceedings, in particular arbitration and criminal proceedings as well as administrative or regulatory proceedings.

Kamalia is admitted to the Paris bar. Prior to becoming a Professor of law, she practiced in the Public International Law and Arbitration Group of Shearman & Sterling in Paris (2007–2014). Kamalia regularly sits as arbitrator, conducting proceedings in French, English, Russian and Turkish and is also a member of the ICC International Court of Arbitration.

Contact: https://lipha.u-pec.fr/membres/membres-permanents/mehtiyeva-kamalia

Alice Meissner is an international partner at Fieldfisher and is heading the Austrian dispute resolution practice in Vienna. Her focus lies in international commercial and investment arbitration as well as corporate litigation. She also advises foreign investors with their direct investment structures. Her clients include multinational cooperations in the energy and automotive sector.

Alice is a dual admitted attorney, with admissions in Austria and in Germany. She is listed as arbitrator with various international arbitration institutions and has been acting as arbitrator under UNCITRAL, ICC and VIAC Rules. Among others, she is also Fellow of the Hong Kong Institute of Arbitrators and Chair of the European Chinese Arbitrators Association (ECCA).

Alice graduated from the law faculty at the University of Hamburg and obtained her phD at the University of Vienna. She has been a visiting lecturer at the Central European University and at the Danube University Krems.

Contact: Fieldfisher Austria
Rotenturmstrasse 5–9
1010 Vienna, Austria
T: +43 1 928 163 40 02
alice.meissner@fieldfisher.com
https://www.fieldfisher.com/en/people/dr-alice-meissner

Maximilian Menz is a partner of the dispute resolution boutique WACH UND MECKES in Munich.

His practice covers a broad spectrum of national and international arbitration and commercial litigation, with a particular focus on cross-border and technology-related disputes. Max has conducted arbitration proceedings as counsel and arbitrator.

His expertise includes corporate and commercial law including post M&A and trade-related conflicts. Max represents clients across a broad range of industry sectors including private equity, banking and financial institutions, investors, trade, engineering, aviation, life sciences, and the automotive industry.

Max has also made significant contributions to the field through publications on arbitral law and participations as a speaker at national and international conferences.

Max was admitted to the German Bar in 2016 and holds an LL.M from the University of Edinburgh (2016).

Contact: WACH UND MECKES und Partner
Rechtsanwälte PartGmbB
Karlstrasse 12
80333 Munich, Germany
T: +49 89 1222 464 0
E: maximilian.menz@wachundmeckes.com
https://wachundmeckes.com/de/why

Ludmila Meszarosova is a counsel at Barnert Egermann Illigasch Rechtsanwälte GmbH in Vienna and a member of its Corporate/M&A and Arbitration practice groups. She has several years of experience in litigation and arbitration and specializes mainly in corporate and post-M&A disputes.

Ludmila Meszarosova has been involved as party representative in various domestic and international arbitration proceedings (both in ad hoc and institutional arbitrations) and in setting aside proceedings before the Austrian Supreme Court.

Ludmila Meszarosova holds a Magistra of Laws (Mag.[a] iur.) degree from the University of Vienna (2013) and was admitted to the Vienna bar in 2021.

Contact: Barnert Egermann Illigasch Rechtsanwälte GmbH
Rosenbursenstrasse 2
1010 Vienna, Austria
T: +43 1 513 80 08
E: meszarosova@beira.at
www.beira.at

Isabelle Michou is a Partner at Quinn Emanuel Urquhart & Sullivan, based in Paris.

Her practice focuses on international arbitration. She acts as counsel for large corporations as well as States or state-owned companies, and has developed substantial expertise in a range of industries including in telecoms, energy, mining, aerospace, large-scale infrastructure projects and hospitality. She has appeared before numerous high-profile arbitral tribunals, under the auspices of the major institutional rules including ICC, ICSID, LCIA, SCC, as well as in ad hoc arbitrations under the UNCITRAL Rules.

Isabelle also appears in arbitration-related proceedings before the French courts in cases involving issues of sovereign immunities, interlocutory, interim or conservatory relief, enforcement and challenges of arbitral awards.

She also acts as arbitrator under the ICC, SCC and LCIA Rules as well as other rules.

She is a board member of the Swedish Arbitration Association (SAA), the Finnish Arbitration Institute (FAI), the French Comité Français de l'Arbitrage (CFA) and the Swiss Foundation of International Arbitration Advocacy (FIAA), as well as a member of the Executive Committee of the Institute for Transnational Arbitration (ITA).

She is a French and Canadian national and is dual qualified as a Paris Avocat and a Solicitor of England & Wales.

Contact: https://www.quinnemanuel.com/attorneys/michou-isabelle

Nazlı Moralı is a Legal Counsel at the Vienna International Arbitral Centre, joining the VIAC Secretariat in April 2024. She holds an LL.B. from Istanbul Yeditepe University, an M.A. in Project Management and EU Law from University of Applied Sciences Burgenland, and an LL.M. in International Law from the University of Vienna.

Previously, she worked as an associate at an international law firm in Vienna and is admitted to the Istanbul Bar.

Contact: VIAC – Internationale Schiedsinstitution der Wirtschaftskammer Österreich
Wiedner Hauptstrasse 63
1045 Vienna, Austria
T: +43 (0)5 90 900-3499
F: +43 (0)5 90 900-113499
E: nazli.morali@viac.eu
www.viac.eu

Alexander Petsche is the managing partner of Baker McKenzie's Vienna office. He specializes in arbitration and compliance. Alexander Petsche acts as party representative in arbitral proceedings under various rules and in adhoc arbitrations. Furthermore, he is regularly appointed as arbitrator in adhoc and institutional arbitrations. He also represents parties before Austrian courts in matters relating to arbitration, including the challenge and enforcement of arbitral awards. He is a member of the Board of the International Arbitral Centre of the Austrian Federal Chamber of Commerce.

He studied Law at the Universities of Vienna and Paris, and studied Business Administration at the University of Economics, Vienna, and the Lyon Graduate School of Business. He holds a doctorate in both disciplines. In 1995/96 he completed post-graduate studies at the College of Europe in Bruges.

Alexander Petsche publishes regularly on international litigation and arbitration and has written more than 150 publications on various business law topics. He is co-editor and co-author of "Austria: Arbitration Law and Practice" (Juris Publishing 2007). He teaches Compliance at the Central European University.

Contact: Baker McKenzie Rechtsanwälte LLP & Co KG
Schottenring 25
1010 Vienna, Austria
T: +43 (1) 24 250
E: alexander.petsche@bakermckenzie.com
www.bakermckenzie.com

Nina Pichler is an attorney-at-law and working as a Partner and Head of Dispute Resolution at Oberhammer Rechtsanwälte GmbH in Vienna. She holds a double degree in law and business administration from the Karl-Franzens-University of Graz, Austria ("Dr. iur", 2021 and "Mag. rer. soc. oec." and Mag. iur, 2009).

MMag. Dr. Nina Pichler studied also abroad at the University of Siena (Italy) and at the Montclair State University (NJ/USA). Until 2025 Nina Picher was a Partner in another renowned law firm in Vienna. Prior to joining this law firm, she has been working for two other multinational law firms located in Vienna in the practice areas Dispute Resolution and Corporate / Mergers & Acquisition. Nina Pichler is specialized in commercial litigation and arbitration, with a particular focus on post-M&A, joint venture and shareholder disputes. Further, she has considerable experience in the fields of corporate transactions, general commercial, corporate and insolvency and restructuring law. She is also a lector in insolvency law at the University of Applied Science in Kufstein.

Nina Pichler speaks fluently German, English and Italian and is also a member of the International Association of Italian Speaking Lawyers ("AIGLI").

Contact: Oberhammer Rechtsanwälte GmbH
Karlsplatz 3/1
1010 Vienna, Austria
E: n.pichler@oberhammer.co.at
www.oberhammer.co.at

Nikolaus Pitkowitz is founding partner and head of dispute resolution at Pitkowitz & Partners and President of the Vienna International Arbitral Centre (VIAC).

Dr. Nikolaus Pitkowitz is considered one of the leading Austrian arbitration practitioners and was recently ranked as the number one dispute resolution lawyer in the leading national ranking of lawyers by the Austrian magazine "trend". He acted as party counsel and arbitrator in over 130 international disputes, in a range from smaller to multibillion cases, located in Europe, the United States, and Asia. Most notable is his role as counsel in the largest ever pending arbitration in Austria, as well as in arbitrations seated across Europe, in the Americas and in Asia. He has also acted as party counsel in a variety of complex litigation proceedings and has handled cases of great public interest, including before the European Court of Justice (ECJ). Dr. Pitkowitz is experienced in a variety of industries, including energy, automotive, telecommunications, arts, (post-)M&A, real estate and construction.

Dr. Nikolaus Pitkowitz holds law degrees from Universities of Vienna (JD and PhD) and Sankt Gallen, Switzerland (MBL) and is also qualified and certified as a mediator.

Dr. Nikolaus Pitkowitz is arbitrator and panel member of all leading arbitration institutions, and Fellow of the Chartered Institute of Arbitrators (FCIArb). He also acts as Court Member of the Casablanca International Arbitration and Mediation Centre (CIMAC) and as Vice-chair of the International Arbitration Committee of the Section of International Law of the American Bar Association (ABA).

Dr. Nikolaus Pitkowitz frequently speaks, lectures and is author of over 50 publications, including a monograph on Setting Aside Arbitral Awards and the Handbook on Third Party Funding in International Arbitration. He is also co-editor of the Austrian Yearbook on International Arbitration and co-organizer of the Vienna Arbitration Days.

Pitkowitz & Partners, based in Vienna, is a leading commercial law firm. The firm is focused on international arbitration and complex litigation, as well as on real estate and construction law and has been regularly ranked by GAR 100 among the world's leading arbitration firms.

Contact: Pitkowitz & Partners
Schwarzenbergplatz 3
1010 Vienna, Austria
T: +43 1 41301-0
n.pitkowitz@pitkowitz.com
www.pitkowitz.com

© Marlene Rahmann

Jessica Puhr is a Legal Counsel at the Vienna International Arbitral Centre ("VIAC"). She joined the VIAC Secretariat in August 2021. Within the VIAC Secretariat, Jessica is responsible for case management, the VIAC Portal and marketing.

Jessica studied law (Mag. Iur.) and English and American Studies (BA) at the University of Vienna. She also holds a business degree (MA) from FH Burgenland.

Contact: VIAC – Internationale Schiedsinstitution der Wirtschaftskammer Österreich
Wiedner Hauptstrasse 63
1045 Vienna, Austria
T: +43 (0)5 90 900-4355
F: +43 (0)5 90 900-216
E: jessica.puhr@viac.eu
www.viac.eu

Peter Rižnik is an arbitrator in independent practice based in Vienna, Austria.

With extensive experience serving as arbitrator, tribunal secretary, and counsel, Peter has participated in commercial and investment arbitrations conducted under the rules of the all-premier European arbitral institutions as well as in ad-hoc cases under the UNCITRAL Arbitration Rules. He is a member of the ICC Court of International Arbitration, one of the founders and board member of ArbCEE (Arbitration Association of Central and Eastern Europe), and Vice-President of the Moot Alumni Association.

Peter is also active in academia and regularly lectures on arbitration throughout the region, including as a habilitated lecturer at the University of Maribor in Slovenia.

As a Slovenian national he is particularly skilled in Central-European, Central-Eastern and South-Eastern European markets. In the past, Peter was active as an arbitration counsel in private practice, as a full-time tribunal secretary, as external counsel of the Ljubljana Arbitration Centre as well as with UN-organizations, including in international commercial law and the law of outer space.

Contact: peter@riznik.eu.

Violeta Saranciuc is a partner in the Dispute Resolution group of Zamfirescu Racoţi Vasile & Partners in Bucharest (Romania), where she specializes in international arbitration and international disputes. She has extensive experience representing clients before arbitral tribunals under various rules, including ICSID, ICC, VIAC, LCIA, UNCITRAL, as well as the rules of the Romanian CICACCIR rules.

Her work includes disputes related to construction and infrastructure projects, M&A and privatization agreements, energy disputes, international sales and general contractual matters, as well as investment protection matters. She also represents clients in arbitration-related court proceedings and is experienced in complex commercial and competition litigations.

She is a VIAC Ambassador for Romania in the framework of the VIAC CAN project, a member of the Rising Arbitrators Initiative's Executive Committee, and a co-founder of YRAP – Young Romanian Arbitration Practitioners.

Contact: Zamfirescu Racoti Vasile & Partners
12 Plantelor Street, District 2,
Bucharest RO-023974, Romania
T: +40 21 311 05 17
E: violeta.saranciuc@zrvp.ro
www.zrvp.ro

Milica Savić is a Partner in the Arbitration and Litigation Practice Group of Karanovic & Partners with 15 years of professional experience. She primarily focuses on arbitration work as she represents clients in major investment arbitration cases under ICSID, ICC and UNCITRAL arbitration rules as well as in commercial arbitration. Milica also focuses on privatization related disputes, complex and high-value M&A and construction disputes, bankruptcy and reorganisation proceedings.

Milica regularly participates at regional and international arbitration conferences as a speaker (ICC Construction Arbitration Conference, Balkan Arbitration Conference, various Young ICCA and ICC YAAF events). She is recognized among the top leading dispute resolution lawyers in Serbia by various relevant legal directories. This year alone she was ranked as "Up and Coming" by Chambers & Partners, Arbitration: Future Leaders by Lexology (former Who's Who Legal) and as "Next Generation Partner" by Legal 500.

Contact: Karanovic & Partners
T: +381 11 3094 214
E: milica.savic@karanovicpartners.com
https://www.karanovicpartners.com

Friederike Schäfer is a partner at ZEILER and works in the field of international dispute resolution with a strong focus on international arbitration.

Before joining the firm as a partner in 2022, Friederike Schäfer worked several years in private practice and as Counsel in the Secretariat of the ICC International Court of Arbitration. In this position, she handled hundreds of ICC proceedings, scrutinized hundreds of awards.

Friederike also has experience with various other arbitration rules, such as VIAC, UNCITRAL and DIS. She advises clients at all stages of a dispute and is active as arbitrator and party representative. Since joining our firm, Friederike has focused on various aspects of the energy sector and financing matters as well as on commercial and corporate matters.

Friederike regularly lectures on international arbitration at international and national conferences. She has authored numerous publications on international arbitration, private international law and other areas of law.

Friederike heads the German Desk of our firm and is admitted to the bar in Austria and Germany. She works in English and German and speaks French fluently.

Contact: Zeiler Rechtsanwälte GmbH
The ICON, Wiedner Gürtel 11
1100 Vienna, Austria
E: friederike.schaefer@zeiler.eu
www.zeiler.eu

Nicol Schneider is an attorney-at-law in the Dispute Resolution Team of DORDA. She assists clients in international and domestic arbitration proceedings as well as litigations. She specializes in commercial and construction disputes, focusing also on distribution, inheritance, and trust law.

Prior to joining DORDA, Nicol was working as an associate for Platte Disputes.Solutions as well as a lecturer at the University of Vienna and the University of Applied Sciences in Vienna.

Nicol passed the Austrian Bar Exam and holds two law degrees from the New York University (LL.M.) and the University of Vienna (Mag. iur.). She also studied at the University of Edinburgh.

Contact: DORDA Rechtsanwälte GmbH
Universitätsring 10
1010 Vienna, Austria
T: +43 1 533 4795-162
E: nicol.schneider@dorda.at
www.dorda.at

Alfred Siwy is a partner at Zeiler Rechtsanwälte and an expert in national and international dispute resolution, with a strong focus on international arbitration and litigation.

Alfred regularly advises clients in commercial and investment arbitration under various rules, including the ICC, VIAC, UNCITRAL and ICSID Rules. Alfred also represents clients before Austrian courts in commercial and corporate matters. Alfred has acted as counsel in disputes across all industries, recently including in particular disputes involving competition law, consumer protection law and international investment law.

Alfred lectures on dispute resolution at international conferences and has authored numerous publications in his and adjacent fields. He was admitted to the Austrian bar in 2011 and as a solicitor in England and Wales in 2019. He is a graduate of the University of Vienna (Mag. iur. 2003, Dr. iur. 2011) and King's College London (LL.M. 2006).

Contact: Zeiler Rechtsanwälte GmbH
The ICON, Wiedner Gürtel 11
1100 Vienna, Austria
M:+43 664 889 287 84
T: +43 18901087-84
E: alfred.siwy@zeiler.eu
www.zeiler.eu

Marina Stanisavljevic is an Australian qualified lawyer and international law specialist. She is a counsel at Schoenherr, where she focuses on investor-state and commercial arbitration. Marina represents clients under various institutional rules, arbitral seats, and applicable laws, including in the pharmaceutical, information & communication, financial services, post-M&A, and telecom sectors.

Marina is recognized by WWL as a Future Leader in Arbitration.

Prior to joining Schoenherr in 2018, Marina practiced as a solicitor in Melbourne, Australia, and worked in the defence counsel team at the International Criminal Tribunal for Former Yugoslavia in The Hague.

Marina speaks English and Serbian-Croatian-Bosnian.

Contact: Schoenherr Attorneys at Law
Schottenring 19
1010 Vienna
T: +43 1 53437 50736
E: M.Stanisavljevic@schoenherr.eu
www.schoenherr.eu

Caroline Strohmeier is an associate in the dispute resolution team of Pitkowitz & Partners, specializing in international arbitration and litigation.

Prior to joining Pitkowitz & Partners, Caroline served as a research assistant at both the Institute for Civil and Civil Procedure Law and the Institute for Corporate Law at Vienna University of Economics and Business. She also gained valuable experience through various internships at prestigious international law firms during her studies.

Caroline holds a Bachelor's and Master's degree in Business Law, along with a Bachelor's degree in Business Administration, from Vienna University of Economics and Business. As part of her Master's program in Business Law, she also studied at ESADE Law School in Barcelona.

During her Master's studies, Caroline competed in the 28th Willem C. Vis International Commercial Arbitration Moot Court, where her team ranked among the top 16 out of nearly 400 universities and received recognition for writing the third-best memorandum for the respondent. Since 2021, she has been coaching the WU Vienna Vis Moot Team.

Contact: Pitkowitz & Partners
Schwarzenbergplatz 3
1010 Vienna, Austria
T: +43 1 41301-0
E: c.strohmeier@pitkowitz.com
www.pitkowitz.com

Irene Welser is the Senior Partner of CERHA HEMPEL and heads the Contentious Business Department. She has been an equity partner for more than 30 years.

Irene is a passionate counsel and team leader in big-scale arbitrations. She is well known for never leaving the big picture out of sight and fiercely fighting for her clients. As an arbitrator, she adopts an efficient approach avoiding unnecessary formalism. Her strong academic background ensures the awards she writes thoroughly tackle the legal issues involved. Irene has participated in more than 70 international and national arbitrations pursuant to the ICC, Vienna and UNCITRAL Rules.

Shareholder disputes, construction, liability, contract, insurance and energy law as well as M&A and oil & gas disputes are key areas of her practice. She is also general counsel to corporate clients and so combines her litigation and arbitration proficiency with a firm understanding of how to avoid or settle disputes. Irene is an author and co-author of numerous books and articles related to arbitration. In 2003, she was appointed the youngest honorary professor ever at the University of Vienna. Irene Welser is a Board Member of the Vienna International Arbitral Centre. In this capacity, she has been involved in the development of the new VIAC Rules 2021.

Irene Welser is a regular speaker at international conferences and recognized educational institutions (*e.g.*, Austrian Attorneys' Academy or the Summer Arbitration Academy of the University of Vienna).

She has lectured on arbitration across the world and is an active part of the international arbitration community. Irene is a proud member of Arbitral Women. Irene is chair emeritus of the Litigation Arbitration & Dispute Resolution working group of LEX MUNDI. She is not only co-editor of the Austrian Yearbook on International Arbitration but is the only author who has contributed to each and every edition of this yearbook since its launch in 2007. Her clients benefit from her strong personality and her devotedness to success that often finds innovative solutions to tricky issues.

Irene is a member of ASA, IBA, LCIA, Arbitral Women and the board of the Chinese-European Legal Association. In recent years, Irene has held lectures on international arbitration in Istanbul, California, Hong-Kong, Beijing, Seoul, Tokyo, Brussels, Romania, Slovakia, Rome and at the Düsseldorf Arbitration School as well as at the Austrian Arbitration Academy.

Irene speaks German, English, French and Italian.

Contact: CERHA HEMPEL Rechtsanwälte GmbH
Parkring 2
1010 Vienna, Austria
T: +43 1 514 35-121
E: irene.welser@cerhahempel.com
www.cerhahempel.com

Gerold Zeiler's practice focuses on international Commercial Arbitration, Investment Arbitration and International Litigation. He regularly sits as arbitrator and acts as counsel of parties in both ad hoc arbitration proceedings as well as administered arbitration proceedings, including proceedings under the VIAC, ICC, UNCITRAL and ICSID Rules.

Gerold Zeiler is a partner with Zeiler Rechtsanwälte. He is a graduate of the University of Vienna (Mag. iur. 1988, Dr. iur. 1996) and Washington University in St. Louis (LL.M. 2016).

In 2018, the ICC World Council appointed Gerold as the Austrian member of the ICC Court. He is a member of the Publications Board of the ABA Section of Dispute Resolution, a Fellow of the Chartered Institute of Arbitrators (FCIArb) and a former president of the Austrian Arbitration Association (ArbAUT). His published work includes a comprehensive commentary on Austrian arbitration law (Schiedsverfahren, 2nd edition, 2014) and he is furthermore the editor of Austrian Arbitration Law (2016).

He regularly speaks at international conferences and guest lectures a university course.

Contact: Zeiler Rechtsanwälte GmbH
The ICON, Wiedner Gürtel 11
1100 Vienna, Austria
T: +43 (1) 890 10 87 – 80
M: +43 664 889 287 80
E: gerold.zeiler@zeiler.eu
www.zeiler.eu

Developments on the Austrian Market

Niam Leinwather/Nazli Morali/Jessica Puhr

VIAC's Annual Report – 2024

A Year of Fruition Anticipation

VIAC's Annual Report – 2024

A Year of Fruition and Anticipation

Niamh Leinwather/Nazli Morali/Jessica Puhr

I. Introduction

2024 marked a year of fruition for many of VIAC's ongoing projects, simultaneously it was a year of anticipation for the upcoming Golden Jubilee year. Nominated for a GAR award for "Regional Institution that Impressed", VIAC continued its trajectory of advancements and solidified further its position as a leading institution in the field of international arbitration and mediation, particularly in the Central and Eastern Europe ("CEE") and South-eastern Europe ("SEE") regions, where its influence continues to expand.

On the case management front, VIAC modernised its model mediation clauses to align with judicature of the Austrian Supreme Court and significantly reduced the cost structure for mediation proceedings. It further adapted its arbitration rules by introducing rules and a model clause for corporate disputes in response to a pivotal Austrian Supreme Court decision. The latter developments underscore its commitment to staying at the forefront of international dispute resolution and legal developments. Building on the reform of the award monitoring policies in 2023, VIAC is now finalising a best practice note for arbitrators in award writing as well as a note on the use of artificial intelligence in arbitration proceedings. These efforts demonstrate VIAC's commitment to thought leadership in dispute resolution globally.

As part of its broader vision, VIAC continued to innovate through its various initiatives, including Expert Focus Groups addressing emerging issues, and the ongoing development of the ADR Wellbeing Toolbox. The VIAC Community Ambassador Network ("VIAC CAN") continued to grow and is becoming a cornerstone of the institution's outreach efforts in the CEE and SEE regions. The initiative has facilitated invaluable connections and further reinforced VIAC's prominence in the region. 2024 marked the first year that the VIAC CAN Congress was made open to the public and was received with astounding enthusiasm.

Institutional collaborations also took centre stage this year, with VIAC strengthening its ties on the investment arbitration front with international institutions such as ICSID, in mediation with the Austrian Franchise Association, and from a commercial arbitration perspective with the Macedonian

Association of Corporate Lawyers and the Arbitration and Mediation Center of Armenia. These initiatives reflect VIAC's enthusiasm and dedication to global thought exchange and collaboration.

VIAC welcomed two new team members, one in a paralegal position. The addition of a paralegal to the case management team for the first time also significantly contributes to the efficiency of case administration. The addition of these two new colleagues has also expanded VIAC's language offering considerably with the Secretariat now boasting language skills in eight languages.[1)]

2024 was also a year of reflection and remembrance for VIAC, as we mourned the loss of distinguished members of our arbitration community. Martin Magál, a valued member of our International Advisory Board, passed away, leaving a profound legacy. We also bid farewell to Alexander Bělohlávek who played an important role in VIAC's history. They will both be deeply missed and fondly remembered.

With the beginning of the preparations for the 50-year celebration of VIAC in 2025, last year was a year of anticipation amongst the VIAC team. The meticulous organisation of various celebratory events began as well as the revision of the much-valued VIAC Handbook kicked off with its publication due in October 2025. 2024 stands as a testament to VIAC's unwavering commitment to excellence, collaboration, and leadership in the field of international dispute resolution. This annual report will provide an overview of VIAC's activities in 2024 including the highlights, statistics and trends observed.

II. Highlights of 2024

A. Continuing to Optimise VIAC's Case Management in Arbitration Proceedings

Efficiency continues to be a cornerstone of VIAC's case management, and 2024 saw significant progress in this regard. Building on the measures introduced in previous years, the VIAC Award Checklist has become an integral tool in facilitating smoother finalisation of awards. This year, VIAC further modernised several key documents, including the Acceptance of Office Forms,[2)] the Checklist for Arbitrators for the Final Determination of Costs, the

---

[1)] In addition to German and English, VIAC team members offer a range of language skills: Vladyslava Donchyk in Russian and Ukrainian, Nazli Morali in Turkish, Ema Potočnik in Slovenian, Ferenc Pöcz in Czech, Hungarian, and Slovak, and Klaudia Sood in Polish.

[2)] The Acceptance of Office Form is available on the VIAC website: https://www.viac.eu/images/documents/Arbitrators%20Acceptance%20of%20Office_workable.pdf [last accessed on January 30, 2025].

Transfer Instructions,[3]) and the Declaration by the Tribunal Secretary. These forms are now more user-friendly providing clearer guidance for arbitrators and the parties.

Looking ahead, VIAC is actively developing a new document entitled Best Practice for Costs, designed to guide arbitrators on structuring and drafting the cost sections of awards. This practical resource will include examples to ensure clarity and consistency in cost decisions. Another project in the pipelines is the Note on the use of Artificial Intelligence ("AI") in arbitration proceedings. This non-binding tool aims at facilitating discussions on incorporating AI while ensuring the integrity and effectiveness of the arbitral process.

Additionally, VIAC published a brochure showcasing its hearing facilities.[4]) Available for both VIAC and non-VIAC arbitrations, the brochure highlights the variety of rooms available at VIAC's office at the Austrian Federal Economic Chamber, which offer day-light, top notch technical equipment, catering facilities on-site as well as very competitive pricing.

B. Improvements of VIAC's Mediation Services

A working group at VIAC comprised of VIAC's President, Nikolaus Pitkowitz, VIAC's Board member, Martin Hauser, members of the Mediation Board, Claudio Arturo und Ulrike Frauenberger-Pfeiler as well as a team from VIAC's Secretariat, Secretary General, Niamh Leinwather, Legal Counsel, Sophie Tesarik and Legal Intern, Stella-Jo Thurner undertook a comprehensive review of the Vienna Rules of Mediation with the objective of enhancing the practice of mediation in Austria and beyond. The focus of the working group was the optimisation of VIAC's mediation services in order to encourage parties to engage more in this underutilised method of alternative dispute resolution.

Key changes include the simplification of the model mediation clauses[5]) while taking into account the latest judgements of the Austrian Supreme Court. There are now two model clauses for mediation that also provide for numerous supplementary provisions. The revision introduced a revised fee schedule for mediation proceedings. The registration fee is now a flat rate set at EUR 500 rather than a maximum amount of EUR 1,500, and the calculation of VIAC's administrative fees has been significantly revised. The administrative fees

[3]) The Transfer Instructions Form is available on the VIAC website: https://www.viac.eu/images/documents/Transfer%20instructions_workable_final.pdf [last accessed on January 30, 2025].

[4]) The brochure "Hearings at VIAC" is available on the VIAC website: https://viac.eu/images/documents/Hearings_at_VIAC.pdf [last accessed on January 30, 2025].

[5]) The model mediation clauses are available on the VIAC website: https://viac.eu/en/mediation/mediation-clauses-vienna-rules-2021 [last accessed on January 30, 2025].

continue to be calculated on the basis of the amount in dispute (as outlined in Annex 3 of the Vienna Rules). However, the following maximum amounts have been introduced: EUR 2,000 for disputes up to EUR 500,000; EUR 5,000 for disputes between EUR 500,001 and EUR 5,000,000; and EUR 10,000 for disputes exceeding EUR 5,000,000.

Registration Fee	
Flat rate	EUR 500
Administrative Fees	
Amount in dispute	*Maximum Rate*
up to EUR 500,000	EUR 2,000
from EUR 500,001 to EUR 5,000,000	EUR 5,000
over EUR 5,000,001	EUR 10,000

At the end of the mediation proceedings, the Secretary General has the discretion to set the administrative fees according to this scale, taking into account the specific circumstances of the case. With this new system, mediation proceedings have become much more cost-efficient at VIAC. Compared with other international institutions VIAC's offering is highly competitive.

In addition, VIAC remained steadfast in its commitment to further expand the use of mediation as evidenced by its cooperation agreement with the Austrian Franchise Association or its ongoing efforts to further develop and grow the Consensual Dispute Resolution Competition in cooperation with the International Bar Association.

C. Reform following the Austrian Supreme Court Decision 18 OCg 3/22y[6])

In April 2024, the Austrian Supreme Court set aside an arbitral award, stating that shareholder disputes are arbitrable under Austrian law only if specific conditions are met. These include ensuring all shareholders agree to the arbitration agreement, and can participate in the arbitration, protecting their rights under fair trial standards, and drafting precise arbitration agreements to avoid enforceability issues.

---

[6]) The decision is available here: https://www.ris.bka.gv.at/Dokumente/Justiz/JJT_20240403_OGH0002_018OCG00003_22Y0000_000/JJT_20240403_OGH0002_018OCG00003_22Y0000_000.pdf [last accessed on January 30, 2025].

In response to this ruling by the Supreme Court, a working group was set up led by VIAC's Vice-President, Franz Schwarz, VIAC's Board Member, Paul Oberhammer, VIAC's National Advisory Board member, Christian Koller, as well as members from VIAC's Secretariat, Niamh Leinwather, Secretary General and Sophie Tesarik, Legal Counsel. Recognising the court's emphasis on ensuring comprehensive binding effects, adequate participation rights, and precise drafting in arbitration agreements, VIAC has introduced a targeted approach to align its rules with these requirements while maintaining user-friendliness and flexibility. The working group has implemented two important updates to its framework to address these developments.

First, VIAC developed a Model Arbitration Clause for intra-corporate disputes, available on the VIAC website since January 2025.[7]) This model clause offers a practical solution for corporations seeking to include or update arbitration provisions in their articles of association or partnership agreements. Designed for clarity and precision, it aims to pre-empt impracticable clauses and provide a straightforward tool for meeting the Austrian Supreme Court's standards.

A second key step was the drafting of a new Annex to the VIAC Rules, specifically tailored to intra-corporate disputes. Annex 7 now ensures compliance with the Austrian Supreme Court's requirements by providing clear guidance for arbitration agreements involving shareholder disputes. It outlines mechanisms to guarantee that all shareholders are bound by and adequately represented in the arbitration process, thus safeguarding fairness and preventing future challenges to arbitral awards.

These updates reflect VIAC's commitment to adapting to evolving legal standards while offering practical resources that uphold the integrity of the arbitral process.

D. VIAC Community Ambassador Network (VIAC CAN), Legal Tech Think Tank (LTTT) and Other Initiatives

In February 2023, VIAC launched VIAC CAN. Since its inception, the VIAC CAN initiative has grown significantly. What began as a regional effort has evolved into a globally established platform for professionals to share knowledge and explore opportunities. The Congress and the plethora of events that have ensued from this network demonstrate the power of cross-border collaboration and how VIAC CAN has acted as a catalyst for positive change in the CEE/SEE region and beyond.

---

[7]) The model arbitration clauses are available on the VIAC website: https://viac.eu/images/documents/vienna_rules/VIAC_schieds_mediationsordnung_2021_e_v4_1812s.pdf [last accessed January 30, 2025].

VIAC's LTTT convened regularly in 2024, to analyse the impact of AI on transparency and disclosure obligations in arbitration proceedings. A particular focus was on the development of a non-binding AI Practice Note, intended to facilitate discussions about the use of AI in VIAC arbitration proceedings. In 2024, an additional workstream was introduced to strengthen collaboration with tech companies by organising joint events that foster closer ties between the legal and technology sectors, enhancing mutual understanding and engagement.

During 2024, VIAC's expert focus groups continued their work on trending topics focusing on investment arbitration, energy, construction, and post-M&A disputes, as well as ESG, succession, and trust. Among their notable achievements, the Energy Expert Focus Group led by Ana Stanic, E&A Law Limited, London and Eric Leikin, Freshfields, Vienna successfully organised a legal workshop in collaboration with OPEC, specifically its General Legal Counsel, Leonardo Sempertegui. Over the course of two days, various representatives engaged in in-depth discussions on key topics, including government considerations, reflections on financing energy contracts, and the pivotal role of dispute settlement in facilitating today's energy agreements. The first day featured a plenary session, fostering dialogue among government officials, and institutional representatives. The second day comprised a series of focused workshops, exploring contractual and legal mechanisms to balance the interests of investors and states, as well as broader dispute resolution frameworks within the energy sector. These initiatives showcase VIAC's commitment to fostering dialogue and innovation within the ADR community, ensuring its continued leadership in the field.

The ADR Wellbeing Toolbox was launched in 2023 by VIAC, ARBalance, and REAL and gained quite some traction in 2024 hosting four events. This initiative underscores our ongoing commitment to supporting the wellbeing of our users and comprises a series of free, recorded webinars designed to provide practical tools and insights. In 2024 an in-person event was organised during the Willem C. Vis International Commercial Arbitration Moot ("Vis Moot") in Vienna, tailored specifically for students. For International Women's Day, the ADR Wellbeing Toolbox hosted a fireside chat with two renowned female practitioners, Patrizia Netal, VIAC Vice-President and Emi Rowse Igusa, Partner and Head of Japan Practice at Kududn and Partners. In the penultimate webinar of the year, Amber Allan, head of Learning and development at Stewarts shared her useful techniques for overcoming imposter syndrome. The final event of 2024 took place during the Kyiv Arbitration Days and focused on Emotional Intelligence in the Workplace, tailored for our colleagues in Ukraine and led by Sara Cook, conflict response specialist. Looking ahead to 2025, the ADR Wellbeing Toolbox will be introducing fresh concepts addressing key topics, including pre-recorded sessions that will deal with various aspects of professional and personal wellbeing, burnout prevention, emotional resilience, conflict fatigue, workplace relationships and female-related challenges such as fertility issues.

E. Events – From Vienna through the Balkans and the Baltics to Tbilisi and beyond: VIAC's Standout Events of 2024

2024 was a significant year for VIAC, marked by a series of impactful events that showcased its leadership in arbitration and mediation. The year began with the first ever VIAC CAN Congress on 9 February 2024, bringing together 40 VIAC CAN Ambassadors. The Congress featured an exclusive programme for VIAC Ambassadors on Thursday, 8 February 2024, including a tailored cross-examination workshop led by Franz Schwarz, VIAC's Vice-President. On Friday, 9 February 2024, the main agenda unfolded with engaging panel discussions on "ADR in Emerging Markets" and "New Trends in Investment Arbitration: What Role Can the Vienna Rules Play in the Region?", a keynote speech on business development, and a workshop on body language. The event concluded on Saturday, 10 February 2024, with a ballroom dancing class and the prestigious Ball of Legal Professionals — an elegant evening of celebration and connection, marking the perfect end to a memorable event.

VIAC was also the proud co-organiser of the Vienna Arbitration Days which took place on 7 to 8 June 2024. The Vienna Arbitration Days 2024 offered dynamic discussions on the latest trends in digitalisation, practical and ethical aspects for arbitration practitioners, and the impact of ESG and human rights policies on dispute resolution. The event was complemented by cultural highlights, including a dinner at Motto am Fluss with a live performance, the first-ever Arbitral Women Breakfast, a guided tour of the Heidi Horton collection, and a performance from the Chorus Juventus of the Vienna Boy's Choir after the infamous World Café.

VIAC actively participated at the 22nd "Exporttag", a trade fair hosted by Advantage Austria of the Austrian Federal Economic Chamber on 18 June 2024. VIAC had its own stand and engaged with trade experts fostering valuable discussions about dispute resolution possibilities in cross-border transactions. Under the theme "Beyond the Box" over 70 international leaders from politics, business, and academia inspired and informed the some 3,000 visitors.

VIAC also made a significant impact at the Vis Moot in March 2024, hosting multiple events, such as an innovative AI-focused session where the Vis Moot problem from the previous year was arbitrated using AI. VIAC also co-organised the launch of the world's first Global Tribunal Secretary Platform, at the University of Vienna along with ASA, Jus Connect, AAA-ICDR, and CIArb, which offers arbitrators an innovative tool to source external tribunal secretaries and access valuable practitioner resources. During the Vis Moot, VIAC partnered with various organisations and institutions. "Running for Resolutions", organised in cooperation with Comitê Brasileiro de Arbitragem, brought together the arbitration community for a unique morning run in the scenic Wiener Prater – an opportunity to strengthen connections in an informal setting and promote a healthy lifestyle. Additionally, in collaboration with CAM-CCBC, VIAC co-hosted a Traditional Viennese Breakfast, where participants enjoyed an authentic Viennese coffee morning alongside an engaging panel discussion on cybersecurity from an institutional perspective. In March 2024, VIAC also had the honour of hosting the IFCAI General Assembly and the IFCAI Councillors' Meeting at its premises, warmly welcoming representatives from ADR centres worldwide to Vienna.

During the summer, VIAC once again participated in academic student programmes such as the Summer ELSA Law School and the Austrian Arbitration Academy. Both programmes give students from around the globe the unique opportunity to interact with arbitration experts. VIAC offered a glimpse into the world of institutional arbitration as well as advice on careers in arbitration.

Under the auspices of the VIAC CAN initiative, in 2024 VIAC organised 19 exceptional events across 15 jurisdictions in CEE/SEE, and beyond. From traditional conferences like the "Arbitration Matinée" in Belgrade and "The Future of Modern International Arbitration" in Warsaw to industry-focused roundtables for the construction sector in Sarajevo. Each occasion addressed unique regional and professional needs. VIAC partnered with local law firms and institutions to host international conferences, including, but not limited to "Arbitration 360: Cutting-Edge Issues and Expert Advice" in Skopje and "Navigating Arbitration: Essential Skills for Lawyers and In-House Counsel" in Ljubljana. VIAC also embraced more creative settings for a smaller group gathering in Zagreb, and even incorporated a musical performance into the programme for "The Art of Arbitration" in Vilnius. 2024 was also a year of expansion for VIAC CAN. For the first time, VIAC organised events in Georgia and Kosovo, and extended its reach to audiences in India and Japan. Additionally, VIAC supported and participated in international arbitration events in the Baltics, Bucharest, Moldova, and Azerbaijan.

In the latter half of the year highlights included VIAC hosting the highly anticipated GAR Live Vienna on 27 September covering energy transition disputes in arbitration, with a focus on key cases and new regulations in the renewable energy sector. The classic "GAR What would you do?" interactive session on "soft skills" in arbitration did not disappoint, where the stellar panel discussed real-life scenarios and compared solutions with the audience. This was followed by the Winds of Change conference at the end of November, co-organised with the University of Vienna and Herbert Smith Freehills, which featured a star lineup of speakers addressing key developments in investment arbitration.

Overall, VIAC significantly enhanced its public presence and outreach in 2024, with a notable increase in activity on LinkedIn and other platforms.

III. 2024 Trends and Statistics

A. Trends Observed in 2024

Since 2021, the Vienna Rules allow VIAC to act as an administrative and appointing authority (Annex 4 and 5). In 2024, there has been a marked rise in cases where parties engage VIAC as an administrative authority. This highlights the growing recognition of the advantages of VIAC arbitration, such as streamlined processes and enhanced oversight, therefore ensuring efficiency and fairness. Requests for VIAC to act as appointing authority have also grown, highlighting the institution's role in ensuring impartial and effective tribunal appointments by its Board. This upward trend underscores the value of VIAC's administrative and appointing authority services, which offer structured case management, transparent cost administration, and expert arbitrator selection. By offering logistical support, secure communication channels, and independent oversight, VIAC enhances the efficiency and integrity of ad hoc proceedings, reinforcing its reputation as a trusted and impartial institution in international dispute resolution.

VIAC also observed an overall rise in more complex cases in 2024. Despite ongoing challenges faced due to sanctions, payment issues and difficulties with document delivery, VIAC ensured equal treatment and access to justice for all parties in 2024 and a smooth case administration. Modern and efficient internal processes and utilising Advantage Austria's services for document logistics have positioned VIAC as a leader in managing such cases and underscore its adaptability. These measures enhance confidence in VIAC-administered arbitrations, particularly in cases with heightened financial or regulatory risks. In addition, and in line with the growing complexity of cases, there was a sharp rise in security for costs applications, presumably reflective of difficulties encountered during enforcement proceedings. Interestingly, no third-party funders were disclosed in 2024 whereas 2023 saw some use of third-party funders.

B. VIAC's Caseload and Consistent Aggregated Amount in Dispute

VIAC's caseload remained high in 2024. With 45 new cases and a total of 71 pending cases, VIAC continued administering one of its highest number of cases in recent years.[8]) The increased aggregated amount in dispute of almost two billion was the highest recorded aggregated amount in dispute in VIAC's history. Of the new cases received in 2024, the highest amount in dispute was approximately EUR 40 million, whereas the lowest amount in dispute was recorded at EUR 14,000.

C. Origin of the Parties – CEE in Focus

VIAC continues to establish itself as the premier institution in the CEE and SEE region, broadening its international position. Consequently, 41 percent of all parties stem from the CEE and SEE region, this is an increase of 36 percent in comparison to last year. Whereas the percentage of parties from Austria decreased from 33 percent to 23 percent. The remaining percentages can be assigned to parties from Northern and Western Europe (15 percent) and beyond (18 percent) with parties originating from, *e.g.*, British Virgin Islands, China, Morocco, USA and Azerbaijan.

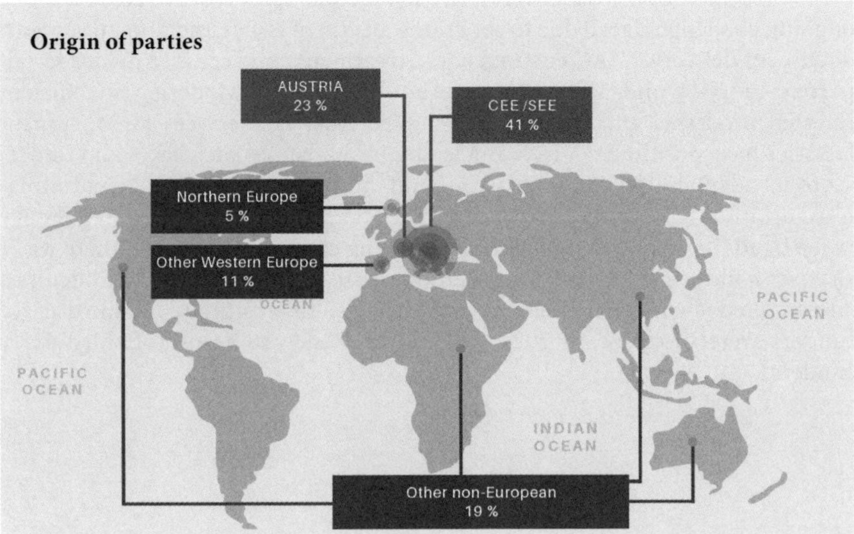

Figure 1: Overview of the origin of parties in VIAC proceedings in 2024.

8) In 2023, the 72 pending cases was already an increase of 32 percent from 2022.

D. Nationality of Arbitrators – Increase in Arbitrators from CEE

Arbitrators confirmed by the VIAC Board vary in nationality and are becoming more international. In the 2024 statistics, 40 percent of arbitrators were Austrian nationals compared to 58 percent in 2023. There was a significant increase in arbitrators appointed from the CEE and SEE region, an increase from 23 percent in 2023 to 33 percent in 2024. Approximately 29 percent of arbitrators were nationals from other Western and Northern European. Ten percent of the arbitrators were from non-European countries, a significant increase in diversity compared to 2023 where only two percent of arbitrators were from non-European countries.

Figure 2: Overview of nationality of arbitrators in VIAC proceedings in 2024.

E. Applicable Law and Seat

Austria is widely regarded as an arbitration-friendly jurisdiction, with a modern and well-developed legal system. As a result, Austrian law is specified as the governing law in a significant proportion of arbitration agreements (40 percent). Reflecting this preference, an impressive 93 percent of cases select Vienna as their seat of arbitration.

As of 31 December 2024, other laws applicable in VIAC cases included the CISG (11 percent), English law (7 percent), Hungarian law (4 percent), Czech law (4 percent), German law (2 percent), Italian law (2 percent), and Ukrainian law (2 percent).

F. Duration of Proceedings and Expedited Proceedings

The Vienna Rules provide that VIAC proceedings shall be conducted in an efficient manner (Art. 28 para. 1 Vienna Rules 2021), and VIAC makes every effort in its administration to ensure that it fulfills the latter. VIAC's effort to increase efficiency is also reflected in the average duration of proceedings in 2024: 12 months. The average duration between the receipt of Statement of Claim and the transfer of file also declined, from five months in 2023 to only four months in 2024.

Art. 45 Vienna Rules 2021 governs supplementary rules for expedited proceedings. If parties choose to opt in, an arbitral tribunal shall render an award within six months of transfer of file. Over the past years, VIAC observed a decrease in expedited proceedings. As of 31 December 2024, eight percent of VIAC cases were conducted as expedited proceedings.

Figure 3: Average duration of VIAC proceedings in 2024.

G. Nature of Disputes

The nature of disputes remained varied in 2024. The leading nature of disputes were "Engineering and Technology" (33 percent) followed by "Investments" (11 percent) and "Wholesale and Retail Trade" (also 11 percent), then "Energy and Resources" (9 percent) and "Construction and Infrastructure" (7 percent). Other disputes included "Telecommunications", "Arts, Entertainment and Recreation" and "Banking and Finance".

H. Gender statistics

VIAC is dedicated to promoting diversity and achieving gender parity in arbitration, and in 2024 VIAC observed a general improvement. 63 percent of arbitrators were male, while only 37 percent were female. When taking only party nominated arbitrators into consideration, the disparity was very visible: 83 percent were male, while 17 percent were female. The VIAC Board continued its effort to balance out this discrepancy. Consequently, this year saw a significant improvement and 64 percent of VIAC appointed arbitrators were female (compared to 52 percent in 2023).

In an effort to increase the presence of female arbitrators in VIAC cases and as a signatory and activist of the ERA-Pledge,[9]) VIAC once again launched an International Women's Day campaign on LinkedIn. Under the theme "Inspire Inclusion" female Board members shared their perspectives on the topic. On a related note, VIAC's Secretary General has been appointed as a member of the ArbitralWomen Board for the 2024–2026 term, serving as Chair of the Educational Programmes Committee and as a member of the Events and Cooperation Committees. This marks her first term on the ArbitralWomen Board of Directors, highlighting VIAC's overall commitment to diversity as well as her own personal dedication to the topic.

In 2024, VIAC continued evaluating the ages of arbitrators, a practice initiated in 2023, and reported notable changes in the distribution of age groups. The proportion of confirmed arbitrators aged 36 to 45 increased to 27 percent, up from 20 percent in 2023, reflecting a growing presence of younger professionals. Similarly, arbitrators under 35 made up 10 percent in 2024, more than doubling from 4 percent the previous year. Meanwhile, 38 percent of arbitrators were in the 46 to 55 age group, and 13 percent were aged 56 to 65. The proportion of arbitrators over 65 declined to 8 percent, further highlighting a shift toward younger age brackets.

IV. 2025 Outlook

As 2025 unfolds, VIAC looks forward to a year of celebration, growth, and continued excellence in international arbitration. In 2025, VIAC will proudly celebrate its 50th anniversary, marking half a century of commitment to the arbitration community as the premiere international arbitral institution in CEE and SEE. New initiatives and ongoing improvements in the arbitration process ensure that VIAC maintains the highest standards of service and efficiency. With a focus on innovation, VIAC continues to improve its case management practices, reinforcing its reputation for excellence in dispute resolution by introducing new arbitrator guidelines, practice notes and an updated edition of VIAC Handbook to provide valuable support to arbitrators and practitioners.

Over the course of 2025, a series of activities will commemorate this milestone, with an anniversary event in October 2025 entitled "VIAC – The Next 50 Years", which will take place the day before GAR Live Vienna. Highlights include the VIAC CAN Congress-Third Edition on 28 February

[9]) The Equal Representation in Arbitration Pledge ("ERA-Pledge") recognises the underrepresentation of women in international arbitral tribunals. The Pledge seeks to increase, on an equal opportunity basis, the number of women appointed as arbitrators in order to achieve a fair representation as soon as practically possible, with the ultimate goal of full parity. Find out more and sign the pledge here: https://www.arbitrationpledge.com/take-the-pledge [last accessed on January 28, 2025].

2025, special events during the Vis Moot in Vienna, events during the Paris Arbitration Week, and the Vienna Arbitration Days in May 2025, all featuring dedicated 50 Years of VIAC theme. A year-long campaign will highlight 12 historical milestones from VIAC's journey, paired with commitments to its future, special merchandise, and other initiatives.

Vienna, as a historic bridge between East and West, continues to serve as a key hub for international arbitration, fostering connections between diverse legal traditions and business cultures. In this ideal framework, VIAC remains dedicated to advancing international arbitration, looking forward to a year of meaningful progress, deeper collaboration, and continued success.

Chapter I

The Arbitration Agreement and Arbitrability

Michael Barnert/Ludmila Meszarosova
Arbitrability of Corporate Disputes under Austrian Law

New Requirements for Arbitration Agreements Established by the Austrian Supreme Court

Arbitrability of Corporate Disputes under Austrian Law

New Requirements for Arbitration Agreements Established by the Austrian Supreme Court

Michael Barnert/Ludmila Meszarosova

I. Introduction

The arbitrability of corporate disputes, especially concerning the challenge of defective shareholder resolutions in limited liability companies, has been an often discussed and highly controversial topic among Austrian scholars.[1]) One of the key questions to be answered was whether – and if so, under which conditions – the binding effect of the award rendered in arbitration proceedings, in which only the company acts as respondent (either based on the provisions

[1]) With regard to the situation before the recent decision of the Austrian Supreme Court, *see, e.g.*, (just to name a few examples): *Martin Auer, Schiedsvereinbarungen bei der GmbH im Lichte des SchiedsRÄG 2005,* in SATZUNGSGESTALTUNG IN DER GMBH – MÖGLICHKEITEN UND GRENZEN 123 (*Kalss & Rüffler*, 2005); *Thomas Garber, Rechtsunsicherheiten im Kontext personengesellschaftsrechtlicher Beschlussmängelstreitigkeiten im Schiedsverfahren,* Zak 188 (2023); *Susanne Kalss, Beschlussmängel in Personengesellschaften vor Gerichten und Schiedsgerichten,* GesRZ 141 (2023); *ead., Gesellschaftsrecht und Schiedsrecht in Österreich,* JBl 205 (2015); *Peter Klein, Arbitrability of Company Law Disputes,* in AUSTRIAN ARBITRATION YEARBOOK 2007, 29 (*Klausegger* et al. eds., 2007); *Christian Koller & Rosanna Wiedermann, Probleme des Mehrparteien-Schiedsverfahrens in gesellschaftsrechtlichen Streitigkeiten,* in SCHIEDSVERFAHREN IM GESELLSCHAFTSRECHT (*Czernich & Rüffler* eds., 2022); *Nikolaus Pitkowitz, The Arbitrability of Corporate Disputes under Austrian Law – Still Open Questions?*, in AUSTRIAN YEARBOOK ON INTERNATIONAL ARBITRATION 2014, 31 (*Klausegger* et al. eds., 2014); *Andreas Reiner, Schiedsverfahren und Gesellschaftsrecht,* GesRZ 151 (2007); *Friedrich Rüffler & Sarah Seper, Gesellschaftsrechtliche Grundlagen: Objektive Schiedsfähigkeit,* in SCHIEDSVERFAHREN IM GESELLSCHAFTSRECHT (*Czernich & Rüffler* eds., 2022); *Bernd Terlitza & Martin Weber, Zur Schiedsfähigkeit gesellschaftsrechtlicher Streitigkeiten nach dem SchiedsRÄG 2006,* ÖJZ 1 (2008); *Wilfried Thöni, Drittschutz im aktien-, GmbH-rechtlichen Beschlußanfechtungsprozeß,* GesRZ 55 (1994); *Martin Trenker & Mathias Demetz, Schiedsfähigkeit von Beschlussmängelstreitigkeiten in der GmbH,* wbl 1 (2013); *Gerold Zeiler, Zur schiedsrechtlichen Anfechtung von Gesellschafterbeschlüssen,* in Festschrift für Gert Delle Karth, 1055 (*Schumacher & Zimmermann* eds., 2013); *id., Zur Schiedsfähigkeit von gesellschaftsrechtlichen Beschlussmängelstreitigkeiten,* RdW 392 (2023).

of applicable corporate law or an agreement in the articles of association), can extend to all shareholders of the company, even if they were not parties to the arbitration proceedings, and, in particular, how to ensure that the rights of all shareholders in such proceedings are respected.

In its previously established case law, the Austrian Supreme Court had in general affirmed on numerous occasions that corporate disputes regarding the validity of shareholder resolutions, in which only the company acts as respondent, are objectively arbitrable, provided that all shareholders have consented to the respective arbitration agreement and were given the opportunity to participate in the arbitration proceedings as so-called intervening parties (*Nebenintervenienten*). Unlike the German Federal Supreme Court (*Bundesgerichtshof* – BGH), which – in its decisions known as the "Arbitrability I-IV" decisions ("*Schiedsfähigkeit I-IV*")[2]) – held that such corporate disputes can only be subject to arbitration if the arbitration clause fulfills certain criteria (in particular, sets out the rights of the shareholders in such disputes), the Austrian Supreme Court has not – up until now – considered the arbitration clause as key to arbitrability.

On 3 April 2024, the Austrian Supreme Court has, however, issued a landmark decision[3]) on the arbitrability of corporate disputes, in which it held – closely following the German Federal Supreme Court's "Arbitrability" decisions – that corporate disputes regarding defective shareholder resolutions in which only the company acts as respondent in the proceedings are only objectively arbitrable if sufficient participation and involvement of all shareholders, even if they are not party to the proceedings, is guaranteed. These rights, however, cannot be left to the conduct of the proceedings, but have to be set out *already in the arbitration agreement itself.* Thus, the arbitration agreement for such disputes has to be drafted accordingly, otherwise the dispute lacks objective arbitrability (with the result of risking that the respective award is set aside).

The recent decision of the Austrian Supreme Court has far-reaching implications, both, for arbitration as well as corporate practice. Some of the most relevant consequences in this regard, such as the need to replace or amend existing arbitration clauses in articles of association by more elaborate arbitration clauses meeting the new standard as set by the Austrian Supreme Court, and implications of the decision on pending arbitration proceedings and already issued awards, will be addressed below.

Furthermore, the recent decision of the Austrian Supreme Court also required an amendment to the Vienna Rules in order to ensure that they reflect

---

[2]) BGH, Mar 29, 1996, docket no. II ZR 124/95 (Germany) ("*Schiedsfähigkeit I*"); BGH, Apr 6, 2009, docket no. II ZR 255/08 (Germany) ("*Schiedsfähigkeit II*"); BGH, Apr 6, 2017, docket no. I ZB 23/16 (Germany) ("*Schiedsfähigkeit III*"); BGH, Sep 23, 2021, docket no. I ZB 13/21 (Germany) ("*Schiedsfähigkeit IV*").

[3]) OGH Apr 3, 2024, docket no. 18 OCg 3/22y (Austria).

the new requirements outlined by the Austrian Supreme Court. The new Supplementary Rules for Corporate Disputes and Model Arbitration Clause for Articles of Association for Arbitral Proceedings under the Vienna Rules published by the Vienna International Arbitral Centre (VIAC) on 1 January 2025 will also be shortly introduced in Section IV. below.

II. The Decision of the Austrian Supreme Court

A. Background of the Underlying Dispute

The decision of the Supreme Court dealt with an application for setting aside of an award issued in arbitration proceedings concerning the validity of a shareholder resolution in a limited partnership under Austrian law (*Kommanditgesellschaft*).

The articles of association of the limited partnership had foreseen that shareholder resolutions shall be challenged according to the rules applicable to limited liability companies (*GmbH* – LLC). Pursuant to Section 42 paragraph 1 of the Austrian Limited Liability Companies Act [*GmbH-Gesetz* – LLCA]), a claim challenging the validity of a shareholder resolution must be raised directly (and exclusively) against the company (and not – as would otherwise be the case in a limited partnership – against all remaining shareholders, *i.e.*, the shareholders not acting as claimants); therefore, only the company acts as the respondent in the proceedings and the remaining shareholders do not participate as parties in such proceedings, but, however, have the right to join the proceedings as intervening parties (*Nebenintervenienten*) (Section 42 paragraph 5 LLCA). According to Section 42 paragraph 6 LLCA, the binding effect of the court decision on the validity of the shareholder resolution issued in such proceedings shall extend to all shareholders – irrespective of whether they joined the proceedings as intervening parties or not; in other words, for the extension of the binding effect of the court decision to all shareholders, it suffices that all shareholders had the possibility to join the proceedings.

In the case at hand, shareholder resolutions that were passed by the general assembly of the limited partnership in October 2020 were challenged by a group of shareholders opposing these resolutions. The respective shareholders initiated *ad hoc* arbitration proceedings as foreseen in the arbitration agreement of the company and directed their claims against the company as the respondent in accordance with the above cited rules. The remaining shareholders, who were not parties to the proceedings, were informed about the arbitration and given the opportunity to join the proceedings, however, they did not participate in the constitution of the arbitral tribunal, which was appointed only by the shareholders acting as claimants and the company acting as respondent in the arbitration proceedings. This was due to the fact that the shareholders were informed by the company about their possibility to join the proceedings only after the arbitral tribunal had been appointed. Despite the opportunity to do so, none of the remaining shareholders decided to join the proceedings.

After the arbitral tribunal issued its award, which declared the respective shareholder resolutions null and void, the company (acting as a respondent in the arbitration proceedings) brought an action before the Austrian Supreme Court to set aside the award, arguing, *inter alia*, that the award issued by the arbitral tribunal cannot have a binding effect on the shareholders who could not properly participate in the arbitration proceedings and the constitution of the arbitral tribunal. In this regard, the company argued – referring to the case law of the German Federal Supreme Court (*Bundesgerichtshof* – BGH) known under the reference "Arbitrability I, II, III and IV"[4]) – that the subject matter of the proceedings, *i.e.*, a dispute regarding the validity of a shareholder resolution, is not objectively arbitrable, unless the right of all shareholders to participate in the proceedings – including the constitution of the arbitral tribunal – is respected; the respective rights of the shareholders to participate and the procedure for granting such participation rights, shall, according to the German Federal Supreme Court, however, already be set out in the arbitration agreement itself, *i.e.*, from the outset, unless such an arbitration agreement shall be deemed null and void.

The shareholders acting as respondents in the set-aside proceedings before the Austrian Supreme Court (the shareholders who had successfully challenged the shareholder resolutions in the arbitration proceedings) argued, *inter alia*, that all remaining shareholders had been informed about the arbitration proceedings and given the possibility to join (which, however, none of the shareholders made use of). In this regard, the shareholders also referred, *inter alia*, to the established case law of the Austrian Supreme Court,[5]) which held in its previous jurisprudence that shareholder disputes regarding the validity of shareholder resolutions in limited liability companies are objectively arbitrable; according to this case law, in order to extend the binding effect of an award issued in such proceedings to all shareholders (as foreseen in Section 42 paragraph 6 LLC), it is sufficient that all shareholders are bound by the arbitration agreement and given the opportunity to join the proceedings as intervening parties (*Nebenintervenienten*) in the same manner as in proceedings

[4]) BGH, Mar 29, 1996, docket no. II ZR 124/95 (Germany) ("*Schiedsfähigkeit I*"); BGH, Apr 6, 2009, docket no. II ZR 255/08 (Germany) ("*Schiedsfähigkeit II*"); BGH, Apr 6, 2017, docket no. I ZB 23/16 (Germany) ("*Schiedsfähigkeit III*"); BGH, Sep 23, 2021, docket no. I ZB 13/21 (Germany) ("*Schiedsfähigkeit IV*").

[5]) OGH, Jun 3, 1950, docket no. 2 Ob 276/50 (Austria); OGH, Dec 10, 2009, docket no. 7 Ob 221/98w (Austria); OGH, Apr 3, 2001, docket no. 4 Ob 37/01x (Austria); OGH, Jun 29, 2006, docket no. 6 Ob 145/06a (Austria); OGH, Oct 22, 2010, docket no. 7 Ob 103/10p (Austria); OGH, Apr 19, 2012, docket no. 6 Ob 42/12p (Austria); OGH Dec 16, 2013, docket no. 6 Ob 43/13m (Austria); OGH Jun 26, 2014, docket no. 6 Ob 84/14t (Austria).

before state courts. With regard to the right to participate in the constitution of the arbitral tribunal, the respondents also put forward that the shareholders, who were informed about the proceedings, had the possibility to join the proceedings and, in case of a joinder, could have raised objections against the constitution of the arbitral tribunal and challenge the appointed arbitrators (Section 589 Austrian Civil Code of Procedure [*Zivilprozessordnung* – ACCP] by way of analogy). Alternatively, the parties and the shareholders joining the proceedings would have had the option to agree on a re-constitution of the arbitral tribunal. By not joining the proceedings despite the opportunity to do so, the shareholders waived these rights with respect to the arbitration proceedings at hand and no violation of the shareholders' right to be heard had occurred. As regards objective arbitrability of the subject matter, the respondents argued that the question of objective arbitrability is an issue to be distinguished from the question of whether the rights of all parties bound by the award had been respected in the arbitration proceedings, as this is a question that depends on the conduct of the respective proceedings and is to be assessed on a case-by-case basis.[6]) For all these reasons the respondents argued that the respective jurisprudence of the German Federal Supreme Court shall not be followed.

B. The Reasoning of the Court

In its decision, the Austrian Supreme Court followed the arguments put forward by the company and – closely relying on the "Arbitrability I – IV" decisions of the German Federal Supreme Court and, thereby, departing from its previously established case law regarding the general objective arbitrability of shareholder disputes – held that such corporate disputes regarding the validity of shareholder resolutions are only objectively arbitrable, if the arbitral award rendered in such proceedings has a binding effect against all shareholders; such binding effect, however, can only be extended to the shareholders not involved in the arbitration proceedings as parties if the shareholders have consented to the arbitration agreement and have been *granted the respective right to participate in the proceedings* and, most importantly, in the *constitution of the arbitral tribunal*, already in the *arbitration agreement itself*. According to the Supreme Court, the arbitration agreement, therefore, has to be drafted accordingly.

In its reasoning, the Austrian Supreme Court strongly relied on the respective case law of the German Federal Supreme Court (the decisions known as "Arbitrability I-IV")[7]) regarding the minimum requirements for the

---

[6]) *See also* the similar reasoning of the appellate court referred to in the decision OGH, Apr 19, 2012, docket no. 6 Ob 42/12p (Austria).

[7]) *See* BGH, Mar 29, 1996, docket no. II ZR 124/95 (Germany) ("*Schiedsfähigkeit I*"); BGH, Apr 6, 2009, docket no. II ZR 255/08 (Germany) ("*Schiedsfähigkeit II*");

validity of arbitration agreements in limited liability companies, which cover disputes regarding defective shareholder resolutions. According to the reasoning of the German Federal Supreme Court, the minimum requirements for arbitration agreements in such disputes shall serve the purpose to protect the shareholders against the risk of being put at a disadvantage and deprived of the necessary legal protection. Apart from corporations, such as limited liability companies, these minimum requirements for arbitration agreements shall also apply in principle to partnerships such as limited partnerships (if the application of the principles applying to corporations on a given partnership is justified, which is to be assessed on case-by-case basis), *e.g.*, in cases where the application of the respective rules for the challenging of shareholder resolutions in corporations (such as limited liability companies) has been agreed and, therefore, the arbitration claim is to be directed against the company and not against the remaining shareholders and the remaining shareholders, therefore, run the risk of being put at a disadvantage and deprived of the necessary legal protection in the same way as in disputes regarding shareholder resolutions in corporations such as, *e.g.*, limited liability companies. In its case law, the German Federal Supreme Court also noted that the risk of the remaining shareholders of being deprived of their rights also cannot be eliminated by merely postulating a duty of the company to inform the remaining shareholders of the arbitration proceedings, as this information alone cannot guarantee that the remaining shareholders would be able to participate in the selection and appointment of the arbitrators and at least join the proceedings as intervening parties.

In its reasoning in the present case, the Austrian Supreme Court sided with the arguments of the German Federal Supreme Court: It held that in order to preserve the principles of a fair trial within the meaning of Art 6 of the European Convention on Human Rights (ECHR), the shareholders must be involved in the arbitration proceedings to a sufficient extent and in good time and be given the opportunity to exercise their rights and interests already at the stage of the formation of the arbitral tribunal. In particular, the court held that all shareholders must be involved in the arbitration proceedings in such a timely manner allowing them to participate in the selection of the arbitrators and the constitution of the arbitral tribunal. Moreover, these participation and involvement rights of all shareholders have to be enshrined already *ex ante*, *i.e.*, stipulated *in the arbitration agreement* itself.

According to the Austrian Supreme Court's opinion, the procedural rights of the shareholders, thus, have to be guaranteed by the appropriate drafting of the arbitration agreement and cannot be left to the actual organization of the arbitration proceedings. The court also explicitly held that, in order to safeguard the rights of all shareholders with regard to the composition of the

BGH, Apr 6, 2017, docket no. I ZB 23/16 (Germany) ("*Schiedsfähigkeit III*"); BGH, Sep 23, 2021, docket no. I ZB 13/21 (Germany) ("*Schiedsfähigkeit IV*").

arbitral tribunal, it is not sufficient that the parties are free to agree on a new constitution of the arbitral tribunal if the shareholder joining the proceedings does not accept the already constituted arbitral tribunal; nor would it mean a sufficient participation in the selection of the arbitrators and constitution of the arbitral tribunal if the joining shareholders were to be granted a (mere) right to challenge the (already appointed) arbitrators in application of Section 589 ACCP (by analogy). The objective arbitrability of the dispute must be assessed on the basis of the arbitration agreement and cannot be decided subsequently on a case-by-case basis depending on the procedural arrangements of the parties and the arbitral tribunal in the specific arbitration proceedings.

The court further outlined its reasons for qualifying the issue of insufficient wording of the arbitration agreement as a problem of objective arbitrability, closely following the arguments put forward especially by *Zeiler*.[8]) The starting point for the Austrian Supreme Court in its assessment of the objective arbitrability, *i.e.*, the question of whether a certain matter can be effectively brought before an arbitral tribunal, is the claim in question. Such assessment is, therefore, of a "claim-related nature". Further, the Austrian Supreme Court holds that the legislator has set limits to the ability of the parties to settle disputes between them in arbitration proceedings; some areas of law are generally excluded from the scope of an arbitration agreement, or a claim may be arbitrable only subject to the fulfillment of certain "conditions" or "prerequisites" (*Kautelen*). This means that in some cases the state will "give up its monopoly" on jurisdiction only subject to the fulfillment of certain conditions. In the Austrian Supreme Court's view, this shall also apply with regard to the arbitrability of corporate disputes. A precondition for the arbitrability of corporate disputes is in the court's view the extension of the binding nature of the arbitral award on all shareholders. An arbitration award that does not have the effect of a legally binding court judgment on all shareholders, due to the lack of party status of the non-participating shareholders, cannot, in the view of the Austrian Supreme Court, fulfill the "peace function" (*Friedensfunktion*) assigned to it. Only the participation of all shareholders in the proceedings can prevent that differing decisions regarding the same subject matter will be issued, leading to an unmanageable fragmentation of the legal relationships within the partnership. Therefore, in the court's view, the state's monopoly on jurisdiction with regard to disputes over defective shareholder resolutions can only be given up in so far as the structure of the arbitration proceedings – starting with the structure of the arbitration agreement – ensures that the conflict within the company is resolved in a uniform way by extending the binding effect of the arbitration award to all shareholders. In order to ensure this, appropriate "prerequisites" must be provided for. The question of whether a corporate law claim is

[8]) *See Gerold Zeiler, Zur Schiedsfähigkeit von gesellschaftsrechtlichen Beschlussmängelstreitigkeiten*, RdW 392 (2023).

objectively arbitrable is, in the court's view, therefore, closely linked to the binding effect of the award and cannot be answered separately from the binding effects of the arbitral award and the structure of the arbitration agreement which determines it. Even though, in principle, corporate disputes are objectively arbitrable, a specific claim may lack objective arbitrability because the arbitration award – due to the lack of fulfillment of the minimum requirements to ensure the shareholders' participation and participation rights – could not achieve the binding effect on all shareholders, although the subject matter of the dispute requires this. The court, therefore, sees the extension of the binding effect of the award (also) as a problem of objective arbitrability. The claim to challenge a shareholder resolution of a partnership is, thus, only objectively arbitrable if the arbitral award rendered in such proceedings can achieve a binding effect on all shareholders. In the case of disputes over defective shareholder resolutions, this is only the case if the shareholders who were not involved in the arbitration proceedings as parties are guaranteed the same legal protection as in state proceedings. In order to achieve this, however, the arbitration agreement must be drafted accordingly, otherwise, the dispute lacks objective arbitrability.

Since the arbitration agreement in the present case did not fulfill the above requirements, the Austrian Supreme Court concluded that the present dispute was not objectively arbitrable and set-aside the award rendered by the arbitral tribunal in the present proceedings.

III. Key Implications for the Arbitration and Corporate Practice

The present decision of the Austrian Supreme Court has far-reaching implications both on the arbitration as well as on the corporate practice. Some of the most relevant aspects to be considered will be addressed below.

A. Review of Existing Arbitration Clauses

The decision of the Austrian Supreme Court requires a review – and possibly amendment – of existing arbitration agreements applying to shareholder disputes concerning defective shareholder resolutions in statutes or articles of association of corporations, partnerships, and other entities, which provide for a seat of the arbitral tribunal in Austria and, thus, are subject to the Austrian *lex arbitri*. It is to be assumed that most of the (standard) arbitration clauses as contained in statutes and articles of association, which generally also include disputes between the shareholders and the company regarding defective shareholder resolutions, may not meet the new requirements established by the recent decision of the Austrian Supreme Court.

In this regard, it shall be noted that, even though the Austrian Supreme Court's decision related to a challenge of shareholder resolutions in a limited partnership, the new standards for arbitration agreements will have to be met by all companies to which similar rules regarding claims for challenging shareholder resolutions apply, stipulating that only the company (and not all other remaining shareholders) shall act as respondent in the proceedings, either by applicable law or by way of a respective agreement in the articles of association of the respective company. By virtue of applicable law, this specifically relates to limited liability companies (*GmbH*), stock corporations (*Aktiengesellschaften*), flexible companies (*FlexCo*) and cooperative societies (*Genossenschaften*).[9]) Whether the requirements shall also apply to Austrian Private Foundations (*Privatstiftung*), is in discussion.[10]) Furthermore, the respective requirements for arbitration clauses will also apply to any other companies, such as, *e.g.*, (limited) partnerships, if the article of associations of these companies foresee that claims in connection with the validity of shareholder resolutions shall be directed (only) against the company (and not against the remaining shareholders), *e.g.*, by way of referring to the application of rules pertaining to corporations (as in the present case that was decided by the Austrian Supreme Court).

The amendment of arbitration clauses providing for respective disputes to be resolved in an *ad hoc* arbitration will require very careful and specific drafting, considering that any inaccuracy or incompleteness of the clause will pose a risk of the award rendered in such *ad hoc* arbitration proceedings being set aside by the Austrian Supreme Court. When drafting an amendment to an arbitration agreement or a new arbitration agreement, practitioners may seek guidance from the new Model Arbitration Clause for Articles of Association published by VIAC following the decision of the Austrian Supreme Court.[11])

Alternatively, the shareholders of companies, whose articles of association provide for dispute resolution in an *ad hoc* arbitration proceeding, may choose to opt for the application of the Vienna Rules instead, and include the new Model Arbitration Clause for Articles of Association in their articles of association. Considering that the amendment of the Vienna Rules and the new Model Clause for Articles of Association has been drafted by a specialized working group convened by VIAC, which was comprised of experts from both academia and practice, in order to ensure that they reflect the new prerequisites

---

[9]) *See* OGH Jun 26, 2014, docket no. 6 Ob 84/14t (Austria).

[10]) *See Brian Gabriel-Oiwoh & Philipp Peters, The Crystal Standard: Quo Vadis for the Arbitrability of Corporate Disputes in Austria?* Kluwer Arbitration Blog, Sept 9, 2024 (https://arbitrationblog.kluwerarbitration.com/2024/09/09/the-crystal-standard-quo-vadis-for-the-arbitrability-of-corporate-disputes-in-austria/) (last accessed on January 20, 2025).

[11]) *See* in more detail Section IV. below.

outlined by the Austrian Supreme Court,[12]) choosing arbitration under the Vienna Rules may, for shareholders wishing to resolve their disputes through arbitration, be the most efficient and safe way forward.

B. Practical Implications for Pending Shareholder Disputes and Previously Issued Awards

The decision of the Austrian Supreme Court also creates an imminent risk of setting-aside of any awards rendered in pending shareholder disputes regarding the validity of shareholder resolutions, if the arbitration proceedings are based on an arbitration agreement which does not fulfill the new criteria stipulated by the Austrian Supreme Court (which, as mentioned above, will likely be the case in most shareholder disputes).

In this respect, it shall especially be noted that the risk of setting aside of the award due to a deficient arbitration agreement is imminent in such proceedings irrespective of how diligently the arbitration proceedings had been conducted by the parties and the arbitral tribunal: According to the decision of the Austrian Supreme Court, the objective arbitrability of the claim depends on the wording of the respective arbitration agreement and, as explicitly stated by the court, it is, therefore, not sufficient if the remaining shareholders were merely granted the respective rights to participate in the proceedings and the constitution of the arbitral tribunal in the course of the proceedings. Based on the reasoning of the Austrian Supreme Court, this would, therefore, mean that an arbitral award issued in proceedings, which were initiated on the basis of a deficient arbitration clause which does not fulfill the new standards set out by the court, could be set aside by the Austrian Supreme Court even if the rights of all (remaining) shareholders were in fact respected in the course of the proceedings.

Furthermore, parties of such proceedings also have to bear in mind that the lack of objective arbitrability of the subject matter of the proceedings must be considered by the Austrian Supreme Court in a setting aside proceedings not only upon the assertion of a party, but also *ex officio* (Section 611 paragraph 3 ACCP). The lack of objective arbitrability also cannot be healed in the proceedings, nor waived by the parties, and does not require a respective objection by the parties to be considered by the arbitral tribunal or the Austrian Supreme Court in its decision.

In addition, according to Section 613 ACCP, the lack of objective arbitrability also is to be considered by courts and administrative authorities in other proceedings, *e.g.*, in enforcement proceedings or by the commercial courts in connection with applications for the registration of certain changes

[12]) Available for download on the VIAC homepage (https://www.viac.eu/en/arbitration/rules-of-arbitration-and-mediation). *See* in more detail Section IV. below.

in the business registry (*e.g.*, for changes of the articles of association including changes regarding the registered capital), which is especially relevant in connection with shareholder resolutions on subject matters which for becoming legally effective require a registration in the business registry. This applies even if an action to set aside the respective award was not brought before the Austrian Supreme Court and the respective deadline for challenging the award (three months from the date of receipt of the award) had already expired. The provision under Section 613 ACCP shall ensure that arbitral awards that are defective due to the lack of arbitrability are not subject to enforcement or otherwise afforded any legal effect in other court or administrative proceedings.[13])

C. Other Consequences and Remaining Questions

The decision of the Austrian Supreme Court raises further questions, which – although they have not all been explicitly addressed by the court – will be relevant for the arbitration and corporate practice.

In connection with the amendment of the respective arbitration agreement in the articles of association, the question arises whether the amendment of the clause, in order to adapt it to the requirements outlined by the recent decision of the Austrian Supreme Court, requires the consent of all shareholders. According to case law, the inclusion of an arbitration agreement in the articles of association shall require the consent of all shareholders. However, it is disputed whether the requirement of consent of all shareholders applies also in a case, in which the shareholders had already in the past submitted to arbitration (*i.e.*, in principle) and (only) agree on an amendment of an existing arbitration clause to include additional rules, which actually serve to protect their interests and rights in the arbitration proceedings. Based on these arguments, *Trenker* argues that the amendment of the arbitration clause, only to adapt it to the new requirements set out by the Austrian Supreme Court, shall not require the consent of all shareholders, but only a shareholder resolution under the general principles with the quorum generally applicable to changes of articles of association (*e.g.*, the statutory quorum, *i.e.*, three quarters, according to Section 50 LLCA for limited liability companies, or an otherwise agreed quorum in the articles of association).[14])

Another question that is relevant and to be considered by practitioners when drafting amendments to existing arbitration agreements (as well as when drafting new arbitration agreements not previously included in the articles of association or the statutes) is the applicability of the consumer protection

---

[13]) *See Stefan Riegler*, Section 611, in ARBITRATION LAW OF AUSTRIA: PRACTICE AND PROCEDURE (*Riegler* et al., 2007) at mn 79.

[14]) *See Martin Trenker*, *Schiedsfähigkeit von Beschlussmängelstreitigkeiten nach 18 OCg 3/22y*, NZ 87 (2024) at page 303.

provision of Section 617 of ACCP to arbitration agreements. The respective provision of the ACCP, which entered into force on 1 July 2006 and applies to arbitration agreements concluded after that date providing for a seat of the arbitral tribunal in Austria, outlines additional requirements for arbitration clauses concluded between entrepreneurs, on one hand, and consumers, on the other hand, and stipulates *inter alia* that arbitration agreements between entrepreneurs and consumers may only validly be concluded for disputes that have already arisen. In a landmark decision rendered in 2013, the Austrian Supreme Court held that Section 617 ACCP also applies to disputes relating to "corporative matters" (*aus dem Gesellschaftsverhältnis*)[15]) and that shareholders of a company may also qualify as consumers (depending on whether the respective shareholder can exert a controlling influence on the management of the company). As a consequence, the requirements of Section 617 ACCP may also apply to arbitration agreements in articles of association or statutes, if only a single shareholder qualifies as a consumer. However, in this regard, it shall be considered that Section 617 only applies if the seat of the arbitral tribunal is in Austria. Some authors,[16]) therefore, suggest, as a solution to avoid the application of Section 617, which would only allow the conclusion of an arbitration agreement after the dispute had arisen (and, thus, render general arbitration clauses extending to all future disputes invalid), to foresee that the seat of the arbitral tribunal shall be outside of Austria (*e.g.*, in Germany or Switzerland, which do not contain similarly strict consumer protection provisions with regard to arbitration agreements). Furthermore, with regard to the necessary amendment of the already existing arbitration agreements, only with the purpose to adapt it to the requirements outlined by the recent decision of the Austrian Supreme Court, one could argue that Section 617 ACCP shall not apply, since the adaption of the clause only constitutes an amendment of an already existing arbitration agreement concluded before 1 July 2006, and not the conclusion of a new arbitration agreement. However, this question has not been addressed by the court in its recent decision. It, therefore, remains to be seen whether such interpretation would be accepted by the Austrian Supreme Court.

Furthermore, it is to be noted that the reasoning of the Austrian Supreme Court which links the objective arbitrability to the wording of the arbitration agreement has also received critical reception in the Austrian literature and

---

[15]) *See* OGH Dec 16, 2013, docket no. 6 Ob 43/13m (Austria) (with further references to the case law regarding the qualification of a shareholder as a consumer); *see also Markus Schifferl* & *Venus Valentina Wong*, *Decisions of the Austrian Supreme Court on Arbitration in 2013 and 2014*, in AUSTRIAN YEARBOOK ON INTERNATIONAL ARBITRATION 2015, 335 (*Klausegger* et al. eds., 2015) with the report on the respective decision of the Austrian Supreme Court under Section V. (at page 348 *et seqq*.).

[16]) *See, e.g., Andreas Reiner, Rechtssicherheit für gesellschaftsrechtliche Schiedsverfahren – auch ohne Korrektur des § 617 ZPO durch den Gesetzgeber,* GesRZ 101 (2019), at page 104.

raises additional issues which will need further clarification. In this regard, it has in particular been criticized that the objective arbitrability depends on the wording of the arbitration agreement and, if the arbitration agreement does not fulfill the requirements set out by the Austrian Supreme Court, the subject matter would also lack objective arbitrability, even if all shareholders were, in fact, granted sufficient rights to participate in the proceedings and the constitution of the arbitral tribunal. According to *Koller*, in such cases, it would constitute an "excessive formalism" if one would require that a new arbitration agreement shall be concluded.[17])

A similar problem also arises in the reverse situation: In its reasoning, the Austrian Supreme Court also held that the objective arbitrability of such corporate disputes depends on the extension of the binding effect of the award to all shareholders; in other words, this would mean that if the binding effect of the award cannot be extended to all shareholders, the subject matter would lack objective arbitrability. If one strictly follows the reasoning of the Austrian Supreme Court, this would lead to the conclusion that even if the wording of the arbitration agreement fulfills the criteria set out by the court, but the shareholders were (contrary to the wording of the arbitration agreement) not granted the respective rights in the proceedings, the award issued in such proceedings could be set aside due to the lack of objective arbitrability, since, in such cases, the binding effect of the award cannot be extended to all shareholders. As mentioned above, the lack of objective arbitrability is an *ex officio* ground for setting aside the award, does not require an objection of the parties, cannot be healed in the proceedings and must also be considered by other courts and authorities in other proceedings (such as, *e.g.*, enforcement proceedings or registrations in the business register). As a result, such an award could, therefore, be set aside or deemed irrelevant by other courts or authorities, even if none of the parties or the remaining shareholders raise any objections against the award nor challenge the award in a setting-aside proceeding.

Finally, it shall be noted that the court also did not answer the question whether it is permissible to agree in the statutes of partnerships that an action challenging the validity of shareholder resolutions shall be brought only against the company (and not against all other shareholders, which would otherwise be the case). To date, there is no case law of the Austrian Supreme Court regarding the admissibility of such agreements.[18]) The Austrian Supreme Court left this question open also in its recent decision and, unfortunately, did not bring clarification to this issue, which is highly relevant both in arbitration and state court proceedings, considering that the validity of such an agreement

[17]) *See Christian Koller, Zur (mangelnden) objektiven Schiedsfähigkeit von Beschlussmängelstreitigkeiten bei Personengesellschaften*, ecolex 337 (2024).

[18]) For arguments regarding the admissibility of such agreements, *see, e.g., Paul Oberhammer, Die OGH im Zivilprozeß* 350 *et seqq.* (1997).

is decisive for the question which party (the company itself or all remaining shareholders) has a standing to be sued in such proceedings.

IV. New Supplementary Rules for Corporate Disputes and Model Arbitration Clause for Articles of Association for Arbitral Proceedings under the Vienna Rules

Following the decision of the Supreme Court, the Vienna International Arbitral Centre (VIAC) has convened a specialized working group comprised of experts from both academia and practice, including VIAC Vice President Franz Schwarz, Prof. Christian Koller and Prof. Paul Oberhammer, to draft an amendment to the VIAC Rules of Arbitration and Mediation 2021 (Vienna Rules), ensuring they reflect the prerequisites outlined by the Austrian Supreme Court, including the proper involvement of all shareholders in the formation of the arbitral tribunal and throughout the arbitration proceedings.[19])

The work of the expert group resulted in VIAC issuing a new Annex 7 to the Vienna Rules setting out Supplementary Rules for Corporate Disputes (Supplementary Rules) and a new Model Arbitration Clause for Articles of Association.[20])

A. Supplementary Rules for Corporate Disputes[21])

The Supplementary Rules set out in Annex 7[22]) to the Vienna Rules shall apply if the parties have agreed on the application of the Vienna Rules, in particular through an arbitration clause contained in articles of association. The Supplementary Rules shall apply only to corporate disputes in which the binding effect of the arbitral award is intended to extend to shareholders or the company itself, even if they are not named as parties to the arbitration, such as, in particular, disputes concerning shareholder resolutions, including disputes concerning their contestability, defectiveness or nullity, unless otherwise agreed (Article 1 paragraph 1).

---

[19]) *See* https://www.viac.eu/de/news/austrian-supreme-court-decision-prompts-viac-to-amend-vienna-rules-for-arbitration-agreements (last accessed on January, 15 2025).

[20]) Available for download on the VIAC homepage (https://www.viac.eu/en/arbitration/rules-of-arbitration-and-mediation).

[21]) References to Articles in this section without further specification refer to the relevant Articles of the Annex 7 to the Vienna Rules (Supplementary Rules for Corporate Disputes).

[22]) The Annexes are an integral part of the Vienna Rules (Vienna Rules, Part III Annexes to the Rules of Arbitration and Mediation, Footnote 1).

1. Information of the Affected Entities

The Supplementary Rules contain detailed provisions ensuring that all persons or companies to whom the binding effects of the arbitral award shall extend to (so-called "affected entities"), either by virtue of the nature of the legal relationship in dispute or by virtue of statutory provisions, are informed about the commencement (and, upon their request, about the further progress) of the arbitral proceedings in a timely manner and are granted the right to join the arbitral proceedings.

According to Article 2 paragraph 1, the claimant shall include in its statement of claim the full names and contact details of the affected entities ("named affected entities"). In such case, the Secretary General shall then transmit the statement of claim not only to the respondent, but also to the affected entities named by the claimant (Article 2 paragraph 3). In this regard, the claimant is required to submit additional hard copies (including exhibits) of the statement of claim in the number of copies necessary to provide each named affected entity with a copy (Article 2 paragraph 2).

In addition to the claimant, both the respondent (in its answer to the statement of claim) and the named affected entity (in its declaration to join) may name additional affected entities who were not already named by the claimant, stating their full names and contact details (Article 2 paragraph 4). The Secretary General shall then transmit the statement of claim (and the answer to the statement of claim, if applicable) also to the additional named affected entities (Article 2 paragraph 7). In order to ensure that sufficient copies of the statement of claim and answer to the statement of claim, respectively, are made available, the Secretary General may request the parties to submit within a time limit set by the Secretary General additional copies of the statement of claim respectively the answer to the statement of claim in hardcopy form for subsequently named affected entities, and, if the parties fail to do so, may declare the proceedings terminated (Article 2 paragraph 6).

In proceedings in which the company is the respondent (such as, *e.g.*, in disputes concerning shareholder resolutions in limited liability companies according to Section 42 LLCA), the above provisions regarding the naming of the affected entities are complemented by the obligation of the company to take every appropriate measure to ensure that all affected entities are included. In this regard, at the request of the Secretary General, the company shall provide information on the measures taken within a time limit set by the Secretary General (Article 2 paragraph 5). This rule is a welcomed clarification – considering that the applicable provisions of the LLCA in disputes concerning shareholder resolutions in limited liability companies do not explicitly impose an obligation on the company (acting as respondent in such proceedings) to ensure that all shareholders are adequately (and in a timely manner) informed about the commencement of the proceedings.[23]) The explicit provision included by VIAC in the new Supplementary Rules will, therefore, help to prevent guerilla tactics of the company acting as a respondent in such corporate disputes, which could, *e.g.*, by omitting (or refusing) to name additional shareholders of the company not already named by the claimant or by refusing to provide respective contact details of all shareholders in order to include them as affected entities in the respective proceedings, obstruct the proceedings and thereby prevent that the binding effect of the award extends to all shareholders, which could lead to an annulment of the award issued in such proceedings according to the recent ruling of the Austrian Supreme Court.

In order to enable the company to fulfill its obligation to take appropriate measures to ensure that all affected entities are included, it is recommended to include a provision in the articles of association stipulating that all shareholders are obliged to provide the company with a current postal and electronic address for service or the address of a representative for service, and that receipt of any written communication at such address will be deemed to have occurred after the expiry of a reasonable period of time.[24])

2. Possibility of the Affected Entities to Join the Arbitral Proceedings

Following the naming of the affected entities by the parties, the Secretary General shall request the named affected entity to submit a declaration to join the arbitral proceedings within 30 days of receipt of the statement of claim respectively answer to the statement of claim (Article 3 paragraph 1) and, in addition, inform these entities about their right to information pursuant to Article 8. The declaration to join shall be submitted to the Secretariat in electronic form and shall contain, apart from personal data and contact details of the affected entity, in particular, a declaration whether the affected entity wishes to join the proceedings on the side of the claimant or on the

[23]) The prevailing doctrine in Austria is in favor of such an obligation of the management of the company (by way of analogy) to inform the shareholders of the commencement of the proceedings. *See, e.g., Peter Klein, Arbitrability of Company Law Disputes*, in Austrian Arbitration Yearbook 2007, 29, 43 (*Klausegger* et al. eds., 2007)*; Martin Auer, Schiedsvereinbarungen bei der GmbH im Lichte des SchiedsRÄG 2005,* in Satzungsgestaltung in der gmbh – Möglichkeiten und Grenzen 123, 130 (*Kalss* & *Rüffler*, 2005); *Andreas Reiner, Schiedsverfahren und Gesellschaftsrecht,* GesRZ 151, 156 (2007); *Hans G. Koppensteiner* & *Friedrich Rüffler, GmbHG* § 42 para. 11 (3rd ed. 2007); *Wilfried Thöni, Drittschutz im aktien-, GmbH-rechtlichen Beschlußanfechtungsprozeß* GesRZ 55, 59 (1994).

[24]) *See also* the respective recommendation of the German Arbitration Institute (*Deutsche Institution für Schiedsgerichtsbarkeit* – DIS) in the Model Clause for Articles of Incorporation for Arbitrations Pursuant to the Supplementary Rules for Corporate Disputes (available at https://www.disarb.org/en/tools-for-dis-proceedings/dis-model-clauses) (last accessed on January 20, 2025).

side of the respondent and whether the affected entity wishes to join the proceedings as a *party* (*i.e.*, with full party status, *cf* Article 6 paragraph 1.1 Vienna Rules) or as an *intervening party* according to Article 5 (Article 3 paragraphs 2 and 3).

As already mentioned above, in its declaration to join the proceedings, the named affected entity may also name further affected entities that were not already named by the claimant (Article 2 paragraph 4). If a declaration to join lists additional named entities, the statement of claim and the answer to the statement of claim as well as a copy of the declaration to join naming them will be transmitted in hardcopy form to the newly named affected entity, with the request to submit a declaration to join within 30 days of receipt in accordance with Article 3 (Article 3 paragraph 4).

By submitting the declaration to join within the set time period, the named affected entity joins the proceedings ("joined affected entity") (Article 4 paragraph 1). The joinder of the affected entity as a *party* to the proceedings, however, requires the consent of the claimant and the respondent (Article 4 paragraph 2).

If a named affected entity does not submit its declaration to join within the set time period, it is deemed to have *waived the right to participate in the constitution of the arbitral tribunal*. The named affected entity, however, retains the option to join the arbitration proceedings as an intervening party according to Article 5 (Article 4 paragraph 4).

Pursuant to Article 5, the affected entities may join the proceeding as an intervening party at any time until its termination. The request to join as an intervening party must contain the information specified in Article 3 paragraph 3.1 (*i.e.*, the full name and contact details of the affected entity). The arbitral tribunal shall decide on such joinder pursuant to Article 14 paragraphs 1 and 2 Vienna Rules, however, taking into account that the named affected entity has the right to participate in the proceeding as an intervening party and that the discretion of the arbitral tribunal is limited in this respect (Article 5 paragraph 2). The explicit clarification included in the Supplementary Rules stating that the discretion of the arbitral tribunal is limited in such cases is in line with the case law of the Austrian Supreme Court, which held that the shareholders have a right to participate in the arbitration proceedings concerning disputes regarding shareholder resolutions as intervening parties and therefore, such intervention requests by the shareholders must be accepted by the arbitral tribunal and the arbitral tribunal does not have any discretion regarding the admissibility of such intervention.[25])

---

[25]) OGH, Dec 10, 1998, docket no. 7 Ob 221/98w (Austria) (The discretion of the arbitral tribunal regarding the admission of the intervention of the shareholders in such cases is "reduced to zero"); OGH, June 26, 2014, docket no. 6 Ob 84/14t (Austria); also referred to in the recent decision of the Supreme Court, OGH Apr 3, 2024, docket no. 18 OCg 3/22y (Austria) at mn 45.

Finally, with regard to such intervening parties, the Supplementary Rules provide that if the named affected entity joins the proceedings only after the time limit to submit the declaration to join according to Article 3 paragraph 1 has elapsed, this shall be deemed as (i) consent to the constituted arbitral tribunal, and (ii) acceptance of the proceeding as it stands at the time of joining (Article 4 paragraph 5).

Irrespective of whether the affected entities join the proceedings or not, they have a right to request information according to Article 8. Upon request, the arbitral tribunal shall inform the named affected entities of the status of the proceeding by transmitting to them the parties' or intervening parties' submissions as well as the arbitral tribunals' decisions and orders (Article 8 paragraph 1). In addition, the arbitral tribunal may also inform the affected entities about other aspects of the case file, if they have filed such a request and if the arbitral tribunal considers that this information may be relevant for the affected entities to exercise their right to participate in the proceedings as intervening parties (Article 8 paragraph 2).

3. Constitution of the Arbitral Tribunal

The *joined affected entities, i.e.,* the affected entities which have submitted a declaration to join the arbitration proceedings within the time period set by the Secretary General (Article 4 paragraph 1), have a right to participate in the constitution of the arbitral tribunal.

Article 6 of the Supplementary Rules sets out the procedural rules for the joint nomination of the arbitrators by the parties and the joined affected entities as follows:

- If the dispute is to be resolved by a sole arbitrator, the parties and the joined affected entities shall jointly nominate a sole arbitrator within 30 days after receiving the Secretary General's request; if such nomination is not made within this time period, the sole arbitrator shall be appointed by the Board (Article 6 paragraph 1).
- If the dispute is to be resolved by a panel of arbitrators, the parties and the joined affected entities on claimant's and respondent's side shall each jointly nominate an arbitrator. In such cases, the nomination of an arbitrator in the statement of claim or the answer to the statement of claim will only be considered as a non-binding proposal. The Secretary General shall request the parties and the joined affected entities on the claimant's and respondent's side to jointly nominate an arbitrator within 30 days after receiving the request (Article 6 paragraph 2).
- If a joint arbitrator is not nominated within this time period, the Board shall appoint the arbitrator for the defaulting party (or parties). In exceptional cases, after granting the parties the opportunity to comment, the Board may revoke appointments already made and appoint new co-

arbitrators or all arbitrators (Article 6 paragraph 2 Annex 7 and Article 18 paragraph 4 of the Vienna Rules).

The procedure for the joint appointment of the arbitrators foreseen in the new Supplementary Rules for Corporate Disputes is, thus, in principle identical with the general provisions regarding the constitution of the arbitral tribunal in multi-party proceedings set out in Article 18 of the Vienna Rules, with the difference that the *joined affected entities* have the right to participate in the constitution of the arbitral tribunal in any case (irrespective of the manner of joinder). For the purpose of the nomination of the arbitrators in disputes to be resolved by a panel of arbitrators, the party/parties on the claimant's side and the joined affected entities on the claimant's side form one group and have to nominate together the arbitrator for the claimant's side. The same applies for the party/parties on the respondent's side and the joined affected entities on the respondent's side. If either the claimant's or the respondent's side fails to nominate the arbitrator on time, the Board will appoint a substitute arbitrator – in general, only for the defaulting party (*i.e.*, the appointment of the arbitrator of the other, non-defaulting side remains unaffected). In exceptional cases, and after granting the parties the opportunity to comment, the Board may, however, decide to revoke also the appointments already made and to appoint new co-arbitrators or even all arbitrators including the chairman. This allows for flexibility to consider special circumstances of the case, in which the appointment could result in unequal treatment of the parties. This could, for example, be the case if deviating interests of several respondents, who are obliged to jointly nominate an arbitrator, exist, or if the affected entities only join on the respondent's side and the joinder leads to a result that the parties and the joining affected entities are unable to agree on a candidate.[26])

The declarations of the nominated arbitrators regarding their impartiality and independence, availability, qualification, acceptance of the office and submission to the Vienna Rules (Article 16 paragraph 3 Vienna Rules) as well as the disclosures regarding any circumstances that could give rise to doubts as to the arbitrator's impartiality, independence or availability or that conflict with the agreement of the parties (Article 16 paragraph 4 Vienna Rules) will be forwarded also to the joined affected entities, who may, if deemed necessary by the Board, be also requested to provide comments (Article 19 paragraph 1 and 2 Vienna Rules). The joined affected entities may also challenge arbitrators pursuant to Article 20 Vienna Rules (Article 6 paragraph 3 Annex 7).

In summary, under the new Supplementary Rules, the joined affected entities, *i.e.*, the affected entities which have submitted a declaration to join the arbitration proceedings within the time period set by the Secretary General, enjoy the same rights with regard to the constitution of the arbitral tribunal as

---

[26]) *See, e.g.*, examples in *Stefan Riegler & Filip Boras*, *VIAC Handbook* (2019) Article 18 mn 12 *et seqq.* (with regard to the appointment of arbitrators in multi-party proceedings).

the initial parties (the initial claimant and respondent) of the arbitration proceedings.

4. Concentration of Proceedings through Consolidation

The new Supplementary Rules also deal with the question of consolidation of two or more proceedings concerning the same shareholder resolution. Although this aspect has not been explicitly addressed in the recent decision of the Supreme Court,[27]) the respective judgments of the German Federal Supreme Court (*Bundesgerichtshof* – German Federal Supreme Court), which served the Supreme Court as model in its decision, stipulate as one of the requirements for the validity of arbitration clauses in corporate disputes regarding shareholder resolutions that it has to be ensured that all disputes concerning the validity of a shareholders' resolution and relating to the same subject matter are consolidated before the same arbitral tribunal.[28]) The new Supplementary Rules address the consolidation of proceedings, and, in connection therewith, the question of the constitution of the arbitral tribunal(s) in the consolidated proceedings, in Article 7.

According to Article 7 paragraph 1, two or more proceedings concerning the same resolution shall be consolidated by the Board at the request of a party, a joined affected entity or at the proposal of the Secretary General, applying Article 15 Vienna Rules *mutatis mutandis*. Contrary to the consolidation under Article 15, the consolidation is also admissible even if not all parties and joined affected entities agree.

If the request for consolidation is made prior to the confirmation of the nomination or the appointment of an arbitrator, the constitution of the arbitral tribunal shall be governed by Article 6. If the request for consolidation is made after the confirmation of the nomination or the appointment of an arbitrator, the proceedings shall be consolidated into the proceedings first commenced, unless the parties and joined affected entities agree otherwise. In this case, the Board may revoke arbitrator appointments already made and order the renewed constitution of the arbitral tribunal in accordance with the procedure set out in Article 6 (Article 7 paragraph 2).

5. Arbitral Award

One of the key elements of the new Supplementary Rules is the provision of Article 9 which addresses the extension of effects of the arbitral award issued

[27]) The reasoning of the Supreme Court focused mainly on the question of the right of the shareholders to participate in the proceedings and in the constitution of the arbitral tribunal (*see* OGH Apr 3, 2024, docket no. 18 OCg 3/22y [Austria] at mn 60 *et seqq.*).

[28]) BGH, Apr 6, 2009, docket no. II ZR 255/08 (Germany) ("*Schiedsfähigkeit II*") at mn 20 and 24.

in corporate dispute proceedings conducted under the new Supplementary Rules.

Apart from the parties, the arbitral award issued in such proceedings will be also transmitted to the joined affected entities and intervening parties of the proceedings (Article 9 paragraph 1).

Furthermore, according to Article 9 paragraph 2, the obligation to comply with the terms of the award (Article 36 paragraph 7 Vienna Rules) extends to *all affected entities named, and those invited to participate in the proceedings pursuant to Article 3 paragraph 1, irrespective of their actual participation.* The effects of an award issued in such proceedings shall, thus, extend to all affected entities which were named by the parties (or by other affected entities) and invited by the Secretary General to submit a declaration to join according to Article 3 paragraph 1, irrespective of whether these have actually joined the proceedings or not. Since these named affected entities were given the opportunity to participate in the proceedings, including the constitution of the arbitral tribunal, their right to be heard in the proceedings was respected, which justifies the extension of the effects of the award to these persons, irrespective of whether or not they actually exercised their right to be heard and participated in the proceedings.

6. Costs

Finally, the new Supplementary Rules also address additional aspects in connection with the costs of the proceedings.

Considering the various notifications and transmission of documents to the affected parties required under the new Supplementary Rules, it is to be expected that such proceedings will require a much higher administrative effort than proceedings administered under the general provisions of the Vienna Rules. In this regard, one has to especially bear in mind that a company acting as respondent in disputes regarding shareholder resolutions might have more than a hundred shareholders, which would all have to be named as affected entities in the proceedings, served with the respective documents (such as the statement of claim or the answer to the statement of claim, respectively, including all exhibits and declaration to join naming them as affected entities, if applicable) and informed by the Secretary General about their possibility to join the proceedings.

Against this background, Article 10 paragraph 1 stipulates that if the transmission costs prior to the transmission of the file exceed the registration fee due pursuant to Article 10 Vienna Rules, the claimant shall bear the actual costs incurred. In addition, the Secretary General may fix an advance on costs, at any time according to his own discretion, to cover the transmission expenses.

With regard to the calculation of procedural costs in accordance with Article 44 paragraph 4 Vienna Rules (which provides for an increase of the administrative fees and arbitrators' fees listed in Annex 3 in case of multi-party proceedings by 10 percent for each additional party up to a maximum increase of 50 percent), Article 10 paragraph 2 clarifies that for this purpose, all parties, joined affected entities and other intervening parties shall be considered as additional parties.

B. New Model Arbitration Clause for Articles of Association

In addition to the new Supplementary Rules, VIAC has also issued a new Model Arbitration Clause for Articles of Association (Model Clause), which may be included in the articles of association if the parties wish to agree on an arbitration clause with the intention of extending the binding effect of the arbitral award to shareholders or the company itself, even if they are not named as parties to the arbitration proceedings. The respective Model Clause reflects the prerequisites outlined by the Supreme Court in its recent decision, in particular regarding the proper involvement of all shareholders in the formation of the arbitral tribunal and throughout the arbitration proceedings. According to the recommendation of VIAC, the clause must be included in its entirety. This is conclusive, considering that the Supreme Court held in its recent decision that the respective rights of the shareholders to participate in the proceedings, including the constitution of the arbitral tribunal, must be included already in the arbitration clause itself as a prerequisite for the objective arbitrability of the dispute.[29]) Consequently, the Model Clause suggested by VIAC outlines the respective rights of the shareholders in connection with such arbitration proceedings (in line with the procedure foreseen in the Supplementary Rules) in the wording of the Model Clause itself.

[29]) OGH Apr 3, 2024, docket no. 18 OCg 3/22y (Austria), Section 2.4, in particular mn 67.

Chapter II

The Arbitrator and the Arbitration Procedure

Irene Welser/Samuel Farokhnia-Mimnagh/Daniel Dibon
Interim Relief and the Prima Facie Standard in Commercial Arbitrations

Nina Pichler/Maria Bejan
Halting the Clock
Different Aspects of Staying Proceedings in International Arbitration in Austria

Maximilian Menz/Marios Kourtis
Unlocking the Potential of Institutional Expedited Procedures

Nikolaus Pitkowitz/Johanna Kathan-Spath and the 22 contributors
The Vienna Propositions:
Setting a New Beat in Resolving ESG Disputes, Embracing Innovation, and Tackling Legal Challenges in a Changing World

Interim Relief and the Prima Facie Standard in Commercial Arbitrations

Irene Welser/Samuel Farokhnia-Mimnagh/Daniel Dibon

I. Introduction

It is a well-established prerequisite to obtain interim relief that the applicant party must show it has a prima facie case. This gives rise to the question whether the existence of a prima facie case on the part of the applicant automatically means that the opposing party cannot have a prima facie case of its own.

The situation becomes even trickier in case of claim and counterclaim as, in such a situation, both parties may be inclined to seek interim relief. For example, if both the claim and the counterclaim depend on the question whether a contract may be terminated, rescinded, avoided or declared void/voidable, can the prospect of success for the claim or counterclaim diminish the extent to which a party has a prima facie case when seeking interim relief? In other words, does the putting forward of a prima facie case by a counterclaimant automatically exclude a claimant's establishment of a prima facie case and the other way round? In addition, is the establishment of a prima facie case a question of fact or a question of law? These are the issues considered in this contribution.

II. In General: The Test for Provisional Measures

According to established doctrine, the general requirements for provisional measures are that the applicant must show:

a) a prima facie case on jurisdiction;
b) risk of serious or irreparable harm to the applicant;
c) urgency;
d) a prima facie case on the merits;
e) a balance of hardships weighing in its favour; and
f) no prejudgment of the merits.[1])

---

[1]) Chapter 17: Provisional Relief in International Arbitration (Updated December

In addition, the severity or gravity of the requested relief may elevate the threshold when establishing the elements for interim relief (*i.e.*, the degree to which a prima facie case must be established).[2]

III. The Prima Facie Case on the Merits Standard

The prima facie standard is a generally accepted element in the test for interim relief.[3] However, it may not be a mandatory standard.[4] *Born* suggests that even if a party does not establish a compelling prima facie case, or its prima facie case seems significantly weaker than that of the opposing party, then a tribunal may still (although it would be rare) grant interim relief.[5]

According to many civil procedure laws that apply in court litigation cases, prima facie is mainly a standard of (diminished) proof, *i.e.*, that facts do not have to be evidenced *beyond any doubt*, but only a certain degree of probability has to be attested. For example, in "ordinary" court proceedings that require a full degree of proof under Section 272 Austrian Civil Procedure Act, the judge, unless otherwise specified, is to assess, with careful consideration of the results of the entire proceedings and evidence, based on his free conviction, whether a factual statement is to be regarded as true or not. As a result, the judge has to be *fully convinced* whether a fact could, as a result of the evidence proceedings, be established or not, and if it could *not* be established, burden of proof rules apply.

2023), in *G. Born*, International Commercial Arbitration (3rd Edition) 2021, at §17.02.5[G][3][b].

[2]) Chapter 17: Provisional Relief in International Arbitration (Updated December 2023), in *G. Born*, International Commercial Arbitration (3rd Edition) 2021, at §17.02.5[G][3][b]; *see* also *PNG Sustainable Development Program Ltd. v. Independent State of Papua New Guinea* (Decision on a preliminary objection that a claim is manifestly without legal merit), ICSID Case No. ARB/13/33, October 28, 2014, Public Source Awards, Kluwer Law International at 115.

[3]) *See* Chartered Institute of Arbitrators, International Arbitration Practice Guideline: Applications for Interim Measures 5–6 (2015), Article 2.1.ii); *see* also *M. Grando*, The Coming of Age of Interim Relief in International Arbitration: A Report from the 28th Annual ITA Workshop (July 20, 2016) Kluwer Arbitration Blog.

[4]) *A. Yesilirmak*, Provisional Measures in International Commercial Arbitration, International Arbitration Law Library, Volume 12 (2005), at 5.28, p. 177; the author only says that it "*may be necessary*". Conversely, in Chapter 8: Preliminary, Interim and Dispositive Determinations, in *J. Waincymer*, Procedure and Evidence in International Arbitration (2012) at 626, it is suggested that the "*reasonable possibility*" of success is a threshold requirement.

[5]) Chapter 17: Provisional Relief in International Arbitration (Updated December 2023), in *G. Born*, International Commercial Arbitration (3rd Edition) 2021, at §17.02.5[G][3][b][iv].

Even in ordinary court proceedings, one of the means of easing the burden of proof is prima facie evidence (so called presumptive evidence), which is primarily applied in tort law, in particular when there is a typical, formulaic connection between a proven fact and another fact that is necessary to establish an element of the statutory offense. Reliance on prima facie evidence, in such cases, leads to a reduction of the standard of proof.

While the standard of proof under the Austrian Civil Procedure Act is high probability or, in fact, full conviction of the judge, in contrast, for prima facie evidence, the *preponderance* of the evidence ("preponderant reasons") is sufficient.[6]) A respondent would then have to raise serious doubts by refuting the presumptive evidence against its case.

This standard of full conviction of the judge is, just like before arbitral tribunals that are to grant interim relief, also lowered in preliminary injunction proceedings before the court, where facts do not have to be *fully proven*, but only to be *attested by immediately available means of certification*, also known as "prima facie evidence".

According to Section 389 Austrian Enforcement Act, when applying for the issuance of an interim injunction before an ordinary court, the applicant party must provide a truthful and detailed presentation of the facts supporting the application and attach the necessary certification in documentary form or other readily available evidence. Prima facie evidence is therefore, under Austrian law and many other civil procedure rules, a question of proof of facts and not a question of probability of success.

International arbitration practice seems to take a different view: Prima facie is often described as "*fumus boni iuris*" and includes a rough legal evaluation of whether the applicant party is – at least to some degree – likely to succeed also on legal issues.

Some academics argue that, in granting interim measures, the tribunal must first assess whether the asserted claim has a reasonable chance of success.[7]) Others say that the basic requirement is to satisfy the tribunal that "*the moving party has, with reasonable probability, a case or, alternatively, to determine that the claim is not frivolous or vexatious*".[8]) "*An arbitral tribunal should make an 'overall assessment of the merits of the case' in question in order to determine whether the moving party's case is 'sufficiently strong to merit protection*'". The requesting party is also required to provide prima facie

[6]) *Brenn* in *Fasching/Konecny*³ II/3 § 178 ZPO mnr 30.

[7]) *I. Welser,* Lahmlegung des Geschäftsbetriebs durch schiedsgerichtliche einstweilige Verfügungen, in FS Reich-Rohrwig (2014), p. 343; *M. Nueber*, Einstweilige Maßnahmen eines Schiedsgerichts, in *Czernich/Deixler-Hübner/Schauer*, Handbuch Schiedsrecht (2018), p. 434 mnr 12.9; *G. Zeiler* in *Liebscher/Oberhammer/Rechberger*, Schiedsverfahrensrecht I mnr 7/41.

[8]) *A. Yesilirmak*, Provisional Measures in International Commercial Arbitration, International Arbitration Law Library, Volume 12 (2005), at 5.28, p. 177–178.

evidence that its claim is justified on the merits.[9]) This is, maybe, owed to the fact that "*iura novit curia*" is not the generally accepted principle in international arbitration, but that the parties must also prove the law. Some argue that this means, in order for a preliminary injunction to be successful before an arbitral tribunal, there must be "*a reasonable possibility on a prima facie basis that the requesting party will succeed on the merits of the claim*".[10]) Others say there must be a realistic possibility that the requesting party will prevail on the merits.[11]) This implies that the applicant party may prove a prima facie case of success, even if the responding party has credible defenses against the claims.[12])

Waincymer suggests that the standard is flexible and requires "*something akin to a prima facie successful or at least tenable case on the merits*".[13])

The UNCITRAL Model Law and the UNCITRAL Arbitration Rules 2021 both stipulate that interim measures require a party to show that "*there is a reasonable possibility that the requesting party will succeed on the merits of the claim*".[14]) *Petrochilos* argues that this can be best described as an affirmative requirement that the applicant party must demonstrate a prima facie good case in order to meet the threshold for interim relief.[15]) He also states that the strength of the case that must be demonstrated requires judgment based on the circumstances of each case, especially in light of the specific interim measure being sought: "*The more far-reaching the measure, the higher the threshold will be*".[16])

The LCIA User's Guide chapter on interim measures suggests that the UNCITRAL standard can "*serve as a basis for commonly accepted requirements*".[17])

---

[9]) *S. Pfisterer* and *A. Schnyder*, International Arbitration in Switzerland, Volume 2 (2023), at § 27 3. b).

[10]) *D. Girsberger* and *N. Voss*, International Arbitration, 4th Extended Edition (2021), mnr 1089; *see also A. Rab*, Interim Measures in International Commercial Arbitration: A Comparative Review of the Indian Experience (2022), p. 215.

[11]) *C. Jermini/L. Castiglioni*, Vorsorgliche Massnahmen im Bereich der Schiedsgerichtsbarkeit (2023), p. 228.

[12]) *J. Sanchez*, Applying the Model Law's Standard for Interim Measures in International Arbitration, Volume 37 (2020), Journal of International Arbitration, p. 75.

[13]) Chapter 8: Preliminary, Interim and Dispositive Determinations, in *J. Waincymer*, Procedure and Evidence in International Arbitration (2012) at 632.

[14]) UNCITRAL Model Law, Article 17A(1)(b); UNCITRAL Arbitration Rules 2021, Article 26(3)(b).

[15]) *G. Petrochilos*, "Interim Measures under the Revised UNCITRAL Arbitration Rules", ASA Bulletin, (2010) Vol 28, Issue 4, p. 881.

[16]) *G. Petrochilos*, "Interim Measures under the Revised UNCITRAL Arbitration Rules", ASA Bulletin, (2010) Vol 28, Issue 4, p. 882.

[17]) *M. Scherer*, Chapter 19: Interim and Conservatory Measures, in *M. Scherer, L. Richman, et al.*, Arbitrating under the 2020 LCIA Rules: A User's Guide (2021) at 23.

Other academics interpret the UNCITRAL standard as being equivalent to needing to show "*a reasonable chance of succeeding on the merits*",[18]) although it is simultaneously noted that this requirement "*must not be overstretched*". It is also argued that arbitrators should not set the bar too high and that, depending on how complex the case is, it may be better to approach the question from the perspective whether "*it is clear that the underlying claim is not groundless on the merits*".[19]) This, however, in the opinion of the authors, seems to be a rather low hurdle that could make it too easy to be awarded interim relief in international arbitration.

Ultimately, there is variance in the standard applied by tribunals when determining whether a party has met the threshold of a prima facie case.[20]) The LCIA User's Guide (written by academics) suggests that "*the more far-reaching the requested interim measure is, the higher the threshold for the prima facie case should be*".[21])

To sum it up, the prima facie case as seen as a prerequisite for interim measures in arbitration is not limited to (a reduced degree of) evidence on facts, but also includes *legal issues*, including some probability of winning the case on the merits.

IV. How Comprehensively Do the Facts Need to be Assessed in order to Reach Legal Conclusions?

While the arbitral tribunal may consider the legal sufficiency and respective strengths of the parties' cases, this assessment must only be performed on a prima facie basis without a detailed assessment of the merits.[22]) ICSID arbitral awards indicate that a party may only need to show "*a reasonable case* [...] *which, if the facts alleged are proven, might possibly lead the*

[18]) *L. Beisteiner*, Chapter 5: Provisional Measures Specific to Construction Arbitration: Focus on the Austrian Legal Framework and Jurisprudence, in *C. Baltag* and *C. Vasile* (eds), Construction Arbitration in Central and Eastern Europe: Contemporary Issues (2019) at 71; the author cites *G. Zeiler* in *Liebscher/Oberhammer/Rechberger*, Schiedsverfahrensrecht I (2016), para 7/58 for this proposition.

[19]) Article 22: Interim Measures of Protection, in *F. Schwarz* and *C. Konrad*, The Vienna Rules: A Commentary on International Arbitration in Austria (2009) at 22-069. For this case, they actually relied on the Dutch award (NAI Case 1694) addressed in the body of this contribution.

[20]) *M. Scherer*, Chapter 19: Interim and Conservatory Measures, in *M. Scherer*, *L. Richman*, et al., Arbitrating under the 2020 LCIA Rules: A User's Guide (2021) at 29.

[21]) *Eadem*.

[22]) *A. Yesilirmak*, Provisional Measures in International Commercial Arbitration, International Arbitration Law Library, Volume 12 (2005), at 5.29, pp. 177–178.

Tribunal to the conclusion that an award could be made in favour of Claimants".[23])

In fact, *Born* argues that this is a "*very limited prima facie inquiry*" and that it is a rare case where a party fails to advance a plausible basis for a prima facie case.[24]) This approach is also reflected in the ICSID case *Paushok v Mongolia*, where the tribunal adopted the standard that "*the Tribunal needs to decide only that the claims made are not, on their face, frivolous or obviously outside the competence of the Tribunal"*.[25]) This suggests a very high bar to deny the existence of a prima facie case.

In an ICSID arbitration (chaired by *Born*), the Tribunal found that "*in practice, the requirement to demonstrate the prima facie success on the merits will ordinarily lead to a rejection of a request for provisional measures only in rare circumstances, where the requesting party has failed to advance any credible basis for its claims"*.[26]) Furthermore, "*it is essential, in this regard, that a tribunal not pre-judge, either consciously or unconsciously, the resolution of any aspect of the parties' respective claims and defenses"*.[27])

This standard is not applied universally, however. The CIArb Practice Guideline on Applications for Interim Measures[28]) (the "CIArb Guideline") confirms that a prima facie case on the merits should be shown for a successful request for provisional measures. However, in the explanatory note, the guideline suggests that a requesting party must only show "*a reasonably arguable case*" that "*on a very preliminary review of the applicant's case* [...] *has a probability of succeeding on the merits of its claim*". This suggests that some test on the balance of probabilities must be undertaken as to the strength of an applicant's case. This is also supported by the practice by some SCC tribunals, which require the applicant to show their case appears *more likely to succeed* than that of the responding party.[29]) The guideline does state that the tribunal must not prejudge the merits, but it is difficult to see how determining a

---

[23]) *Sergei Paushok et al. v. Government of Mongolia*, UNCITRAL, Order on Interim Measures, September 2, 2008 at 55; and *C. Mouawad* and *E. Silbert*, A Guide to Interim Measures in Investor-State Arbitration, in W. Park (ed), Arbitration International, Oxford University Press 2013, Volume 29, Issue 3, pp. 381–434 at 399.

[24]) Chapter 17: Provisional Relief in International Arbitration (Updated December 2023), in *G. Born*, International Commercial Arbitration (3rd Edition) 2021, at §17.02.5[G][3][b][iv].

[25]) *Sergei Paushok et al. v. Government of Mongolia*, UNCITRAL, Order on Interim Measures, September 2, 2008 at 55.

[26]) *PNG Sustainable Development Program Ltd. v. Independent State of Papua New Guinea*, (Decision on a preliminary objection that a claim is manifestly without legal merit), ICSID Case No. ARB/13/33, October 28, 2014 at 120.

[27]) *Ibidem*, at 121.

[28]) Chartered Institute of Arbitrators, International Arbitration Practice Guideline: Applications for Interim Measures 5–6 (2015), article 2.

[29]) *A. Havedal Ipp*, SCC Practice Note: Emergency Arbitrator Decisions Rendered 2015–2016 at 18.

probability of succeeding does not involve some testing of the applicant's case (including against any defenses).

As mentioned, Article 2(3) of the CIArb Guideline states arbitrators should not prejudge a case. While the explanatory note does not assist in determining how this is avoided, it does state: "*Where arbitrators consider that the interim measure cannot be granted without making a decision on the merits of the case as a whole, they may refrain from granting such a measure*".[30])

In *Constellation Overseas Ltd. v. Alperton Capital Ltd., ICC Case No. 23856/MK*[31]) an ICC tribunal considered the question whether provisional measures should be granted. The case concerned a dispute over which one party owned certain shares in a Brazilian drilling (for oil) company. On the topic of the prima facie case on the merits, the tribunal said the respondent had made out a "*reasonable probability of success in proving ownership of the* [shares]" and "*a prima facie valid claim*" concerning other relevant facts about a contested board meeting existed.[32])

It is not clear whether the tribunal required the respondent to establish a "*reasonable probability of success standard*" or the, presumably, lower "*prima facie valid claim*". This ICC award does show that the tribunal engaged in a review of the facts available to it.[33]) The parties also made detailed factual submissions on the prima facie standard and these were weighed against each other. The tribunal did explicitly note that some issues did not need to be considered entirely at this preliminary stage and that its assessment did not prejudge the merits. It is also noted that the claimant in this case was entering voluntary insolvency proceedings, so there was a serious risk to the respondent's ability to recover the funds. This element was, however, assessed only in the context of the severity/imminence of the harm alleged to justify the provisional measure.

The example of a NAI arbitration shows that some tribunals do engage in a detailed assessment of the legal claims taken at face value. In NAI Case 1694,[34]) the tribunal conducted a detailed assessment of the contract to determine whether the contract, on its face, supported the type of claim put forward by the claimant. This merely involved an assessment of whether the type of failure alleged against the respondent was explicitly listed as a warranty in the contract. In this case, the claimant relied on a warranty that a good

---

[30]) In so doing, the CIArb Guideline refers to the following ICC awards as precedent: ICC Case No. 6632, ICC Second Partial Award 8113 of 1995 and ICC First Partial Award 8540 of 1999.

[31]) *Constellation Overseas Ltd. v. Alperton Capital Ltd., et al.* (Interim Award), ICC Case No. 23856/MK, April 26, 2019.

[32]) *Ibidem*, para 192.

[33]) *Ibidem*, paras 191–200.

[34]) NAI Case No. 1694, Interim Award, December 12, 1996, in *A. van den Berg* (ed), ICCA Yearbook Commercial Arbitration 1998 – Volume XXIII, Yearbook Commercial Arbitration, Volume 23 (ICCA & Kluwer Law International 1998), pp. 97–112.

delivered had to be of marketable quality and alleged that this had not been met. The tribunal argued that, since the specific standard required of the material for the purpose of the claimant's case was not included as an express warranty, the claimant had failed to make out a prima facie case.

The tribunal in that case seemed to stray very far into an assessment of the merits and arguably imposed a very different standard on the applicant than legally appropriate. Specifically, the applicant was not entitled to rely on broad, ambiguous standards for marketable quality (merchantable quality) and had to prove a potential breach based on only a narrow and literal reading of the contract. Such a heavy weight of burden on the applicant does not seem to find support in international practice or academic work.

V. Arbitration Institution Summary Reports on the Prima Facie Standard as applied by Arbitral Tribunals

The following is a schedule of examples of arbitral practice under a variety of institutional arbitration rules.

Decisions by Tribunals under the ICC Rules	
Report of the ICC Commission on Arbitration and ADR Task Force on Emergency Arbitrator Proceedings 2019 Emergency Arbitrator ("**EA**")	← It is the applicant's burden to establish a prima facie compelling case that the requested measures are justified and required. This, in turn, suggests that it is the applicant who bears the burden to prove – at least to a prima facie standard – the facts upon which the Application relies. **Many ICC EA cases so far have merely sought to protect or restore the status quo** for the duration of the arbitration on the merits or seek to prevent (irreparable) harm from being suffered, and as such have **not essentially relied or depended on the veracity of extensive factual allegations** (para 131). ← The condition of likelihood of success on the merits (*fumus boni iuris*) requires the party requesting interim relief to show a reasonably arguable case or a reasonable probability of prevailing on the merits (para 152). ← In 25 of the 31 ICC EA cases in which likelihood of success on the merits was considered, the EA required the applicant to establish a prima facie case. One EA mentioned that the request is justified

Decisions by Tribunals under the ICC Rules	
	on the merits "*if there is, on a prima facie basis, a reasonable possibility that the requesting party will succeed on the merits of the claim*". In another case, the EA showed concern about prejudging the merits stating "*some issues at stake depend on a deeper debate, not admissible in an urgent measure proceeding*" and that "*this leads to the conclusion of absence of fumus bonis iuris*" (para 154).
Decisions by Tribunals under the SCC Rules	
SCC 2015-2016 Practice Note – There is prolific reference to Article 17 of the UNCITRAL Model Law as the basis for the tribunal's power to grant provisional measures.	← **Case No. EA 2016/046** – the tribunal said the prima facie test required an assessment of whether there is "*no reasonable prospect of success*"; only then is there *no* basis to assert a tangible right worthy of protection. ← **Case No. EA 2016/050** – the tribunal found there was no prima facie case because the applicant failed to identify a contractual right to the measure requested as a provisional measure (*i.e.*, the right to perform a due diligence). ← **Case No. EA 2016/067** – the tribunal assessed all five arguments that had been put forward (on a preliminary basis) to determine whether at least one of these arguments had a "*reasonable possibility of success*". ← **Case No. EA 2016/090** – the tribunal assessed (on a preliminary basis) the argument that a particular contractual clause should not apply. Finding that it was not convinced by this argument, the tribunal found there was no prima facie case on the merits. ← **Case No. 2016/139** – the merits of the applicant's case depended on whether the tribunal **found the contractual interpretation of the applicant more convincing than that of the responding party**. The tribunal performed this assessment and found *both* parties had equally compelling arguments (on a preliminary basis) so the tribunal found there applicant's case did *not* meet the prima facie standard. – It is to be noted that this also requires the tribunal to find that a reasonably possibility of success = a probability (50.01%) of success. Whether

Decisions by Tribunals under the SCC Rules	
SCC 2015-2016 Practice Note – There is prolific reference to Article 17 of the UNCITRAL Model Law as the basis for the tribunal's power to grant provisional measures.	this is appropriate, remains an open question, but it does fall within the tribunal's discretion. ← **Case No. EA 2016/142** – the tribunal said that the threshold for a prima facie assessment should not be "*too high*". The tribunal relied on a more literal reading of the contract, which was clear and strict, to determine the responding party had not shown a case to rebut the applicant's position that was supported by the literal reading. ← **Case No. EA 2016/150** – the tribunal invoked the balance of probabilities to deny the existence of a prima facie case for the applicant.
SCC 2019-2022 Practice Note	← **Case 2** – the tribunal assessed the applicant's arguments and found that, either way, the applicant would be entitled to some compensation. As such, it affirmed a prima facie case. ← **Case 5** – The tribunal seemed only to assess whether the applicant had a case for a legal claim to the provisional measure requested. Once the applicant could establish this on a preliminary basis, the tribunal felt this was enough for a prima facie case. There does not seem to have been an assessment of the case on the substantive merits. ← **Case 8** – to establish a prima facie case, the tribunal needed to be convinced that the responding party was responsible for the delay at issue. On a preliminary review of the facts, the tribunal found there to be evidence suggesting the responding party *might* be at fault and found the applicant had established a prima facie case. ← **Case 11** – the tribunal engaged in a legal assessment of the contractual terms and their interpretation under the substantive law of the contract in order to assess whether the legal arguments of the applicant concerning the merits were compelling. Having found they were not persuaded, there was no prima facie case. ← **Case 14** – the tribunal considered the facts alleged and applied a reading of the contract and the legal implications of its terms to decide whether a prima facie case was established.

VI. Prima Facie in case of Claim and Counterclaim

In "normal" cases, it is usually the claimant who files for interim measures in order to secure its claim and respondent (simply) rebuts it with substantial arguments. In such cases, it is hardly thinkable that a respondent can file for preliminary measures as well. The situation is totally different if the respondent also files a counterclaim, combined with an injunction to secure this counterclaim (only). One could therefore ask whether the tribunal must look *prima facie* into *both* claims – the claim and the counterclaim – that, in most cases, exclude each other. To put the question differently: Would an arbitral tribunal prejudge the counterclaim, if it comes to the conclusion that claimant has a prima facie claim? Alternatively, does the argument that respondent has a prima facie counterclaim prejudge claimant's claim? Or, is it possible that both claimant and respondent have a prima facie claim?

To solve this issue, it is essential to keep in mind that it is the party *requesting the injunction* that must show that its claim is, prima facie, valid, not without merit, not frivolous, has "*fumus boni iuris*". Only if *both* parties apply for interim measures excluding each other would it be for the tribunal to decide *which* of the mutual claims has, *prima facie*, more likelihood of being successful. If only the respondent applies for interim measures in order to secure its counterclaim, it is sufficient and, in fact, the only relevant issue for the tribunal to decide whether *respondent* has a prima facie case. This does not exclude that claimant may have a prima facie case as well. In such a constellation, the finding that respondent has a prima facie claim does not prejudge the merits (or even a prima facie existence of claimant's claim), but is the only relevant factor to decide on respondent's request.

VII. Conclusion

The prima facie standard in the test for provisional measures is generally recognised as a prerequisite element for granting interim relief. However, there is no strict agreement among tribunals as to the strength of the applicant's facts and legal arguments that is required to make it a "prima facie case". In general, most tribunals seem to rely on the UNCITRAL regime for the provisional measure standard, which requires that "*there is a reasonable possibility that the requesting party will succeed on the merits of the claim*". Prima facie is therefore, unlike in many local civil procedure laws, and probably also because, in international arbitration, parties must also prove the substantive law, not limited to a question of mere facts, but also includes a certain degree of probability of success on legal issues.

There is no agreement in international practise on whether a "reasonable possibility" means that the applicant's claim must be more likely to succeed than the responding party's submissions. This is at the discretion of the tribunal, and there are arguments either way.

In terms of the scope of legal/factual review required, all tribunals and academics consistently say the review should only be conducted on a prima facie/preliminary basis. Tribunals should, in their orders, always mention that the decision is only provisional, on the basis of the facts taken at face value and subject to change pending the full hearing of the party's cases. The tribunal must, in any case, not prejudge the outcome of the case.

However, even within a prima facie assessment of the merits, tribunals conduct the assessment of the merits of a claim very differently. Some tribunals think they should accept/assume all the factual assertions by the *applicant* are correct and see whether, on that basis, claimant would legally have a successful claim. Other tribunals have conducted extensive assessments (based on the preliminary information submitted by the parties) as to the validity of the applicant's arguments both based on the facts as well as on the law.

In case of a claim and counterclaim, the prima facie case of the *applicant for interim measures* is decisive. If only one party has applied for a preliminary injunction, the tribunal merely has to look at that party's prima facie case, including both facts and a chance to succeed on the merits. Such evaluation does not exclude the possibility of the other party having a prima facie case as well. Only when both parties apply for interim measures, must the tribunal assess whether both parties have prima facie cases. Depending on how a tribunal chooses to apply the prima facie standard (and the degree of relevance given to the likelihood of success), this may, and will normally, include an assessment of whether one claim is more likely to be successful than the other. Only in very rare cases both parties will be successful in receiving interim relief before arbitral tribunals.

Halting the Clock
Different Aspects of Staying the Proceedings in International Arbitration in Austria

Maria Bejan/Nina Pichler

I. Introduction

A stay of proceedings is generally defined as the temporary or definite suspension of arbitration proceedings. Different events during the arbitration process can lead to the stay of arbitration proceedings. For instance, when there is a pending decision in another forum that might affect the outcome of the arbitration, or when a party has failed to comply with procedural requirements, but also when the opposing party runs out of funds during the arbitration process and therefore files for bankruptcy.

The power to stay proceedings is widely accepted both in civil law and common law jurisdictions as part of the inherent powers of arbitrators.[1]) Accordingly, most international arbitration rules such as those of the ICSID,[2]) UNCITRAL and ICC support this view and acknowledge that arbitrators have ample procedural powers, which include the power to stay proceedings where the tribunal has jurisdiction.[3])

In Austria, a stay of proceedings in international arbitration is determined by national laws, the rules of arbitration institutions such as the Vienna International Arbitral Center ("VIAC") of the Austrian Federal Economic Chamber and international principles of law. Austrian courts and arbitral tribunals seated in Austria recognize the power to stay proceedings as part of the procedural discretion of arbitrators. VIAC's Rules of Arbitration and Conciliation ("Vienna Rules") provide a framework for the administration of arbitration proceedings, including – at least in specific circumstances – the potential for stays when necessary to ensure fair and efficient resolution of

---

[1]) International Law Association Committee on International Commercial Arbitration, *Report on Inherent and Implied Powers of Arbitral Tribunals – the 76th Conference in Washington* 14 (2014).

[2]) However, under ICSID the parties may not unilaterally suspend the arbitration proceedings.

[3]) ICC International Arbitration Rules 2021, Article 1; UNCITRAL Arbitration Rules 2013, Article 17; ICSID Convention Article 44 which grants tribunals the authority to decide procedural questions not covered by the Convention.

disputes.[4]) Moreover, the Austrian Supreme Court has addressed issues related to the stay of proceedings in various cases.[5])

When a stay is not mandated by law but based on the request of a party, the decision to stay proceedings is typically at the discretion of the arbitral tribunal, which must weigh the interests of justice, the potential impact on the arbitration process, and any relevant legal principles such as the right to be heard.[6]) In practice, the decision to stay arbitration proceedings in Austria would involve considerations such as the need to resolve preliminary issues, the existence of parallel proceedings, or other factors that might affect the arbitration process. Principles of fairness and efficiency guide the tribunal's discretion in this regard, meant to ensure that the stay does not unduly delay the resolution of the dispute.

However, staying arbitration proceedings is considered an exceptional remedy and should not be employed lightly if it would unduly delay the arbitration or prejudice one of the parties.

The discretion of the arbitral tribunal is reduced to a minimum when the stay of proceedings is mandated by law. For instance, when insolvency proceedings are commenced over the assets of a party involved in the arbitration proceedings, most state laws – including the Austrian insolvency laws – require the stay of any pending proceeding regardless of the state or progress of the resolution of the dispute. Given the massive worldwide increase in insolvencies across many jurisdictions – driven by global economic uncertainties and turbulence, coupled with the effects of the COVID-19 pandemic, and the associated financial challenges – this issue is becoming more relevant for international arbitration and has been the subject of countless publications.[7])

[4]) The Vienna Rules grant the arbitral tribunal ample powers to manage the proceedings, primarily through Article 28.

[5]) OGH, November 30, 2018, docket no. 18 ONc 2/18s (Austria); OGH, March 17, 2015, docket no. 18 ONc 1/15i; OGH, March 17, 2015, docket no. 18 ONc 7/14w; OGH, March 17, 2015, docket no. 18 ONc 6/14y; OGH, August 19, 2015, docket no. 18 OCg 2/15s.

[6]) Commission Import Export S.A. (Commisimpex) v. Republic of the Congo, ICC Case No. 16257/EC/ND/MCP/AZO/SP October 4, 2023 (Award on the Admissibility and the Merits of the Respondent's Application for Revision).

[7]) Jennifer L. Permesly et al., Overview: The IBA Toolkit on Insolvency and Arbitration, in *IBA Toolkit on Insolvency and Arbitration (2021)*, March 2021; Fulham Football Club Ltd v Richards [2011] EWCA Civ 855 (England & Wales); Decision 5A_910/2019 (Switzerland); Quicksilver Greater China Ltd v Quicksilver Glorious Sun JV Ltd and another [2014] 4 HKLRD 759 (Hong Kong); WDR Delaware Corporation v Hydrox Holdings Pty [2016] FCA 1164 (Australia); Tomolugen Holdings Limited v Silica Investors Ltd [2015] SGCA 57 (Singapore); Booz Allen & Hamilton v SBI Home Finance (2011) 5 SCC 532 (India); Vesna Lazic, Insolvency Proceedings and Commercial Arbitration 43 (1998); Robert von Mehren, From Vynior's to Mitsubishi: The Future of Arbitration and Public Law, 12 Brook J Intl L 583 (1986).

The principles of international arbitration and insolvency law are somewhat conflicting in this regard. Insolvency law is primarily based on the principle of equal treatment of creditors, follows a strict procedure, and is subject to strict control by an insolvency administrator and state courts. In contrast, the parties in arbitration seek to largely free themselves from state jurisdiction, intending to resolve potential disputes independently, efficiently, and confidentially. The different aims of these systems seem to be at odds with each other.

Specifically, in cross-border contexts, insolvency can have significant effects on pending arbitration proceedings and has been one of the most contentious issues in the last couple of years. On the one hand, the procedural rules of international institutions such as VIAC, ICC, LCIA, or even the UNCITRAL rules differ regarding the fate of pending arbitration proceedings when insolvency proceedings are initiated.[8]) On the other hand, national laws also diverge significantly concerning whether and under what conditions arbitration proceedings should be suspended and whether they can resume. The article will examine the general standards for staying an arbitration proceeding, then focus on the Austrian legal framework for such a stay and will finally explore the different approach taken when one party files for insolvency.

II. Staying Arbitration Proceedings and International Standards

It is well-established that courts are required to stay proceedings or deny jurisdiction when a valid arbitration agreement is in place.[9]) In cases of jurisdictional conflict between courts and arbitral tribunals, the New York Convention on the Recognition and Enforcement of Foreign Arbitral Awards (New York Convention) provides guidance. Specifically, Article II (3) mandates that courts of contracting states refer parties to arbitration when a valid arbitration agreement exists, effectively implying a stay of court proceedings in favor of arbitration.[10]) The principle of competence-competence, which empowers arbitrators to determine their own jurisdiction, further supports staying court proceedings to allow arbitrators the first opportunity to address jurisdictional issues.[11])

[8]) For the last couple of years Working Group V at UNCITRAL has been working on a project dedicated to the applicable law in insolvency proceedings.

[9]) G. Born, International Commercial Arbitration 1278-82 (2d ed. 2014).

[10]) The Convention on the Recognition and Enforcement of Foreign Arbitral Awards, Article II (3).

[11]) JGC Constructors BC Ltd., Fluor Canada Ltd., Operating as a Joint Venture under the name and style of JGC Fluor BC LNG Joint Venture, LNG Canada Development Inc. and Rio Tinto Alcan Inc. v. Vancouver Pile Driving Ltd. and Travaux Civils &

However, the issue of staying arbitration proceedings due to parallel court or arbitration proceedings, or other procedural or material issues, lacks a universally applicable rule in international arbitration. This absence is understandable, given that one of the primary interests in international arbitration is the swift resolution of disputes, and a stay would counteract this interest.

Despite this, halting proceedings is not as uncommon as one might assume, since no rule prohibits parties from filing claims in multiple forums simultaneously. Consequently, a party can file more than one arbitration claim on the same or substantially similar issues against the same opponent and pursue both proceedings concurrently.[12]) These situations pose significant challenges for the parties and the arbitral tribunal because they can lead to delays,[13]) increased expenses and the risk of inconsistent decisions.[14])

In international arbitration, the *lis pendens* doctrine addresses this challenge by granting the party facing parallel proceedings the right to request that the arbitral tribunal stay the proceedings pending before it. Still, the application of the *lis pendens* doctrine is contentious, and its use varies due to differing approaches by state courts.[15]) When searching for a rule on the application of *lis pendens* one will discover that there are no relevant provisions to be found in the New York Convention, the UNCITRAL Model Law, or the rules of major arbitral institutions. Despite the lack of specific binding rules, arbitral tribunals have relied on the doctrine of *lis pendens* to resolve in favor of effective case management and procedural fairness.[16]) Invoking the doctrine has ensured legal certainty by avoiding the risk of contradicting decisions, has protected the parties against forum shopping and has the benefit of minimizing the risk of costly parallel proceedings.

Several factors would be considered by the arbitral tribunal when applying the doctrine in an international arbitration case such as, whether: the arbitral tribunal or court has jurisdiction; the existence of material prejudice to the party opposing the request; the parallel proceedings are between the same parties and relate to the same subject matter; the applicable law precludes the

---

Marins Besix Canada Inc., Operating as a Joint Venture under the name and style of Besix-Vanpile Joint Venture, Judgment of the Supreme Court of British Columbia 2024 BCSC 344, February 27, 2024.

[12]) A party may also use this in an oppressive manner and attempt to intentionally delay the resolution of a dispute.

[13]) Alicja Zielińska-Eisen, Kiran N. Gore, 'Practical Insights on Lis Pendens', Practical Insights on Arbitral Procedure (Kluwer Law International, 2024), § I.

[14]) CME v. Czech Republic, para 207, March 14, 2003 (Ad hoc Arbitration, Final Award); Lauder v. Czech Republic, para 176 *et seq.*, September 3, 2001 (Ad hoc Arbitration, Award).

[15]) In common law jurisdictions it is a factor considered in forum non conveniens and in civil law jurisdiction it is mostly a question of priority of the first called upon court which implies the obligation of the second court to decline its jurisdiction.

[16]) International Law Association, Recommendations on Lis Pendens and Arbitration, Resolution No. 1/2006.

arbitral tribunal from staying the proceedings; the outcome of the parallel proceedings is material for the outcome of the arbitration.[17])

III. Staying Arbitration Proceedings in Austria

When determining whether to stay proceedings, an arbitral tribunal in Austria typically considers the arbitration agreement, applicable law, and the rules selected by the parties as well as soft law instruments. Arbitration proceedings in Austria are governed by sections 577 *et seq.* of the Austrian Code of Civil Procedure (ACCP).[18]) Two instances when a stay should be considered are contained in the relevant provisions of Austrian arbitration law. Accordingly, a tribunal may decide to stay proceedings if a state court is already addressing jurisdictional issues in a parallel proceeding or if a state court is examining a potential conflict of interest involving an arbitrator.[19]) These are two particularly relevant situations that might lead to a stay of arbitration proceedings. In addition, there are more instances when the proceedings are halted (which are discussed below).

Apart from the legal framework of the arbitration, tribunals may also consider general principles of civil procedure applicable in state court proceedings, although the specific context of arbitration or international enforcement typically introduces additional factors. One of these factors considered by courts and tribunals alike is the principle of procedural fairness.[20]) This includes ensuring that parties have adequate access to a forum to present their case and that proceedings are conducted in a manner that respects the rights of all parties involved, with a focus on the speedy resolution of a dispute. This also implies that the parties have a right to comment on a prospective stay of the proceedings. Tribunals may also consider the potential for conflicting decisions, especially in cases involving parallel proceedings, especially when dealing with different jurisdictions. This ensures consistency and coherence in legal outcomes.

When dealing with the efficient administration of justice tribunals may weigh the benefits of a stay against the need to resolve disputes expeditiously, particularly when there are pending proceedings that could impact the outcome of the case.

Although Austrian arbitration law does not specifically regulate the requirements for a stay in all relevant instances, such a stay is permissible and falls within the tribunal's discretion. The decision to grant a stay is ultimately at the discretion of the tribunal and will be decided on a case-by-case basis.

---

[17]) *Ibid.*, Recommendation 5 and 6.

[18]) Katharina Plavec, *§ 577 ZPO,* in Kodek/Oberhammer, ZPO-ON, 2 *et seq.*

[19]) § 584 Abs 1 ZPO letzter Satz; § 589 Abs 3 ZPO letzter Satz.

[20]) Ziehensack in Höllwerth/Ziehensack (eds.), ZPO-Praxiskommentar (2019) § 190 ZPO mn 5.

This discretion, however, is broad, as even if the tribunal denies a non-mandatory stay, it does not constitute grounds for annulment.[21])

In contrast, when one party files for insolvency, the relevant provisions demand that any legal dispute in which the debtor is the claimant or defendant shall be interrupted by the commencement of insolvency proceedings.[22]) A stay due to insolvency proceedings is generally related to the broader legal implications of insolvency on arbitration proceedings, which may override the arbitration agreement. Insolvency proceedings are collective, court-based processes that aim to resolve the interests of multiple parties and usually prohibit individual enforcement actions against the insolvent party. A stay in this context is to protect the collective interest and ensure that the insolvency process is not disrupted by ongoing arbitration. When staying proceedings because of insolvency proceedings there is no consideration of the parties' interest, efficiency and delays. The stay might also be introduced abruptly because of the presumed non-arbitrability of insolvency claims.[23])

A. Instances of Staying the Proceedings

Instances in which a court or an arbitral tribunal may consider a stay of proceedings related to arbitration proceedings are:

1. Recognition and Enforcement of Foreign Arbitral Awards: Under the New York Convention, Austrian courts may stay proceedings for recognition and enforcement if there is a pending application to set aside or suspend the award in the country where it was issued. The court may also require a security payment.

2. Legal Succession or Hindrance: Proceedings may be stayed in case of legal succession affecting the parties or if the arbitration is hindered for reasons beyond its control. This ensures that the proceedings can continue effectively once these issues are resolved.

3. Procedural Issues: A failure of a claimant to provide security for the costs of the respondent (so-called *cautio judicatum solvi*) may also give rise to a stay or termination of arbitral proceedings. Accordingly, Article 33 (7) of the Vienna Rules foresees that if a party fails to comply with an order by the arbitral tribunal for security for costs, the arbitral tribunal may, upon request, suspend in whole or in part, or terminate the proceedings.

4. Preliminary Issues: A stay may be ordered if there is a preliminary issue that affects the outcome of the proceedings on the merits which needs to

[21]) OGH, August 19, 2015, docket no. 18 OCg 2/15s (Austria).

[22]) § 7 IO.

[23]) Christoph Liebscher, Insolvency and Arbitrability, in Arbitrability 178 (Mistelis & Brekoulakis eds., 2009).

be decided by another tribunal or court. This allows for the resolution of critical issues that could impact the arbitration's outcome.

5. Joint Request by Parties: The arbitral tribunal may stay proceedings upon a jointly submitted request by the parties.

These examples demonstrate that stays are generally granted under specific legal conditions, often taking into account fairness and procedural efficiency. Halting proceedings is most suitable when it significantly serves the interest of a swift resolution of the dispute, such as when the parties mutually agree to pause proceedings to negotiate a settlement agreement.[24])

B. Impact of Parallel Proceedings on Pending Arbitrations in Austria

1. Parallel Proceedings

"Parallel proceedings" are not universally defined, but the use of the term varies depending on the applicable legal regime. The International Law Association (ILA) considers parallel proceedings to be:

> *"[P]roceedings pending before a national court or another arbitral tribunal in which the parties and one or more of the issues are the same or substantially the same as the ones before the arbitral tribunal in the Current Arbitration".*[25])

Although the ACCP does not specifically address the issue of a stay of proceedings based on the request of a party in arbitration proceedings, it does address the issue of parallel proceedings in section 584. This article prohibits further legal action before a court or arbitral tribunal in respect of the same parties and claims asserted if arbitration proceedings are pending. As an example of strict application of the principle of *lis pendens,* the rule does not mandate a stay of proceedings when parallel claims are filed but rather requires the court or the arbitral tribunal called on afterward to dismiss the case (*ex officio*).[26]) The main interest in this case is to prevent parallel proceedings over the same claim between the same parties, promoting efficiency and preventing delays or oppressive behavior.[27])

---

[24]) Christian Dorda in Torggler (ed.), Praxishandbuch Schiedsgerichtsbarkeit, 152 *et seq.*

[25]) International Law Association, Resolution No.1/2006, Annex 1: International Law Association Recommendations on Lis Pendens and Arbitration, para. 1

[26]) Rechberger/Hofstätter in Rechberger/Klicka (eds.), Kommentar zur ZPO[5] (2019) zu § 584 ZPO mn 5.

[27]) Katharina Plavec, *§ 584 ZPO,* in Kodek/Oberhammer, ZPO-ON, 15.

The issue of parallel proceedings and whether or not the tribunal or the state court can proceed is, in practice, also closely linked to the question of whether the claim filed is the same claim or a different claim. Like most other civil law jurisdictions, Austria used a version of the 'triple identity test', which requires the following elements of the dispute to be identical: (1) the parties, (2) the subject matter and (3) the relief sought. In practice, this question can be a difficult topic to decide on since the opinions on the application of the definition of the subject matter of a case are many as well as hard to define. Although the issue may initially seem trivial, it is anything but. For the purpose of this article, the issue can be summarized as follows: if the claim filed in another arbitration or court proceeding is the same as the one in the already pending arbitration, the case cannot lead to questions of a stay of proceedings since the claim must be dismissed by the tribunal or the state court in question unless the party submits on the merits of the case without objecting to the court's jurisdiction.[28]) Hence, for a stay of proceedings to be relevant, the case must involve two distinct claims litigated between the same parties.[29])

2. Counterclaims During Pending Arbitration Proceedings

In the complex landscape of international arbitration, the issues of parallel proceedings and counterclaims present unique challenges that require careful navigation. Parallel proceedings can arise when parties initiate multiple arbitration claims concerning the same or substantially similar issues in different forums, potentially leading to delays, increased costs, and inconsistent decisions. The doctrine of *lis pendens* often comes into play, allowing arbitral tribunals to consider staying proceedings to ensure procedural fairness and avoid contradictory outcomes. On the other hand, counterclaims, which are generally admissible under various arbitration rules, add another layer of complexity. They must be closely connected to the main proceedings and are subject to the tribunal's discretion regarding their admissibility and handling. The interplay between these elements necessitates a nuanced approach, balancing the need for efficient dispute resolution with the principles of fairness and legal certainty. This section explores the intricacies of managing parallel proceedings and counterclaims within the framework of international arbitration, highlighting the considerations and strategies employed by arbitral tribunals to address these challenges effectively.

A counterclaim is generally admissible in all arbitration rules and occurs quite frequently in practice, but – as in the case of set-off – only if the claim is

[28]) Dietmar Czernich/Astrid Deixler-Hübner/Martin Schauer, Handbuch Schiedsrecht mn 14.7 *et seqq.* (2018).

[29]) OGH, April 19, 2021, docket no. 4 Ob 43/21h (Austria).

covered by the arbitration agreement.[30]) In Article 5 ICC Rules 2017, Article 7 para 5 to 9 DIS Rules 2018 and Article 19 Swiss Rules, counterclaims are also generally admissible, whereby a connection to the main proceedings should exist. Moreover, the Vienna Rules expressly require a connection, between the pending arbitration and the counterclaim.[31]) It lays within the tribunals discretion to decide on the admissibility of the counterclaim. However, in arbitrations under the Vienna Rules it is possible to deal with related counterclaims, which are filed after the first steps of the proceedings, separately if a decision on the counterclaim would lead to a considerable delay.[32]) The Vienna Rules, allow the tribunal to decide whether to hear the counterclaims within the existing proceedings or as a separate claim if the counterclaims are filed after the answer to the statement of claim.[33])

If the proceedings are separated into two different arbitrations, one of them might be stayed if there are jurisdictional challenges related to the counterclaim, or the separate proceeding is depending on the outcome of the first arbitration proceeding. This is a particularly curious situation, because of the potential for an intentional delay by a party who wishes to prolong the dispute and entangle the opponent in another arbitration.

Therefore, when deciding whether to stay a separate arbitration proceeding produced by the separation of the main claim and the counterclaim, the tribunal must rigorously assess whether the counterclaim is sufficiently connected to the main proceedings and consider factors such as procedural efficiency and fairness to the parties involved. Within the discretionary power of the tribunal this instance of suspension of the proceedings should be requiring a higher standard of proof for the delay of the main proceedings to ensure that the counterclaim does not unduly disrupt the resolution of the dispute and propel the parties into a new arbitration on similar issues.

In summary, whether an arbitrator should stay the proceedings to address in case of separate counterclaims depends on, timeliness, procedural efficiency, jurisdictional considerations, and fairness to the parties but should be evaluated carefully to prevent oppressive behaviors of participants.

C. Impact of Insolvency Proceedings on Pending Arbitrations

The leading question when dealing with arbitration proceedings, in case one party files for bankruptcy, is which national insolvency law applies. The

[30]) Czernich/Deixler-Hübner/Schauer, Schiedsrecht mn 8.99.

[31]) Article 9 Vienna Rules which contrary to Article 5 ICC Rules allow the filing of a counterclaim throughout the proceedings.

[32]) *Killias* in *Torggler et al*, HB Schiedsgerichtsbarkeit^2 mn 1028.

[33]) *Pitkowitz/Dobosz* in VIAC Handbuch Schiedsordnung Art 9 mn 7.

European Insolvency Regulation (EUInsRe)[34]) provides guidelines within the European Union (except Denmark) in this regard. According to this regulation, the law of the country where the insolvency proceedings commenced, generally applies to those proceedings, including legal actions by individual creditors (Article 7 EUInsRe).

However, if an arbitration proceeding is already pending at the time and insolvency proceedings are commenced, the effects of the opening of insolvency proceedings are determined by the law of the country where the seat of arbitration is located (Article 18 EUInsRe).

With reference to Austrian literature and case law, the English High Court of Justice decided in *Syska et al v. Vivendi et al*[35]) that, according to Article 18 of the EUInsRe (former Article 15 of the EUInsRe), the effects of the opening of insolvency proceedings on pending legal proceedings, which the court also considered to include arbitration proceedings, are governed by the *lex fori processus, i.e.*, the (procedural) law of the seat of arbitration, and therefore not by the *lex fori concursus*. The same applies to the arbitration agreement itself as the "foundation" of the (already) pending arbitration proceedings.[36])

Therefore, if arbitration proceedings are pending with the seat in Austria, the effects of an insolvency opening will be governed by Austrian law, even if the insolvency procedure commenced before a court in another member state.

If the arbitral tribunal fails to observe mandatory insolvency laws, the arbitral award may be subject to annulment.

1. When the Seat of the Arbitration is in Austria

The commencement of insolvency proceedings under Austrian law has several legal consequences for the affected party, particularly regarding ongoing proceedings. With the opening of insolvency proceedings concerning a party's assets, the insolvency administrator takes over all the rights and obligations of the debtor and assumes control over the debtor's assets, including the authority to manage pending proceedings. In Austria, insolvency administrators are, according to the consistent case law of the Austrian Supreme Court, also bound by arbitration agreements that the insolvent party entered into with third parties before the opening of the insolvency proceedings.[37])

[34]) Regulation (EU) 2015/848 of the European Parliament and of the Council of May 20, 2015 on insolvency proceedings.

[35]) Vivendi Universal S.A., Vivendi Telecommunication and others v. Elektrim S.A. and others (II) (2009).

[36]) Christian Koller, Auswirkungen der Insolvenzeröffnung auf ein anhängiges Schiedsverfahren in einem anderen EU-Mitgliedstaat, ZIK 2009, 52 (54); Trenker in Laimer, IPR Praxiskommentar, Art 18 EuInsVO 2015 mn 10.

[37]) OGH, November 30, 2018, docket no. 18 ONc 2/18s (Austria); OGH, March 17, 2015, docket no. 18 ONc 1/15i (Austria); OGH, March 17, 2015, docket no. 18 ONc

a) Unconditioned Stay of the Arbitration Proceedings

According to section 6 para 1 of the Austrian Insolvency Code (AIC), proceedings that serve to enforce or secure claims against the assets belonging to the insolvency estate may neither be initiated nor continued after the opening of the insolvency proceedings.

Section 7 subsection 1 of the AIC further states that "*all pending legal disputes*", in which the debtor is the claimant or defendant, are suspended upon the commencement of the insolvency proceedings.[38])

Section 7 of the Austrian Insolvency Code only refers to legal disputes in general. However, the Austrian Supreme Court has explicitly clarified that this provision also applies to pending arbitration proceedings with a connection to the insolvency estate.[39]) Therefore, such arbitration proceedings are also suspended upon the opening of insolvency proceedings concerning a party's assets.[40])

The characteristics of arbitration proceedings, which differ from state court procedures – particularly the potentially preceding appointment of arbitrators – lead to a distinct interpretation of the concept of "pending legal disputes." In arbitration, a dispute is considered pending from the first procedural step. This first step is determined by the content of the arbitration agreement, possibly supplemented by the applicable arbitration rules and the ACCP. This initial step could be, for example, the submission of the statement of claim to the arbitral institution or the agreed-upon arbitrator.[41]) If no such agreement exists, this first step, according to section 587 para 2 no. 4 ACCP, is the claimant's request to the defendant to apply for the appointment of an arbitrator. This request is considered the first procedural step for the claimant in pursuing its claim.[42])

6/14y; OGH, March 17, 2015, docket no. 18 ONc 7/14w (Austria); Alice Fremuth, Schiedsverfahren und Konkurs, ÖJZ 1998, 848.

[38]) Wolfgang Jelinek, *§ 6 IO,* in Koller/Lovrek/Spitzer (eds.), IO – Insolvenzordnung^{2} mn 12; Buchegger in Bartsch/Pollak/Buchegger (eds.), Österreichisches Insolvenzrecht I^{4} § 7 KO, mn 10; Koller, Auswirkungen der Insolvenzeröffnung auf ein anhängiges Schiedsverfahren in einem anderen EU-Mitgliedstaat, ZIK 2009, 52 (54); Schubert in Konecny/Schubert, KO § 7 mn 10; Schumacher/Köchl, Insolvenzeröffnung unterbricht Schiedsverfahren: Fortsetzung als Prüfungsprozess? RdW 2012, 388 (389); Zeiler, Schiedsverfahren^{2} 581 ZPO mn 120.

[39]) OGH, March 17, 2015, docket no. 18 ONc 1/15i (Austria).

[40]) Buchegger in Bartsch/Pollak/Buchegger (eds.), Österreichisches Insolvenzrecht I^{4} § 7 KO, mn 10.

[41]) OGH, November 30, 2018, docket no. 18 ONc 2/18s (Austria); OGH, March 17, 2015, docket no. 18 ONc 1/15i (Austria); OGH, March 17, 2015, docket no. 18 ONc 6/14y; OGH, March 17, 2015, docket no. 18 ONc 7/14w (Austria); Alice Fremuth-Wolf, Zur Unterbrechung des Schiedsverfahrens bei Insolvenzeröffnung, ecolex 2015, 564; Christian Koller, Eintritt und Sperrwirkung der Schiedshängigkeit, ecolex 2014, 1056.

[42]) Alice Fremuth-Wolf, Zur Unterbrechung des Schiedsverfahrens bei Insolvenzeröffnung, ecolex 2015, 564

Upon commencement of the insolvency proceedings and in accordance with the applicable insolvency regulations, the following proceedings will be suspended:[43])

- Arbitration proceedings concerning a claim requiring registration in the insolvency process: Whether (and to what extent) the arbitration proceedings should continue as an examination process is to be discussed in relation to sections 110 and 113 of the AIC.
- Other pending arbitration proceedings related to the insolvency estate (*e.g.*, claims, segregation, separation, and competition processes) must be continued before the arbitral tribunal, due to the insolvency administrator's obligation to respect the arbitration agreement.
- Estate-related proceedings concerning annulment claims (section 611 ACCP), the existence or non-existence of an arbitral award (section 612 ACCP), and ancillary proceedings (such as those related to the appointment of arbitrators under section 587 ACCP and challenge procedures under section 589 para 3 ACCP).

If the commencement of insolvency proceedings over a party's assets is published in the Austrian Insolvency Register (*Ediktsdatei*)[44]) and therefore a stay of the arbitration proceedings is mandated by law, the arbitral tribunal should still record the stay of the pending arbitration proceedings with a procedural order and communicate this to the parties and the insolvency administrator.

The suspension must be affected at any stage of the proceedings. This also applies to cases in which the arbitrator has already closed the proceedings and is in the process of issuing the award. In any case, the issuance of the arbitral award must be suspended due to the stay.

b) Continuation of the Stayed Proceeding

The Austrian Supreme Court[45]) has clarified that in the presence of an arbitration agreement concerning the disputed claim, the insolvency-related claims examination process must, "*in any case*", be conducted by the arbitral tribunal if the claim is contested solely by the insolvency administrator.[46])

However, Austrian insolvency law stipulates that the competent insolvency court is exclusively responsible for the claims' examination procedure (*Prüfverfahren*) in accordance with section 111 para 1 AIC.[47])

---

[43]) Wolfgang Jelinek, *§ 7 IO*, in Koller/Lovrek/Spitzer (eds.), IO – Insolvenzordnung[2] mn 13.

[44]) Publicly available under https://edikte.justiz.gv.at/.

[45]) OGH, November 30, 2018, docket no. 18 ONc 2/18s (Austria).

[46]) Andreas Konecny, Fortsetzung des Schiedsverfahrens als Prüfungsprozess jedenfalls bei Bestreitung durch den Insolvenzverwalter, ZIK 2019, 65.

[47]) OGH, November 30, 2018, docket no. 18 ONc 2/18s (Austria).

To initiate this examination process, the party must first file their claim in a timely manner with the insolvency court in accordance with section 102 AIC, referencing the ongoing arbitration proceeding.[48]) If the insolvency administrator does not acknowledge a claim or its existence is disputed by creditors entitled to do so, a clarification must be made by court. The AIC differentiates for jurisdiction: If no legal procedure has been initiated yet, the insolvency court is exclusively responsible, except for labor law matters and certain legal issues (para 111 AIC). However, a procedure interrupted according to section 7 para 1 AIC must be continued at the respective court (in accordance with section 7 para 3 and section 113 AIC.[49])

As mentioned at the outset, Austrian case law has clarified, that in the event that an arbitration proceeding is already pending before the commencement of insolvency in relation to the defendant, it can be continued as an examination process before the arbitral tribunal. The separate filing of an examination claim with the insolvency court is not required. The examination procedure will then take place before the arbitral tribunal.[50]) The claimant has to convert its claim for relief into a request for a declaratory judgment.

2. Impact on Arbitration Proceedings with the Seat of Arbitration Located in Germany

Even in purely domestic arbitration proceedings between German parties with the seat of arbitration in Germany, the impact of insolvency on the procedure is dealt with similarly. Neither the German Insolvency Code nor the provisions in section 1025 *et seqq.* of the German Code of Civil Procedure (GCCP) concerning arbitration, nor the arbitration rules of international institutions like the ICC or DIS, contain specific provisions regarding this issue. However, the impact of insolvency on an arbitration proceeding largely mirrors the effects of a state court procedure in Germany.[51])

With the commencement of insolvency proceedings, section 80 para 1 of the German Insolvency Code (GIC) transfers the administration and disposal authority over the debtor's assets to the insolvency administrator. As a result, the administrator also exclusively assumes the authority to manage legal proceedings from that point onward.

However, the insolvency administrator is generally bound by existing arbitration agreements in both active and passive proceedings.

[48]) Andreas Konecny, Fortsetzung des Schiedsverfahrens als Prüfungsprozess jedenfalls bei Bestreitung durch den Insolvenzverwalter, ZIK 2019, 65.

[49]) OGH, November 30, 2018, docket no. 18 ONc 2/18s (Austria).

[50]) OGH, November 30, 2018, docket no. 18 ONc 2/18s (Austria); Andreas Konecny, Fortsetzung des Schiedsverfahrens als Prüfungsprozess jedenfalls bei Bestreitung durch den Insolvenzverwalter, ZIK 2019, 65.

[51]) Vivendi Universal S.A., Vivendi Telecommunication and others v. Elektrim S.A. and others (II) (2009).

If an insolvency procedure is opened over a party's assets during ongoing arbitration proceedings, the insolvency administrator takes over the conduct of the proceedings at the stage that has already been reached and remains bound by the procedural steps taken up to that point. Unlike in state civil procedures, however, the commencement of insolvency proceedings does not automatically lead to a suspension of the arbitration proceeding under section 240 GCCP. The arbitral tribunal must still provide the insolvency administrator with an opportunity to be heard and, therefore, cannot simply continue the proceedings without considering the administrator's position.

In a passive action against the insolvent debtor, the creditor must, just like in state procedures, first file and register the claim with the insolvency table (*Insolvenztabelle*) and, in the event of a dispute, convert its claim for relief into a request for a declaratory judgment.

3. Complexity in Cross-Border Scenarios in International Arbitration Proceedings

In international arbitration proceedings, where the parties are based in different countries and the seat of arbitration is located even in a third country, assessing the concrete impact of insolvency over the assets of one party on the arbitration proceedings becomes significantly more complex.[52])

Such scenarios present considerable potential for surprises, as demonstrated *inter alia* by previous decisions from the English Court of Appeal and the Swiss Federal Court in the Elektrim/Vivendi[53]) dispute in 2007. In that case, the Swiss Federal Court rejected the continuation of an arbitration proceeding with the seat in Switzerland after the opening of insolvency proceedings in relation to a Polish party, citing a provision in Polish insolvency law, while the Court of Appeal in a parallel case with the seat of arbitration in England did not consider the Polish provision applicable concerning the same party. Although Poland has since then adopted its insolvency law to be more arbitration-friendly, national insolvency laws continue to show significant differences across Europe. The initiation or continuation of an arbitration proceeding after a party's insolvency can be very problematic in certain jurisdictions (*e.g.*, Bulgaria or Portugal).[54])

As already set out above, if an arbitration proceeding is already pending at the time, insolvency proceedings are opened, the effects of the insolvency are determined by the law of the country where the seat of arbitration is located

[52]) Christian Koller, Auswirkungen der Insolvenzeröffnung auf ein anhängiges Schiedsverfahren in einem anderen EU-Mitgliedstaat, ZIK 2009, 52 (54).

[53]) Vivendi Universal S.A., Vivendi Telecommunication and others v. Elektrim S.A. and others (II) (2009).

[54]) Roland Kläger, Internationale Schiedsverfahren und Insolvenz, ICCGermany, https://www.iccgermany.de/magazin-post/internationale-schiedsverfahren-und-insolvenz/ (2021), last access January 17, 2025.

(section 18 EUInsRe).[55]) In an arbitration proceeding seated in Austria, the effects of the opening of an insolvency are to be governed by Austrian law, even if the insolvency procedure is opened before a court in another member state.

If a non-EU country is involved in an arbitration proceeding seated in Austria, section 240 para 1 AIC applies, stating that insolvency proceedings and decisions from a third (non-EU) country are to be recognized in Austria, if:

- the debtor's center of main interests (COMI) is in that other country; and
- the insolvency proceedings are comparable to those in Austria.

Recognition occurs *ipso iure*, meaning that a separate recognition procedure is only required if the debtor opposes it. The Austrian Supreme Court has not specifically addressed the question of whether a foreign party to an arbitration seated in Austria could be subject to insolvency proceedings in a non-EU country. Also, in this case, it is to be assumed that the arbitration proceedings would likely be suspended.

IV. Practitioners Indication

When a party seeks to stay arbitration proceedings, several efficient measures can be taken to enhance the likelihood of success and ensure the process is handled effectively. The party should provide a clear and compelling justification for the stay. This includes demonstrating how the stay will contribute to a fair, speedy, and cost-effective resolution of the dispute, as outlined in arbitration rules such as the ICDR's.[56]) It is crucial to apply for the stay at the earliest possible stage, ideally before taking any substantive steps in the arbitration proceedings. This helps to avoid any implication that the party is acquiescing to the arbitration process. Delays are a critical consideration when deciding whether to grant a stay of proceedings in arbitration or court settings. This is more significant when considering that the filing of counterclaims can be used by parties as part of aggressive tactics to ensure the proceedings will not be concluded most efficiently. Engaging with the arbitral tribunal and providing comprehensive submissions on the reasons for the stay can help in persuading the tribunal of the necessity and benefits of the stay.

If the stay is sought on jurisdictional grounds, the party should clearly outline any jurisdictional challenges or issues that necessitate the stay, ensuring these are well-documented and supported by evidence. Additionally, if there are related court or arbitration proceedings, the party should highlight how these might impact the current arbitration and justify the need for a stay to avoid conflicting outcomes or duplicative efforts. Furthermore, the party

[55]) Trenker in Laimer, IPR Praxiskommentar, Art 18 EuInsVO 2015 mn 10.

[56]) ICDR Arbitration Rule and Procedure L-3.

would most likely succeed with its request for a stay of proceedings if a joint request for a stay from all parties involved can be obtained as it demonstrates consensus and reduces the likelihood of opposition.

When a stay of arbitration proceedings is implemented due to insolvency proceedings, reasonable measures should be taken to ensure that the rights of all parties are protected and that the proceedings can resume efficiently once the stay is lifted. It is advisable to engage with the insolvency administrator to understand the status of the insolvency proceedings and any potential impact on the arbitration. This can help in coordinating efforts and ensuring that the arbitration can proceed smoothly once the stay is lifted. Additionally, regularly monitoring the progress of the insolvency proceedings to anticipate when the arbitration might be able to resume is advisable. This includes staying informed about any developments that might affect the arbitration. It is also advisable to take steps to preserve all relevant evidence and documentation related to the arbitration. This ensures that the case can be effectively resumed without loss of critical information. However preparation should start at the earliest stage of the arbitration, the drafting of the arbitration proceeding when considering which seat would be appropriate in case insolvency proceedings will be an issue during any future dispute.

Unlocking the Potential of Institutional Expedited Procedures

Maximilian Menz/Marios Kourtis[*])

I. Introduction

Specific provisions for expedited procedures ("**EPP**") have become a standard feature of the rules of most arbitration institutions.[1]) As the recently updated rules of the Netherlands Arbitration Institute[2]) and the Singapore International Arbitration Centre[3]) show, this trend continues. It is therefore unsurprising that the ICC has reported a record number of cases administered under its EPP in 2023.[4])

EPP aim to address the primary drawback of conventional arbitration proceedings, namely their perceived length and complexity (and the associated costs resulting from both). While the EPP of the various institutions differ in their details, their solution to achieve this goal typically rests on three cornerstones: a shorter deadline to issue the final award, the appointment of a sole arbitrator as the default rule, and limitations on the procedural steps of the arbitration (*e.g.*, restrictions on the number of written submissions and limitations regarding the hearing). However, the application of EPP requires a fine balancing act by the arbitral tribunal in order to avoid compromising the

---

[*]) *Maximilian Menz*, LL.M. (University of Edinburgh) is a partner and *Marios Kourtis*, LL.M. (Munich) an associate of WACH UND MECKES und Partner Rechtsanwälte PartGmbB. This article is based on a panel discussion held at the ASAb40 Spring Conference 2024 in Geneva. The authors wish to express their gratitude to the conference organizers, Nadja Al Kawanati, Dr. Daniel Durante, and Dr. Nino Sievi, as well as co-panelists, Roxane Schmidgall and Fabio Santacroce, for their valuable insights and inspiration.

[1]) *E.g.*, the following arbitration rules: VIAC Rules (2021), DIS Rules (2018), ICC Rules (2021), Swiss Rules (2021), SCC Expedited Arbitration Rules (2023), HKIAC Rules (2024), ICDR Rules (2021), WIPO Expedited Arbitration Rules (2021), CIETAC Rules (2024), ACICA Expedited Arbitration Rules (2021), Abu Dhabi International Arbitration Centre's Arbitration Rules (2024). A notable exception are the LCIA Rules (2020).

[2]) NAI Rules (2024).

[3]) SIAC Rules (2025).

[4]) ICC Dispute Resolution 2023 Statistics (2024) [ICC Publication No.: DRS991E], 14 (available under https://iccwbo.org/news-publications/news/icc-dispute-resolution-statistics-2023/).

quality of the adjudicatory process and the fundamental rights of the parties (*e.g.*, their right to be heard).[5]

This article provides an overview of the key procedural tools available under the existing EPP and offers practical guidance to practitioners on how to optimize their use and, ultimately, strike the right balance. It will follow the course of the proceedings, beginning with the application of the rules (*see* below, II.), continuing with the constitution of the arbitral tribunal (*see* below, III.) and the conduct of the proceedings (*see* below, IV.), before concluding with the award (*see* below, V.).

II. Application of EPP

A. Application Modes

Arbitral institutions employ different approaches for the application of their EPP. Understanding these differences is crucial for parties to set up expedited procedures correctly from the outset and avoid surprises.

Most EPP automatically apply if the amount in dispute is below a certain threshold, unless both parties opt out ("**Opt-Out EPP**").[6] The relevant thresholds differ between the various institutions.[7] In contrast, a few rules make the applicability of the EPP subject to a decision of the relevant arbitral institution.[8] Such a decision is issued upon an application of a party if the dispute meets certain requirements (*e.g.*, that the amount in dispute is below a certain threshold or that there is an exceptional urgency; "**Application EPP**").[9] Finally, some institutions provide that the EPP only apply if the parties agree on them ("**Opt-In EPP**").[10] What all EPP have in common is that they will always apply if both parties agree on them.

---

5) *See Christophe Seraglini* & *Patrick Baeten*, *Chapter 2: Expedited Rules and the Possibility of Immediate Measures once a Tribunal is Constituted*, in *Laurent Lévy* & *Michael Polkinghorne* (eds.), *ICC Dossier No. 16: Expedited Procedures in International Arbitration*, Dossiers of the ICC Institute of World Business Law, Volume 16 (2017), 34, 37 *et seq*.

6) *E.g.*, Art. 30(2)(a) in connection with Art. 1(2) Appendix VI ICC Rules; Art. 42(3) Swiss Rules; Art. 56(1) CIETAC Rules; Art. 1(4) ICDR Rules; Art. 42(1)(a) NAI Rules; Art. 36(1) Abu Dhabi Rules.

7) *E.g.*, ICC Rules (USD 3 million for arbitration agreements concluded on or after 1 January 2021); Swiss Rules (CHF 1 million); CIETAC Rules (RMB 5 million); ICDR Rules (USD 500,000); NAI Rules (EUR 1 million); Abu Dhabi Rules (AED 9 million).

8) Art. 42.1 HKIAC Rules; Art. 14.2 *et seq*. SIAC Rules.

9) Art. 42.1 HKIAC Rules; Art. 14.2 SIAC Rules.

10) *E.g.*, Art. 45(1) VIAC, Art. 1.4 DIS Rules, Art. 11 SCC Expedited Arbitration Rules, Art. 2 WIPO Expedited Arbitration Rules.

Each of these three approaches presents distinct challenges but several noteworthy points stand out:

Parties subject to Opt-Out EPP are sometimes taken by surprise that the EPP apply automatically. Arbitration clauses are often inserted into the contract as *"midnight clauses"*. Parties often fail to consider all their implications, in particular the application of the EPP and what this might entail. Counsel should therefore advise their clients on these implications when drafting the arbitration agreement and consider whether the application of the EPP is actually in the client's best interest. If it is not, expressly opting out from the application of the EPP in the arbitration agreement or choosing institutional rules that provide for Opt-In EPP could be an option. Additionally, under certain rules, Opt-Out EPP will not apply if the arbitral institution and/or the arbitral tribunal determines that it is inappropriate given the specific circumstances of the case.[11]) Parties seeking to apply for this option should provide justification as to why the application of EPP is inappropriate, *e.g.*, by demonstrating that, despite the low amount in dispute, the case presents complex factual or legal issues that cannot be handled with within the strict timeframe of EPP.

Furthermore, parties seeking to initiate proceedings under Opt-Out EPP (or Application EPP) should be aware that the amount in dispute may change during the course of the proceedings. *E.g.*, the respondent may file a counterclaim in its answer to the request for arbitration that causes the amount in dispute to exceed the institution's applicable threshold. This could result in the non-application of the EPP, as under many rules the applicability of the EPP is based on the aggregate amount of all quantified claims and counterclaims[12]) and determined between the filing of the answer to the request for arbitration and the constitution of the tribunal.[13]) A change of the amount in dispute at a later stage may also be relevant. Several EPP contain a provision that allows either the institution[14]) or the arbitrator(s)[15]) to decide that expedited procedures should no longer apply due to a change of circumstances.[16])

[11]) *E.g.*, Art. 30(3)(c) ICC Rules; Art. 1(4), Art. E-4 ICDR Rules.

[12]) *See*, for the ICC Rules, ICC Rules, Note to Parties and Arbitral Tribunals on the Conduct of the Arbitration under the ICC Rules of Arbitration (January 1, 2021), para. 131 (available under https://iccwbo.org/news-publications/arbitration-adr-rulesules-and-tools/note-parties-arbitral-tribunals-conduct-arbitration; all online sources last accessed on January 17, 2025).

[13]) *E.g.*, Art. 30.2(a) in connection with Art. 1.3 Appendix VI ICC Rules, Art. 5.1 SIAC Rules; for further examples *see* Andreas Wehowsky, *Expedited Procedures in International Commercial Arbitration – Swiss and International Perspectives* (2023), para. 472.

[14]) *E.g.*, Art. 1.4 Appendix VI ICC Rules, Art. 42.3 HKIAC Rules, Art. 5.4 SIAC Rules.

[15]) *E.g.*, Art. E-5 ICDR Rules.

[16]) Wehowsky, Expedited Procedures, *supra* note 13, para. 476.

However, parties should be aware that some rules limit the submission of new claims after the constitution of the arbitral tribunal, requiring the tribunal's authorization for their admission.[17]) In making a decision, the arbitral tribunal should especially consider the expedited nature of the procedure and potential delays that would follow from admitting additional claims.[18])

For Opt-In EPP, the timing of the agreement is an important factor. The parties may agree on the application of the EPP in the arbitration agreement or at a later stage. Some rules provide that the arbitral tribunal should discuss with the parties at the first case management conference whether the EPP should be applied.[19]) Other rules provide for specific cut-off dates by which such an agreement must be made (*e.g.*, the submission of the answer to the statement of claim).[20])

As a general rule, parties should try to agree on the EPP as early in the proceedings as possible. If they agree at a later stage, it may already be too late to implement certain measures of the EPP (*e.g.*, restrictions on submissions).[21]) In addition, parties should be aware that it is often difficult to reach an agreement on the EPP once a dispute has arisen. In the best-case scenario, the parties will still have the common interest of solving their dispute expeditiously. However, by that time it may already be clear which party will benefit (or be disadvantaged) from the application of the EPP (*e.g.*, if one party wants to drag out the proceedings as long as possible). In addition, once a dispute has arisen, the parties often seem more concerned that their ability to present their case is not limited by the measures contemplated by the EPP.[22]) In any event, if parties wish to agree on the application of the EPP after the constitution of the arbitral tribunal, and particularly after the procedural timetable has been set, they should consider that this may affect the tribunal's position (*e.g.*, due to the shorter time limit for rendering the award). Therefore, they should seek the tribunal's approval before reaching such an agreement.[23])

Given these difficulties in reaching an agreement after the dispute has arisen, parties might want to consider the option of already agreeing on the EPP in the arbitration agreement. Some institutions provide specific model clauses in this respect.[24]) Such an agreement on EPP in the arbitration agreement can be an effective option if the parties are certain that all potential

---

[17]) Art. 3(2) Appendix VI ICC Rules; Art. 5 ICDR Rules; Art. 20 ACICA Expedited Arbitration Rules.

[18]) *Cf. Seraglini & Baeten, Expedited Rules and the Possibility of Immediate Measures, supra* note 5, 57 *et seq.*

[19]) Art. 27.4(ii) DIS Rules.

[20]) Art. 45(1) sentence 2 VIAC Rules.

[21]) *Cf. Wehowsky*, Expedited Procedures, *supra* note 13, para. 454.

[22]) *Seraglini & Baeten, Expedited Rules and the Possibility of Immediate Measures, supra* note 5, 36.

[23]) *Cf. Wehowsky*, Expedited Procedures, *supra* note 13, para. 454.

[24]) *E.g.*, DIS Rules, 4; *see* also Annex 1 VIAC Rules.

disputes under the respective contract are suitable for expedited procedures. Difficulties arise, however, if the parties want the EPP to apply only to certain types of disputes. Inflating the arbitration agreement with a detailed description of the relevant disputes generally does not seem advisable and will usually also not be negotiable in practice. Instead, the parties may take inspiration from the Opt-Out EPP and include a monetary threshold up to which the EPP shall apply.

B. Suitable Disputes

This raises the related question: what types of disputes are suitable for EPP? There is no universal answer, as much depends on the specific circumstances of the dispute. However, parties should particularly take the following factors into account:

- Need for speed: EPP, as their name suggests, are designed for disputes that require a faster resolution than under ordinary arbitration proceedings (*e.g.*, to preserve ongoing business relationships in a joint venture or supply chains). This need for speed should outweigh the potential trade-offs of EPP (*e.g.*, fewer opportunities for the parties to present their case and a potentially less detailed scrutiny by the arbitrators).
- Costs: Expedited procedures are typically less costly than ordinary arbitration proceedings due to their shorter time frame and more lean procedure (particularly with respect to counsel fees). The client's resources are also tied up for a shorter period of time. EPP are therefore attractive for low-value disputes for which it would not be economically viable to conduct ordinary arbitration proceedings. This is precisely the rationale behind the monetary thresholds used in some EPP (although the amount in dispute does not necessarily correlate with the actual economic interests of the parties).
- Complexity: Generally, disputes concerning complex factual and legal issues are less suitable, particularly if they require an extensive document production or the input of experts. The same applies to multi-party proceedings. The tight timeframe of EPP creates the risk that such complex issues may not be addressed in sufficient detail and may lead to incorrect decisions.
- Strategy: Parties should also consider strategic aspects, including whether they have sufficient capacity to comply with the tight deadlines of the EPP. Additionally, they should assess whether expedited dispute resolution aligns with their interests in the specific case.

III. Constitution of the Arbitral Tribunal

The arbitral tribunal plays a crucial role in the arbitration proceedings. It not only organizes and conducts the proceedings, but also renders the award. The proper composition of the arbitral tribunal is therefore a decisive factor for the success of expedited procedures, both in terms of the number and the qualifications of the arbitrator(s).

A. Number of the Arbitrators

EPP typically provide as a default rule that the arbitral tribunal will consist of a sole arbitrator.[25]) However, most rules provide that this does not apply if the parties have agreed otherwise.[26])

A sole arbitrator is often the right choice for expedited procedures and parties should consider very carefully whether they want to deviate from this option: A multi-member tribunal undoubtedly has its benefits, which can also be helpful in expedited procedures. It may allow for a better scrutiny of the case and a reduced risk of mistakes in the adjudication, as it is (generally) less likely that multiple arbitrators will overlook the same issue. Multi-member tribunals may also be able to divide the workload. However, these benefits often tend to be outweighed by the advantages of a sole arbitrator in expedited procedures. The appointment of a sole arbitrator typically leads to a faster constitution of the tribunal, particularly given that it can be difficult to find several members for a tribunal that all have sufficient availabilities to accommodate the short deadlines of an expedited procedure. A sole arbitrator can also make (procedural) decisions more swiftly because there is no need for a time-consuming coordination with the other members of the arbitral tribunal. Finally, a sole arbitrator is less expensive because only fees for one arbitrator are incurred.

In practice, parties often do not pay special attention to EPP when agreeing on the arbitration clause. Therefore, arbitration clauses often provide for a three-member tribunal without distinguishing between ordinary and expedited procedures. This can lead to uncertainty, especially under EPP based on an opt-out mechanism (*see* above, II.). Did the parties intend for a three-member tribunal in all instances? Or does the reference in the arbitration agreement to the institutional rules (including their EPP) suggest that the

---

[25]) *E.g.*, Art. 2 Appendix IV ICC Rules, Art. 42(2)(a) Swiss Rules, Art. 45(5) VIAC Rules, Art. 17 SCC Expedited Arbitration Rules, Art. 1 Schedule 3 SIAC Rules, Art. 42.2(a) HKIAC Rules. In contrast, the EPP of the DIS Rules do not contain a specific provision on the number of arbitrators, i.e., the provisions of the ordinary proceedings under the DIS Rules apply.

[26]) *E.g.*, Art. 42(2)(a) Swiss Rules, Art. 45(5) VIAC Rules, Art. 42.2(a) HKIAC Rules.

parties actually wanted the default rule of a sole arbitrator to apply in expedited procedures? To avoid such uncertainty, parties could consider explicitly specifying the number of arbitrators for expedited procedures in their arbitration agreement.

In addition, parties should be aware that some EPP effectively authorize the arbitral institution to appoint a sole arbitrator even if the arbitration agreement provides for a three-member tribunal.[27]) Awards resulting from proceedings where the arbitral institution has overridden the party agreement may be at risk of challenges, as a tribunal composition contrary to the parties' agreement generally provides grounds for setting aside or refusing enforcement of the award.[28]) At least three decisions based on the SIAC Rules demonstrate that the risk of an award being challenged is not merely theoretical.[29]) The institutions also seem to be aware of these risks and only rarely override the parties' agreement.[30]) In any event, parties who want a three-member tribunal also in expedited procedures should explicitly state this in their arbitration agreement to avoid ambiguity. Arbitral institutions are likely to defer to such an explicit party agreement.[31])

B. Qualifications

In addition to the number of the arbitrators, selecting the right person is also important. EPP present specific challenges. In particular, they have to be conducted within a (generally) fixed and shorter timeframe than ordinary proceedings (*see* below, V.A.). This requires that the arbitrator has sufficient

---

[27]) Art. 2(1) Appendix IV ICC Rules; *cf.* also Art. 5(3) SIAC Rules 2016, now Art. 7 Schedule 3 of the SIAC Rules (2025).

[28]) Art. 34(2)(iv) UNCITRAL Model Law, Art. V(1)(d) New York Convention.

[29]) Shanghai No.1 Intermediate Court, in the case of Nobles Resources Pte. Ltd. v. Good Credit International Trade Co. Ltd. (2016); Singapore High Court, AQZ v. ARA [2015] SGHC 49; Singapore International Commercial Court, BXS v. BXT [2019] SGHC(I) 10. For a more detailed discussion of the issue *see, e.g., Daniel Ling Tien Chong & Benjamin F. Hughes, Chapter 11: Whither Party Autonomy? Constitution of the Tribunal under Expedited Procedures,* in *Kaplan, Pryles* et al. (eds.), *International Arbitration: When East Meets West – Liber Amicorum Michael Moser* (2020), 129; *Wehowsky,* Expedited Procedures, *supra* note 13, paras. 524 *et seq.*; *Mohamed S. Abdel Wahab, Chapter 6: Expedited Institutional Arbitral Proceedings Between Autonomy and Regulation,* in *Laurent Lévy & Michael Polkinghorne* (eds.), *ICC Dossier No. 16: Expedited Procedures in International Arbitration,* Dossiers of the ICC Institute of World Business Law, Volume 16 (2017), 133, 140-144.

[30]) Between 2017 and 2022, the ICC overruled the parties' agreement in only 35 of the 524 EPP cases up to that point; *see Elina Zlatanska & Romain Dupeyré, Expedited Procedures – Practical and Comparative Considerations,* in: ICC Dispute Resolution Bulletin 2023 No. 1, 76, 77.

[31]) *Cf. Philipp Schütt, Fast-Track Arbitration: Das neue beschleunigte Verfahren der ICC,* SchiedsVZ 2017, 81, 85.

availability to meet such a tight schedule. In addition, the tight deadlines do not allow for much passivity or distraction. Rather, what is needed is a proactive arbitrator with strong case management skills capable of guiding the proceedings in an efficient manner.[32])

IV. Conduct of the Proceedings

Arbitration proceedings require meticulous planning, organisation, and management, even more so than litigation in state courts. This necessity arises because, generally, arbitration laws and rules do not comprehensively regulate the procedure. Instead, they leave many procedural issues to the discretion of the arbitral tribunal, allowing for proceedings tailored to the specific needs of the parties.[33]) In the context of EPP, the need for efficient case management becomes even more critical. To render an award within the tight deadlines often set by institutional rules on EPP, both arbitrators and parties have to ensure that the proceedings in general are managed efficiently (*see* below, A.). Furthermore, to reduce the duration and cost of arbitration, they should deploy the tools offered by the various EPP for the modification of traditionally time-consuming and cost-intensive aspects of ordinary procedures (*see* below, B.).

A. Case Management

1. Setting the Procedural Framework

Establishing the "rules of the game" at the outset of the proceedings is crucial when conducting arbitration under EPP. This is why some EPP rules expressly stipulate that the arbitral tribunal shall hold a first case management conference ("**CMC**") promptly, or within a specified time, (generally) after the transmission of the file to the tribunal.[34]) Even in the absence of such a requirement, it is crucial that a CMC be held without undue delay.

To make the most out of the opportunity offered by the initial CMC, the arbitral tribunal should familiarise itself with the case file in advance and identify the key factual and legal issues.[35]) This approach – often referred to as

---

[32]) ICC Commission Report, Controlling Time and Costs in Arbitration (March 2018), para. 13 (available under https://iccwbo.org/wp-content/uploads/sites/3/2018/03/861-2-ENG-Techniques-for-Controlling-Time-and-Costs-in-Arbitration.pdf).

[33]) *Gary B. Born, International Commercial Arbitration – Chapter 15: Procedures in International Arbitration* (3rd ed. 2024), § 15.08 [M].

[34]) *E.g.*, Art. 3(3) Appendix VI ICC Rules; Art. D5 NAI Rules; Art. 29 SCC Expedited Arbitration Rules.

[35]) *Seraglini & Baeten, Expedited Rules and the Possibility of Immediate Measures, supra* note 5, 51 *et seq.*; *Klaus Peter Berger & J. Ole Jensen, Due process paranoia and the procedural judgment rule: a safe harbour for procedural management decisions by inter-*

"proactive case management" – will enable the arbitral tribunal and the parties to focus on the key issues at hand, adopt appropriate procedural solutions, and thereby streamline the proceedings.[36]) In practice, this means that, prior to the CMC, the arbitral tribunal should thoroughly review the request for arbitration and the response in order to determine the most appropriate procedural measures for the dispute. If the parties have not submitted a comprehensive request and/or response, the tribunal could consider addressing written questions to the parties in advance of the CMC in order to get a better understanding of the key issues.[37]) In any event, the arbitral tribunal should encourage the parties to make considerations and even proposals on case management and procedure so that these can be discussed at the first CMC.[38]) As with ordinary arbitration proceedings, it is advisable that the arbitral tribunal prepares and provides the parties with an agenda, a draft procedural timetable and a draft procedural order No. 1 on which the parties can comment ahead of the CMC.[39]) Given that proper preparation will take some time, the CMC should not be rushed. Overall, careful planning of the proceedings will lead to a more efficient outcome than a quick but poorly prepared CMC. Arbitral institutions should also consider this when deciding whether to extend the time limit for holding a CMC.[40])

For the sake of efficiency, the arbitral tribunal and the parties should consider holding the first CMC (or any subsequent CMCs) via telephone, videoconference, or other means of electronic communication. Some institutional rules even require that, as a general rule, the first CMC[41]) or all hearings[42]) are held in this way.

The first CMC should ideally determine the procedure for the entire arbitration and outline it in the procedural timetable established at that time.[43]) However, it may sometimes be advisable for the arbitral tribunal to defer certain procedural decisions until later (*e.g.*, whether an oral hearing should be

national arbitrators, in *William W. Park* (ed.), Arbitration International, Volume 32, Issue 3 (2016), 415, 431.

[36]) ICC Commission Report, Controlling Time and Costs in Arbitration, *supra* note 32, para. 28.

[37]) *Seraglini & Baeten*, *Expedited Rules and the Possibility of Immediate Measures*, *supra* note 5, 53.

[38]) *Cf.* ICC Commission Report, Controlling Time and Costs in Arbitration, *supra* note 32, para. 26.

[39]) *Karl-Heinz Böckstiegel*, *Party Autonomy and Case Management – Experiences and Suggestions of an Arbitrator*, SchiedsVZ 2013, 1, 2 *et seq.*

[40]) *Cf.* Art. 3(3) Appendix VI ICC Rules.

[41]) Art. D5 NAI Rules.

[42]) Art. 3 Schedule 3 SIAC Rules (2025).

[43]) *Seraglini & Baeten*, *Expedited Rules and the Possibility of Immediate Measures*, *supra* note 5, 52.

held), especially if it lacks sufficient information at the time of the first CMC.[44]) With respect to the procedural timetable, adhering to a strict timeline is crucial to ensure that the award is rendered within the prescribed deadlines. However, as commentators have correctly pointed out, the arbitral tribunal should avoid being over-ambitious when setting the procedural timetable. Instead, it should adopt a realistic approach, as unrealistic time planning can lead to extension requests by the parties, which may in turn jeopardize the entire timetable.[45]) The arbitral tribunal should exercise foresight and also allow for some flexibility to handle unexpected procedural contingencies, safeguarding the parties' due process rights.[46]) When drafting the procedural timetable, the arbitral tribunal might consider working backward from the deadline for rendering the award.[47]) This approach involves planning adequate time for drafting the award, scheduling the hearing and its preparation, and accounting for any necessary written submissions.

At this juncture, a more general observation is warranted. The success of proceedings under the EPP heavily depends on the cooperation of the parties with the arbitral tribunal. Therefore, the arbitral tribunal should endeavor to build trust with the parties, with transparency being a crucial element.[48]) During the initial CMC, the tribunal should therefore inform the parties about the specific challenges associated with expedited proceedings and its intention to adopt a proactive and firm approach, in order to meet the goals set by the EPP. This transparency is likely to enhance the parties' trust in the tribunal's procedural management and foster acceptance of its procedural decisions. Consequently, it is also advisable for party representatives, alongside their counsel, to participate in the CMC.[49])

2. Parties and their Counsel

Effective case management is also crucial for counsel and parties in EPP, where limited submission opportunities and tighter deadlines significantly

---

[44]) ICC Commission Report, Controlling Time and Costs in Arbitration, *supra* note 32, para. 26.

[45]) *Böckstiegel, Party Autonomy and Case Management, supra* note 39, 3.

[46]) *Seraglini & Baeten, Expedited Rules and the Possibility of Immediate Measures, supra* note 5, 52.

[47]) *Neil Kaplan & Chiann Bao, So, Now You are an Arbitrator: The Arbitrator's Toolkit – Chapter 14: Expedited Proceedings and Early Determination* (2022), 107, 108.

[48]) See *Klaus Peter Berger & Innhwa Kwon, H Streamlining Of The Proceedings And Early Evaluation*, in: *Nikolaus Pitkowitz* et al., *Chapter II: The Arbitrator and the Arbitration Procedure, The Vienna Predictability Propositions: Paving the Road to Predictability in International Arbitration*, in *Christian Klausegger* et al. (eds.), Austrian Yearbook on International Arbitration 2017, 115, 143 *et seq.*

[49]) *Berger & Kwon, Streamlining Of The Proceedings And Early Evaluation, supra* note 48, 143 *et seq.*; ICC Commission Report, Controlling Time and Costs in Arbitration, *supra* note 32, para. 30.

impact the process. Counsel must plan strategically, ensuring that all evidence can be collected within the time limits and anticipating the necessary steps of the proceedings in advance. This is particularly challenging for respondents, who will generally only fully understand the claimant's arguments after the Request for Arbitration is filed.

It is essential to establish clear work streams, allocate tasks efficiently within the team, and, if possible, assemble larger teams to manage unexpected tasks. Counsel should also prepare clients for the constraints of EPP by explaining the expedited nature of the proceedings and ensuring they have sufficient resources to meet tight deadlines, particularly in cases where internal coordination is required. For clients with hierarchical structures requiring internal approvals, such as management boards or government entities, it is particularly crucial to activate these procedures early to avoid delays.[50]) By understanding these dynamics and planning accordingly, counsel can navigate the expedited arbitration process more effectively, ensuring that their clients' interests are well represented within the stringent confines of EPP.

B. Selected Procedural Measures

To reduce the duration and cost of arbitration proceedings, EPP under various institutional rules typically introduce modifications to aspects of the proceedings that are traditionally deemed to be time-consuming and cost-intensive. They achieve this either by directly incorporating provisions that deviate from the rules governing ordinary procedures or by explicitly granting the arbitral tribunal the procedural discretion to implement these measures. Notably, such measures include limitations on the number and length of submissions (*see* below, 1.), a rather restrictive approach on document production (*see* below, 2.), and a tendency in favour of dispensing with oral hearings (*see* below, 3.). The following sections examine these measures in more detail and provide guidance on how arbitrators can use them effectively without compromising the parties' right to present their case.

1. Submissions

a) Rounds of Submissions

One of the perceived sources of delays and high costs in arbitration is the voluminous submissions made by the parties over multiple rounds. Therefore, a common feature of many institutional rules on EPP is the inclusion of provisions that either directly restrict the number of submissions or grant the arbitral tribunal the authority to do so.[51]) Often, the rules provide that after the

---

[50]) *Cf. Böckstiegel, Party Autonomy and Case Management, supra* note 39, 3.

[51]) A notable example for the latter is Art. 3(4) Appendix VI ICC Rules.

request for arbitration and the response, there shall only be one further round of submissions.[52]) Under many rules, a further submission by the claimant is allowed in reply to a counterclaim filed by the respondent.[53]) If the rules do not limit the number of submissions, the arbitral tribunal should after consultation with the parties determine how many rounds of submissions will be required for the parties to exercise their right to be heard and for the arbitral tribunal to establish the facts of the case and render a correct award within the time limits set by the applicable EPP.[54])

If there is a party agreement on the number of submissions, the arbitral tribunal should generally adhere to this arrangement, even if it jeopardizes the timely issuance of the award, as failure to do so may expose the award to challenge.[55]) Agreements between the parties on multiple rounds of submissions typically justify extending the deadline for the award or may be interpreted as a decision to opt out of the expedited procedures altogether.

Restricting the rounds of submissions serves a practical purpose. If an award is to be rendered within the strict time frames stipulated in EPP, the procedural timetable can only accommodate a limited number of submissions. Moreover, the concept behind this restriction is to enhance efficiency. By limiting the opportunities to present their case, parties are compelled to focus on the material factual and legal issues and relevant evidence. Expedited procedures do not lend themselves to surprises or "ever-evolving" cases.[56]) Rather, the parties must lay out their case in a straightforward manner from the outset, *i.e.*, they must present all the facts and evidence they rely on and make their legal arguments. This "front-loading" of EPP has significant implications for the parties' preparation efforts. Given that, in principle, only one further round of submissions will be granted, parties and their counsel are advised to treat the request for arbitration as a full statement of claim and the response as a full statement of defence. Some arbitration rules even explicitly mandate this approach.[57])

---

[52]) *E.g.*, Art. 3 DIS Rules; Art. 42(2)(c) Swiss Rules; Art. 45(9) no. 1 VIAC Rules; Art. 42(2)(d) HKIAC Rules.

[53]) *E.g.*, Art. 3 DIS Rules; Art. 42(2)(c) Swiss Rules.

[54]) *Wehowsky*, Expedited Procedures, *supra* note 13, para. 608.

[55]) *Seraglini & Baeten, Expedited Rules and the Possibility of Immediate Measures, supra* note 5, 54.

[56]) *Cf. Irene Welser & Christian Klausegger, Chapter II: The Arbitrator and the Arbitration Procedure – Fast Track Arbitration: Just fast or something different?,* in *Christian Klausegger* et al. (eds.), Austrian Yearbook on International Arbitration 2009, 259, 272–273.

[57]) *E.g.*, Art. 6 and 9 SCC Expedited Arbitration Rules.

b) Length of Submissions

An additional case management technique discussed in this context are limitations to the length of the submissions.[58]) According to the 2021 International Arbitration Survey, the one procedural option most participants would be willing to do without was the unlimited length of written submissions.[59]) The underlying rationale of this procedural tool is that by limiting the length of submissions, parties will be compelled to be more concise. This conciseness will, in turn, facilitate more efficient decision-making by the arbitral tribunal. With streamlined and focused submissions, the tribunal will be in a better position to comprehend the case and identify the salient issues in dispute.[60])

The majority of the most prominent arbitration rules, however, do not contain strict page limits for submissions. A notable exception are the ICSID Rules which provide for a 200-page limit for the statement of claim and the statement of defence and for a 100-page limits for the reply and rejoinder.[61]) The ICC Rules also confer upon the arbitral tribunal the discretion to limit the length and scope of written submissions.[62]) A similar provision is found in the recently revised 2025 SIAC Rules.[63])

Regardless of explicit provisions, numerous commentators encourage arbitral tribunals to utilize this procedural tool, including providing instructions on the formatting of submissions to prevent circumvention.[64]) Some commentators go further, suggesting that arbitral institutions should consider imposing presumptive page limits for submissions (and even exhibits) in EPP, based on the amount in dispute.[65]) Arbitral tribunals would retain the discretion to increase these limits depending on the circumstances of the case and party agreements. Alternatively, arbitral institutions could set page limits as guidelines, which the arbitral tribunal could then consider when deciding on costs.[66])

---

[58]) *Joshua B. Simmons* & *Natalia Szlarb*, *Chapter 3: Stopping the Arms Race: Page Limits in International Arbitration*, in *Alan M. Anderson* and *Herman Verbist* (eds.), *Expedited International Arbitration: Policies, Rules and Procedures* (2024), 59.

[59]) Queen Mary University of London and White & Case, 2021 International Arbitration Survey, 13 (available under https://www.qmul.ac.uk/arbitration/media/arbitration/docs/LON0320037-QMUL-International-Arbitration-Survey-2021_19_WEB.pdf).

[60]) *Simmons* & *Szlarb*, *Stopping the Arms Race*, *supra* note 58, 62 *et seq.*

[61]) Rule 81.

[62]) Art. 3(4) Appendix VI ICC Rules

[63]) Art. 3 Schedule 3 of the SIAC Rules (2025).

[64]) *Jörg Risse*, *Ten Drastic Proposals for Saving Time and Costs in Arbitral Proceedings*, in *William W. Park* (ed.), Arbitration International, Volume 29, Issue 3 (2013), 453, 456.

[65]) *Simmons* & *Szlarb*, *Stopping the Arms Race*, *supra* note 58, 70 *et seq.*

[66]) *Simmons* & *Szlarb*, *Stopping the Arms Race*, *supra* note 58, 70 *et seq.*

c) The Right Balance

The potential for restrictions on the number and/or length of submissions to lead to savings in time and costs is apparent. However, the primary concern with such restrictions is whether they violate the due process rights of the parties, particularly their right to present their case. This concern often results in what has been described as "due process paranoia", *i.e.*, the reluctance of arbitral tribunals to act decisively for fear that their award might be set aside or refused enforcement due to a perceived violation of due process.[67]) Consequently, some arbitral tribunals may be inclined to be rather lenient, allowing for numerous rounds of submissions or accepting submissions made outside the designated rounds or that exceed the set page limits.

Restrictions on the number and/or length of submissions, in principle, do not constitute a violation of the parties' right to present their case. Arbitration laws and rules do not generally enshrine an absolute right for parties to present their case in any manner they prefer. Instead, the right to be heard implies a reasonable opportunity for the parties to present their case, excluding obstructive or dilatory tactics. Judicial practice generally also shows deference to the arbitral tribunal's procedural discretion, with courts rarely interfering in procedural management decisions.[68]) Consequently, provided that the restrictions on the rounds and length of submissions afford the parties a reasonable opportunity to present their case, taking into account the complexity and value of the dispute, these restrictions should be deemed appropriate and compliant with due process requirements. This is consistent with the practice adopted by different national or international judicial systems.[69])

In light of this, arbitral tribunals should make effective use of these procedural tools in expedited procedures. Limiting submissions to a single round, in addition to the request for arbitration and the answer, is generally appropriate for cases of low value and complexity, as envisioned by EPP. Similarly, page limits could be determined based on the complexity of the case, with commercial arbitration potentially allowing for lower limits than those specified by the ICSID Rules (*see* above, b)). In any event, the arbitral tribunal should discuss these limitations with the parties during the first CMC and seek their approval. In this context, the tribunal may refer to the overarching principle, explicitly stated in some EPP, that it must consider the parties' interest in expediting the proceedings[70]) as a rationale for such restrictions.

When a party makes submissions that deviate from the stipulated restrictions (*e.g.*, unsolicited submissions beyond those provided for in the

[67]) *Berger & Jensen, Due process paranoia, supra* note 35, 419 *et seq.*

[68]) *Berger & Jensen, Due process paranoia, supra* note 35, 421 *et seq.*

[69]) *Cf.* regarding restrictions on the length of submissions *Simmons & Szlar*b, *Stopping the Arms Race, supra* note 58, 66 *et seq.*

[70]) *E.g.*, Art. 4 Annex 4 DIS Rules.

procedural timetable or submissions exceeding page limits), the arbitral tribunal must assess the reasonableness of such actions. Some EPP explicitly provide that the arbitral tribunal may allow the parties to make further written submissions in compelling circumstances.[71]) For instance, an additional submission might be warranted if compelling reasons prevented the party from presenting the relevant facts or evidence earlier, such as the emergence of new evidence. Similarly, if the respondent surprisingly introduces a new aspect in a late submission, the claimant might reasonably want to respond. In any event, whenever possible, parties are advised to seek leave from the arbitral tribunal for such submissions, clearly demonstrating the necessity for doing so.

When there are no reasonable grounds for procedural deviations from the above restrictions, the arbitral tribunal must consider appropriate sanctions. The answer is not straightforward and depends on the specifics of the case. Disregarding unsolicited submissions is a stringent measure which might be justified if the submission is delayed without reason, especially shortly before or after the oral hearing or the issuance of the award. In any event, the tribunal may consider sanctioning dilatory conduct by imposing costs on the non-compliant party.[72]) If the tribunal decides to consider the irregular submission, it must, in principle, for reasons of equal treatment afford the same opportunities to the opposing party, such as allowing an additional submission or extending page limits.

2. Documentary and Written Witness Evidence

The volume of and manner in which documentary and written witness evidence are presented can also significantly affect the duration and cost of the proceedings.

This concerns especially whether and in which way document production is conducted. Document production is a common feature of international arbitration, as evidenced by the IBA Rules on the Taking of Evidence in International Arbitration.[73]) However, it is often criticised for the substantial costs and delays it tends to generate.[74]) Most EPP do not contain restrictions on document production. But some EPP, notably the ICC Rules and the 2025 SIAC Rules, address this concern by explicitly granting the arbitral tribunal the discretion to deny requests for document production.[75]) According to a review of the final awards rendered in ICC expedited procedures between 2017 and

---

[71]) *E.g.*, Art. 30 para. 1 SCC Rules.

[72]) *Cf.* ICC Commission Report, Controlling Time and Costs in Arbitration, *supra* note 32, para. 82.

[73]) Art. 3 IBA Rules on the Taking of Evidence in International Arbitration.

[74]) *Risse*, *Ten Drastic Proposals*, *supra* note 64, 459 *et seq.*; Queen Mary University of London and *White & Case*, 2021 International Arbitration Survey, *supra* note 59, 13–14.

[75]) Art. 3(4) Appendix VI ICC Rules; Art. 3 Schedule 3 of the SIAC Rules (2025).

2022, a document production phase rarely took place (17 %). When it did, it only lasted a few weeks and/or the requests concerned the production of specific documents.[76]) A few EPP go even further, such as the ACICA Rules, which exclude discovery altogether and allow only the production of particular documents,[77]) or the 2025 SIAC Rules on Streamlined Procedures, which generally do not permit requests for document production.[78])

Even when there are no explicit restrictions on document production, arbitral tribunals should be aware of the challenges a document production phase will pose given the strict time schedule under EPP. While an *a priori* exclusion of document production solely based on the expedited nature of the proceedings may not be appropriate – especially where parties with a common law background are involved – extensive document production exercises are generally incompatible with the character of expedited procedures. The arbitral tribunal should highlight this to the parties at the first CMC. If, after hearing the parties, the tribunal decides that a document production should take place, such a procedure should be rather limited. Specific measures to enhance time and cost efficiency include limiting the number of requests, restricting requests to documents that are relevant and material to the outcome of the case, establishing reasonable time limits for document production, and utilizing the Redfern Schedule.[79]) Regarding timing, it will often be appropriate for the document production phase under EPP to take place after the request for arbitration and the response have been filed, as the parties will, in principle, have already set out their cases in detail.[80])

The arbitral tribunal might want to consider adopting further measures to enhance efficiency regarding documentary evidence in general. For example, it could waive the requirement for translations in languages understood by all participants or permit non-certified translations unless an objection is raised.[81]) Additionally, the tribunal might minimize the need for submitting hard copies of documents.[82])

Another cost- and time-intensive measure frequently employed in international arbitration is the preparation of written witness statements. These statements are intended to enhance efficiency by indicating the relevance

---

[76]) *Zlatanska* & *Dupeyré*, *Expedited Procedures*, *supra* note 30, 78.

[77]) Art. 24.4 and 24.5 ACICA Expedited Arbitration Rules.

[78]) Art. 11(b) Schedule 2 of the SIAC Rules (2025).

[79]) ICC Commission Report, Controlling Time and Costs in Arbitration, *supra* note 32, para. 52.

[80]) *Cf. Böckstiegel*, *Party Autonomy and Case Management*, *supra* note 39, 4; ICC Commission Report, Controlling Time and Costs in Arbitration, *supra* note 32, para. 51.

[81]) ICC Commission Report, Controlling Time and Costs in Arbitration, *supra* note 32, para. 56.

[82]) ICC Commission Report, Controlling Time and Costs in Arbitration, *supra* note 32, para. 55.

of the testimony, enabling the other party to prepare for cross-examination,[83]) and saving time during hearings by substituting direct examination.[84]) In practice, however, the efforts required to prepare written witness statements, both by the witness and the assisting counsel, can outweigh the anticipated efficiency benefits. Under EPP, the arbitral tribunal should carefully assess whether written witness statements are justified. It may, *e.g.*, be appropriate in cases where written witness statements make an oral hearing dispensable (particularly if there is no need to assess the witness's credibility by way of an examination in person). It may also be warranted if the complexity of the facts of the case requires the preparation of witness statements in advance.[85]) In such cases, early guidance from the arbitral tribunal on relevant and disputed facts would streamline witness statements, ensuring they focus on pertinent issues and avoid unnecessary detail.

3. Oral Hearings

Oral hearings in arbitration proceedings are often expensive and time consuming, not least because of the significant preparation they require and of their length.[86]) Accordingly, many EPP grant arbitral tribunals discretion to dispense with an oral hearing and conduct the arbitration on a document only basis.[87]) Similarly, some EPP provide that an oral hearing shall be held only at the request of a party or if deemed necessary by the arbitral tribunal.[88]) Many rules also stipulate that, if oral hearings are to be held, they shall be limited to a single oral hearing.[89]) Some EPP, however, such as the DIS Rules, mandate that a single hearing shall take place unless all parties agree otherwise.[90]) This provision aims to balance the limitations on the parties' opportunity to present their case due to the restrictions on the number of submissions.[91])

---

[83]) *Risse, Ten Drastic Proposals, supra* note 64, 459.

[84]) ICC Commission Report, Controlling Time and Costs in Arbitration, *supra* note 32, para. 78.

[85]) *Cf. Florian Haugeneder* & *Patrizia Netal*, Article 45 [Expedited Proceedings], in Vienna International Arbitral Centre of the Austrian Federal Economic Chamber (ed.), Handbook VIAC Rules of Arbitration and Mediation: A Practitioner's Guide (2nd ed. 2019), 346, 353.

[86]) *Nigel Blackaby, Constantine Partasides* & *Alan Redfern, Redfern and Hunter on International Arbitration* (7th ed. 2023), para. 6.167 *et seq.*

[87]) *E.g.*, Art. 3(5) Appendix VI ICC Rules; Art. 42.2(e) HKIAC Rules; Art. 11 UNCITRAL Expedited Arbitration Rules.

[88]) *E.g.*, Art. 45(9.3) VIAC Rules; Art. 33 SCC Rules; Art. 3(a) of Schedule 3 of the SIAC Rules (2025).

[89]) *E.g.*, Art. 45(9.3) VIAC Rules; Art. 42(2)(d) Swiss Rules; Art. D8 NAI Rules.

[90]) *See* Art. 4 Annex 4 DIS Rules.

[91]) *Meike von Levetzow, Art. 4 DIS-BV*, in *Jan Heiner Nedden, Axel Benjamin Herzberg* & *Ulrich Kopetzki, ICC-SchO, DIS-SchO* (2nd ed. 2022), para. 1.

When the arbitral tribunal has discretion to hold an oral hearing, it should generally not hastily dismiss this option for the sake of time and cost savings. Oral hearings are integral to exercising the parties' right to be heard, allowing them to present their factual and legal arguments comprehensively and enabling the arbitral tribunal to develop a clearer understanding of the dispute.[92]) Opening statements by the parties elaborating on the key issues might be particularly helpful in this respect.[93]) Additionally, if witness evidence (both factual and expert) has been submitted in writing, an oral hearing may be essential to evaluate this evidence properly, whether through cross-examination or examination conducted by the arbitral tribunal.[94])

Before dispensing with oral hearings altogether, arbitral tribunals should consider alternative measures to enhance efficiency. Limiting hearings to a single oral hearing, if not already mandated by the EPP, is generally advisable. Additional hearings should only take place under exceptional circumstances, such as the inability of a crucial witness to attend due to illness. Additionally, the duration of the hearing should be reasonable (*e.g.*, depending on the complexity of the dispute, one or two days). In addition, the arbitral tribunal can restrict the time allocated to the parties for their oral arguments and for the cross-examination of witnesses.[95]) In order to focus the evidentiary hearing on essential issues, the arbitral tribunal, in consultation with the parties, may consider selecting specific witnesses to be heard. This process will involve identifying which issues are relevant to the dispute based on the parties' submissions.[96]) Arbitral tribunals should discuss this with the parties in a CMC in preparation for the oral hearing.

Organizational measures can also help save time and costs. Some EPP explicitly provide that oral hearings shall be conducted in electronic form, unless otherwise agreed by the parties or ordered by the arbitral tribunal.[97]) Remote or hybrid hearings can indeed prove useful in promoting efficiency. They avoid time for travelling to the hearing and costs for a hearing location. In-person hearings should generally be reserved for cases requiring extensive examination of witnesses on complex factual questions or where it is important for the arbitral tribunal to have a personal impression of the witness. Regarding the record of the hearing, the arbitral tribunal might consider using an audio recording instead of a transcript produced by a professional court reporter. This approach could result in cost and time savings by eliminating the need to search for and engage a reporter, as well as avoiding the common practice of parties reviewing the transcript and requesting changes. However, a transcript

---

[92]) *Wehowsky*, Expedited Procedures, *supra* note 13, para. 643.

[93]) *Risse*, *Ten Drastic Proposals*, *supra* note 64, 461 *et seq.*

[94]) *Cf. Wehowsky*, Expedited Procedures, *supra* note 13, para. 646.

[95]) *Cf.* ICC Commission Report, Controlling Time and Costs in Arbitration, *supra* note 32, para. 80.

[96]) *Cf. Wehowsky*, Expedited Procedures, *supra* note 13, para. 647.

[97]) *E.g.*, Art. D8 NAI Rules; Art. 3(b) Schedule 3 of the SIAC Rules (2025).

can generally be helpful for the arbitral tribunal in drafting the award, potentially contributing to time savings during this phase of the procedure.

Finally, the question of whether written post-hearing submissions should be allowed requires consideration. Some EPP, such as the VIAC Rules,[98]) explicitly prohibit submissions after the oral hearing. Even where no such restriction exists, post-hearing submissions can delay the proceedings and conflict with strict timelines for issuing the award. Instead, the arbitral tribunal may consider oral closing submissions at the hearing. If written submissions are nevertheless warranted, the arbitral tribunal should set a short deadline for any post-hearing submissions after the hearing.

V. The Arbitral Award

A. Deadlines and Consequences

A key feature of EPP is a short time limit for the arbitral tribunal to issue the final award. The majority of EPP provide for a time limit of six months.[99]) Notable exceptions are, *e.g.*, the SCC and the CIETAC, which provide for a shorter time limit of only three months.[100]) Depending on the EPP, the time limit may start with the constitution of the tribunal,[101]) the transmission of the file to the tribunal,[102]) or the (first) case management conference.[103])

It is important for arbitrators to bear in mind that, depending on the institution, the institution's scrutiny process must also take place within these time limits. The ICC, *e.g.*, expects the arbitral tribunal to submit its draft award within five months of the case management conference in order to effectively comply with the six-month time limit for rendering the award.[104])

If the award is not rendered within the relevant time limit, the arbitrators may be subject to sanctions by the institutions. This is without prejudice to a justified request for an extension (*see* below, D.). Some institutions provide that the arbitrator's fees may be reduced for failure to render the award in time.[105]) Another measure sometimes provided is the replacement of one or more

[98]) Art. 45(9.4) VIAC Rules.

[99]) *E.g.*, Art. 4(1) Appendix VI ICC Rules; Art. 45(8) VIAC Rules; Art. 1 DIS Rules; Art. 42(2)(e) Swiss Rules; Art. 42.2(f) HKIAC Rules; *see* also Art. D11 No. 1 NAI Rules ("five months").

[100]) Art. 43 SCC Rules; Art. 65(1) CIETAC Rules.

[101]) *E.g.*, Art. 5.2(d) SIAC Rules; Art. 16(1) UNCITRAL Expedited Arbitration Rules.

[102]) *E.g.*, Art. 9 VIAC Rules, Art. 42(2)(e) Swiss Rules; Art. 43 SCC ("case was referred to the Arbitrator"); Art. 42.2(f) HKIAC Rules.

[103]) *E.g.*, Art. 4(1) ICC Rules Art. 1 DIS Rules.

[104]) ICC Note to Parties and Arbitral Tribunals, *supra* note 12, para. 159

[105]) ICC Note to Parties and Arbitral Tribunals, *supra* note 12, para. 161.

arbitrators for failing to fulfill their duties within the prescribed time limits,[106]) or, similarly, a challenge for failure to act without undue delay.[107]) Replacing an arbitrator, however, may cause additional delays if procedural steps, such as oral hearings, need to be repeated. Therefore, the appropriateness of this sanction depends on whether the benefits of replacing the dilatory arbitrator outweigh the resulting delays.[108]) Finally, a significant incentive for adhering to time limits is the potential damage to an arbitrator's reputation, which may reduce the likelihood of future nominations by the institution or the parties for subsequent (expedited) proceedings.

In contrast, exceeding the time limit for rendering an award under the EPP will not generally result in the loss of jurisdiction of the arbitral tribunal.[109]) Failure to comply with an express agreement of the parties to issue an award within a certain time may, under certain circumstances, affect the jurisdiction of the arbitral tribunal and, as a consequence, create the risk that the award will be challenged or unenforceable (Art. V(1)(d) New York Convention).[110]) Ultimately, however, the consequences of non-compliance with the time limit will depend on the interpretation of the parties' agreement. Time limits for the issuance of an award in institutional EPP can typically be interpreted as mere administrative provisions aimed at achieving an efficient decision-making process, but not at depriving the arbitral tribunal of its jurisdiction.[111]) To avoid any uncertainty in this respect, some rules expressly state that failure to observe the time limit does not affect the arbitral tribunal's jurisdiction.[112])

Above, this article has provided recommendations on how to structure the proceedings in the phase between the constitution of the tribunal and a (potential) hearing in order to meet the aforementioned deadlines (*see* above, IV.). The following paragraphs will examine how arbitrators (and the parties) can optimize the phase concerning the drafting of the award (*see* below, B. and C.) or at least avoid sanctions by the institution (*see* below, D.).

---

[106]) Art. 15(2) ICC Rules.

[107]) Art. 11.6 HKIAC Rules.

[108]) *Jonas C. Hinrichsen, Reza Shahrokhi & Erin Cronje, Chapter 2: Expedited Arbitration in Action: Is the Practice Making Perfect?*, in *Alan M. Anderson* and *Herman Verbist* (eds.), *Expedited International Arbitration: Policies, Rules and Procedures* (2024), 31, 54–55.

[109]) *Wehowsky*, Expedited Procedures, *supra* note 13, para 767; *Stephan Wilske & Lars Markert, § 1061 ZPO*, in *Volter Vorwerk & Christian Wolf* (eds.), BeckOK ZPO (54th ed. September 1, 2024), para. 37.1; *Schütt, Fast-Track Arbitration*, *supra* note 31, 86 (regarding the ICC Rules); *see* with respect to the deadline to issue the award in ordinary proceedings under the ICC Rules: German Federal Court, judgment dated April 14, 1988 – III ZR 12/87, NJW 1988, 3090, 3092 and Higher Regional Court Karlsruhe, order dated January 4, 2012 – 9 Sch 02/09, SchiedsVZ 2012, 101, 106.

[110]) *Wilske & Markert, § 1061 ZPO*, *supra* note 109, para. 37.1.

[111]) *Wehowsky*, Expedited Procedures, *supra* note 13, para 767.

[112]) *E.g.*, Art. 45.8 VIAC Rules; Art. 5 Annex IV DIS Rules.

B. (Summary) Reasoning

Drafting the arbitral award can often take a considerable amount of time, in particular its reasoning part. This raises the question of whether the reasoning requirements should be modified in EPP to save time and increase efficiency. The EPP take different approaches in this respect. Some provide that the arbitral tribunal may state the reasons in summary form, unless the parties have agreed to an award with no reasons at all.[113]) Some rules go further and provide that the award must contain reasons only if one of the parties so requests.[114]) Other EPP do not contain any specific requirements for the reasoning of the award compared to the ordinary procedures under their rules.[115])

At least in jurisdictions that have enacted arbitration laws faithfully adopting the UNCITRAL Model Law, an agreement by the parties to omit the reasoning of the award would appear permissible.[116]) In principle, the parties may also agree so by reference to institutional EPP.

Given these options, what should the parties agree in relation to the reasoning? At first glance, agreeing on no reasoning might seem to be the best option to increase efficiency by reducing the time needed to render the award. However, the reasoning serves several important functions in the arbitration proceedings that the parties should consider before making such a decision.

The requirement to state reasons can discipline the arbitral tribunal and improve the quality of its decision. Writing a reasoning forces the arbitral tribunal to ensure that its decision is based on a coherent legal analysis supported by the parties' factual submissions.[117]) It helps the tribunal to better spot contradictions and inconsistencies in its argumentation. Furthermore, parties are more likely to accept a decision that provides a reasoning. Even if the party has lost, it may accept that the tribunal has carefully weighed the evidence and arguments presented and made a sound decision.[118]) If a party perceives that the tribunal has issued a well-reasoned decision that does not contain apparent flaws, it will be rather reluctant to initiate risky and expensive set-aside proceedings against the award.[119]) Finally, reasons are also helpful for the court's assessment in enforcement and setting-aside proceedings. Without

---

113) *E.g.*, Art. 42.2(g) HKIAC Rules; Art. 4 Schedule 3 SIAC Rules, Art. 42(2)(f) Swiss Rules.

114) Art. 42(1) SCC Rules, Art. 41.1 FAI Expedited Arbitration Rules 2020.

115) *E.g.*, the EPP of the ICC, VIAC or DIS.

116) Art. 31(2) UNCITRAL Model Law; *see, e.g.*, Section 1054(2) of the German Code of Civil Procedure (*Zivilprozessordnung – ZPO*).

117) *Nikolaus Pitkowitz, Chapter III: The Award and the Courts, On the Ground of Grounds – Reasons for Sound Reasoning of Arbitral Awards*, in *Christian Klausegger* et al., Austrian Yearbook on International Arbitration 2023, 243, 247.

118) *Id.*, at 248.

119) *Id.*, at 248.

reasons, it can be difficult for the courts to understand the basis for the arbitral tribunal's decision. In particular, a reasoning will help the courts to assess issues concerning the tribunal's jurisdiction and public policy and will facilitate the assessment of whether the proceedings have been conducted properly.[120])

In view of these disadvantages, parties should generally be wary of agreeing on an unreasoned award in EPP. While they may initially benefit from a quicker decision, there is a risk that they may later face difficulties in the form of a flawed award that is prone to time-consuming challenges or is unenforceable. Instead, it generally seems to be a sensible middle way for the parties of expedited procedures to agree on summary reasoning.[121]) Summary reasoning can significantly reduce the time needed to prepare the award and can avoid (at least to some extent) the risks mentioned before.

Arbitrators should proactively discuss the options with the parties at the first case management conference and document the parties' agreement on a summary (or no) reasoning in the procedural order No. 1.

C. Proactive Award Writing and Party Assistance

In addition, arbitrators should not leave the drafting of the award until the end of the proceedings. Several parts of the award can usually be prepared already at the beginning or during the course of the proceedings. This applies in particular to the administrative and procedural parts of the award (*e.g.*, names and representatives of the parties, terms of the arbitration agreement), the summary of the parties' submissions and the procedural history. However, it can also apply to facts that are undisputed or legal issues that are already clear after the first round of submissions. Arbitrators should therefore keep track during the proceedings of what they can already put down in writing. This generally also applies to ordinary arbitration proceedings. However, it is all the more important in expedited procedures where efficiency is of the essence.

Arbitrators could also explore more unconventional methods to reduce the time needed to draft the award. One such proposal contemplates the parties assisting in drafting the final award. Under this method, the arbitral tribunal shall identify the main issues of the proceedings immediately after the last round of submissions or, if applicable, the hearing.[122]) The arbitral tribunal

---

[120]) *Id.*, at 249; *Wehowsky*, Expedited Procedures, *supra* note 13, para. 785.

[121]) *Wehowsky*, Expedited Procedures, *supra* note 13, para. 787; *see* also the UNCITRAL Report of Working Group II (Dispute Settlement) on the work of its seventy-ninth session dated February 23, 2024, 6–7 (available under https://documents.un.org/doc/undoc/gen/v24/012/41/pdf/v2401241.pdf). The Working Group decided against amending the model clause for highly expedited proceedings so as to dispense with the requirement to provide reasons for the award.

[122]) *Risse*, *Ten Drastic Proposals*, *supra* note 64, 462.

shall then instruct the parties to summarize their positions in a short Word document, which also contains references to those parts of the parties' previous submissions where the issues are discussed in detail.[123]) The arbitral tribunal can then use these summaries in the final award, rather than drafting them from scratch.[124]) Clearly, this proposal is intended solely to save drafting time and does not absolve the arbitral tribunal from its duty to thoroughly review and consider the submissions.

D. Last Resort: Extension Request

As a last resort, the EPP generally provide that the institutions may extend the aforementioned deadlines in exceptional circumstances.[125]) It is reported that the institutions handle extension requests restrictively.[126]) Arbitrators should therefore be careful to structure the proceedings in such a way as to stay within the time limits imposed in order to avoid being sanctioned by the institutions. However, unforeseen circumstances may arise that are beyond the arbitrator's control. Such reasons, which may justify an extension, are, *e.g.*, procedural and/or substantive complexity or the conduct of the parties.[127]) But also illness of an arbitrator, accidents or other cases of force majeure.[128])

If such an event occurs, the arbitral tribunal should discuss with the parties the implications for the proceedings and, preferably, obtain the consent of both parties to an extension request. The request for an extension should, in particular, set out the reasons why the delay is beyond the arbitrator's control and why an extension is justified.

This also applies where the delay is caused by the parties' own behavior (*e.g.*, by requesting additional submissions). As set out above, EPP provide arbitral tribunals with several tools to limit such delays. However, it is difficult for the arbitral tribunal to conduct the proceedings in a certain way if both parties disagree. In such a case, the arbitral tribunal should clearly document that it has informed the parties of the consequences for the duration of the proceedings (*e.g.*, in a procedural order). While this may not prevent the proceedings from exceeding the initial time limit, it can at least reduce the risk of the arbitral tribunal facing sanctions for such delays.

---

[123]) *Id.*, 462.

[124]) *Id.*, 462.

[125]) *E.g.*, Art. 31(2) ICC Rules, Art. 45(8) VIAC Rules, Art. 42(2)(e) Swiss Rules; *Wehowsky*, Expedited Procedures, *supra* note 13, para. 761.

[126]) *See, e.g.*, in relation to the VIAC Rules: *Haugeneder & Netal, Article 45 [Expedited Proceedings]*, *supra* note 85, 351.

[127]) *Hinrichsen, Shahrokhi & Cronje, Expedited Arbitration in Action*, *supra* note 108, fn. 87.

[128]) *Haugeneder & Netal, Article 45 [Expedited Proceedings]*, *supra* note 85, 351.

VI. Concluding Remarks

EPP provide a powerful toolbox for enhancing the efficiency and cost-effectiveness of arbitration proceedings. By shortening timelines and simplifying the procedure, EPP can effectively address the key concerns associated with ordinary arbitration proceedings, particularly in cases where time and resources are of critical importance.

As set out above, the effective application of EPP requires a careful balance between speed and the procedural rights of the parties. The role of the arbitral tribunal is crucial in this process. Tribunals must proactively manage the proceedings, implementing the necessary measures to adhere to the prescribed timelines while maintaining procedural fairness. The additional powers provided under EPP can bolster the tribunal's confidence, helping to mitigate undue hesitation stemming from concerns about due process.

Ultimately, however, the success of expedited procedures relies on collaboration. Constructive engagement from the parties, combined with a tribunal committed to efficient case management, is essential to realizing the full potential of EPP as a streamlined and effective dispute resolution mechanism.

The Vienna Propositions: Setting a New Beat in Resolving ESG Disputes, Embracing Innovation, and Tackling Legal Challenges in a Changing World

Nikolaus Pitkowitz/Johanna Kathan-Spath and the 22 contributors[1])

I. Introduction

In 2024, Austria's leading arbitration conference, the Vienna Arbitration Days ("VAD"), was held under the dynamic theme *"Rock me arbitration – Tune in to a new beat!"*. The two-day conference explored latest developments and emerging trends in dispute resolution, with a particular focus on the role of arbitration in regard to Environmental, Social and Governance ("ESG") disputes. Since its inception in 2008, the VAD has consistently featured distinguished speakers who share insights into contemporary challenges and future directions in international arbitration and dispute resolution more generally. The conference upholds its tradition of fostering meaningful, high-level discussions among practitioners, academics, and industry experts.

A central feature of the VAD is the **World Café session**, first introduced in 2016 and now a cornerstone of the conference. This interactive format invites participants from diverse professional backgrounds, varying levels of experience, and different legal specializations to actively engage in focused discussions. Designed to mirror the vibrant atmosphere of a traditional Viennese coffee house, the World Café on the second day of the conference featured twelve themed tables, each dedicated to a topic aligned with the overarching theme of the 2024 VAD.

Each table was moderated by two carefully selected experts who facilitated two rounds of in-depth discussions. Participants of the VAD had the opportunity to select tables based on their interests and join in small and dynamic group conversations. In 2024, the topics offered at the World Café tables included:

---

1) *Antje Baumann, Ondrej Cech, Philippa Charles, Marija Dobrić, Brian Gabriel-Oiwoh, Nata Ghibradze, Anne-Karin Grill, Amelie Huber-Starlinger, Katherine Khan, Ilma Kasumagić, Sofia Kovačević, Torsten Lörcher, Arnela Maglić, Kamalia Mehtiyeva, Isabelle Michou, Peter Rižnik, Violeta Saranciuc, Milica Savić, Friederike Schäfer, Nicol Schneider, Marina Stanisavljević, Caroline Strohmeier.*

- Green Arbitration Clauses: A Contractual Commitment to Good Behavior?
- Is Arbitration Generally Suitable to Resolve ESG Disputes?
- Special Features of ESG Arbitrations – What Are They, and What Makes Them So "Special"?
- Climate Change Disputes (and Quantum Issues Relating to "Causation")
- Sanctions and Arbitration: Impact of Sanctions on Disputes and Proceedings
- Energy Disputes and Force Majeure
- ESG: Finding Common Ground – Mediating ESG Disputes
- ESG Defenses in ISDS
- Do We Need Rules to Address AI in Arbitration?
- Ethical and Other Challenges in AI in Arbitration
- Arbitration Transformed: Leveraging AI Tools for Smarter Dispute Resolution
- Transparency in International Arbitration: How Good Is It?

Part II of this chapter provides a comprehensive overview of the key findings and insights gained from these World Café discussions, summarized as the "Vienna Propositions".

Part III presents detailed reports prepared by the World Café moderators, showcasing the diverse perspectives and valuable contributions of the participants. These reports are shared with the explicit consent of all participants and reflect the collective ideas and insights generated during the sessions.

We sincerely thank the moderators for their thorough preparation before the sessions, for leading the discussions, and for their dedication in finalizing the discussion reports afterwards. Our heartfelt appreciation also goes to all VAD 2024 participants, whose engagement and expertise ensured the success of the World Café.

II. Propositions for Resolving ESG Disputes, Embracing Innovation, and Tackling Legal Challenges

Based on the lively discussions held during the 2024 World Café sessions, the moderators and participants collaboratively developed the following key propositions. These insights are organized into three overarching categories: A) Questions concerning the resolution of ESG disputes; B) Approaches to integrating technology and artificial intelligence ("AI") in arbitration; and C) Issues related to current concerns in the field of arbitration and beyond.

A. Propositions for Resolving ESG Disputes

- **Enhance Arbitration's Flexibility to Meet ESG Demands**
One World Café table explored whether arbitration in general is suitable for resolving ESG disputes. The discussion emphasized that arbitration must evolve both procedurally and institutionally to effectively address the complexities of ESG disputes. This evolution should ensure that arbitration not only serves the interests of the disputing parties but also aligns with the broader public interest inherent in ESG matters (*see in more detail Chapter III.A.*)

- **Clarify and Standardize ESG Obligations in Contracts and Law**
Another World Café table examined the unique features of ESG arbitrations. Participants agreed that while arbitration is fundamentally well-suited to resolving ESG-related disputes, the consistent definition of ESG obligations across contractual and legal frameworks is crucial for delivering predictable and fair outcomes (*see in more detail Chapter III.B.*).

- **Balance State Sovereignty and Investor Rights in ESG Regulations**
Focusing on investor-state dispute resolution, one World Café table discussed ESG defenses and reflected on the evolving commitments and implications in the ESG era. The group emphasized the need to balance states' regulatory freedom to pursue public policy objectives (such as ESG regulations) with the protection of foreign investors' rights (*see in more detail Chapter III.C.*).

- **Promote Mediation as a Strategic Tool for Resolving ESG Disputes**
A fourth World Café table on the topic of ESG dispute resolution discussed mediation as an alternative and/or additional dispute resolution method for ESG disputes. In summary, the discussion recognized mediation's potential to offer a collaborative and efficient path to resolve ESG conflicts, often involving diverse stakeholders, and highlighted that mediation in addition may also offer space for broader commitments for future actions, apologies, and the development of new business strategies as part of the dispute resolution process (*see in more detail Chapter III.D.*).

B. Propositions for Harnessing Technology and Artificial Intelligence in Arbitration

- **Leverage AI to Enhance Efficiency and Decision-Making in Arbitration**
One World Café table discussed how arbitration is being transformed through the use of AI and how AI tools can be leveraged for smarter

dispute resolution. The consensus was that AI should be thoughtfully and strategically implemented to streamline processes, enhance legal research, and support data analysis. However, ensuring confidentiality and procedural integrity remains crucial for the broader adoption of AI in arbitration (*see in more detail Chapter III.E.*).

- **Establish Clear and Flexible Regulations for AI Use in Arbitration**
  Another discussion focused on the need for regulation of AI in arbitration. Participants emphasized the importance of a balanced regulatory framework. According to the discussion, it is essential for regulations concerning AI to consider the specific context (*e.g.*, whether used by arbitrators or counsel) and to address key concerns such as confidentiality, transparency, and fairness – without hindering innovation in arbitral proceedings (*see in more detail Chapter III.F.).*

- **Address Ethical Risks and Biases in AI-Driven Arbitration and Bridge the Generational Divide in Perceptions of AI**
  A third World Café table focused on AI explored the ethical and other challenges of using AI in arbitration and whether the discussion participants perceive AI as friend or foe. The participants agreed that ethical challenges, including data bias and accountability, must be proactively managed by every practitioner in this field to ensure that AI upholds fairness and trust in dispute resolution. Additionally, they recognized a significant generational divide in perceptions of AI, underscoring the need for fostering intergenerational dialogue, targeted training, and collaboration to align innovative and ethical AI practices in arbitration (*see in more detail Chapter III.G.).*

C. Propositions for Tackling Legal Challenges in a Changing World: Sanctions, Transparency and Climate Change

- **Practitioners Need to be Aware of Sanctions Regulations and Consider Their Impact on Dispute Resolution**
  One of the topics of global interest discussed at a World Café table was the pressing issue of EU sanctions against the Russian Federation and their potential impact on disputes and arbitration proceedings. Participants emphasized that arbitration must continuously evolve and practitioners must keep up with the complexity of regulatory developments to effectively handle disputes involving affected parties and, more broadly, disputes arising from international sanctions and geopolitical tensions. Preserving legal certainty and access to justice remains essential (*see in more detail Chapter III.H.).*

- **Strengthen Transparency While Preserving the Qualities of Arbitration**
  Another World Café table examined the role of transparency in arbitration and analyzed with the participants whether they consider (increasing) transparency in arbitration to be crucial and a positive development. The discussions revealed that a more nuanced approach would be beneficial. What is required is a *balanced* approach to transparency in order to enhance trust and legitimacy without at the same time compromising arbitration's core values of confidentiality, efficiency, and flexibility – key factors in choosing arbitration as the dispute resolution method in the first place (*see in more detail Chapter III.I.*).
- **Promote Practical Integration of Green Arbitration Practices**
  Two World Café tables addressed climate change-related issues, with one focusing on "Green Arbitration Clauses". Participants emphasized that achieving sustainable arbitration practices requires active engagement from all stakeholders – parties, arbitrators, and institutions. This involves not only flexible contract drafting (*e.g.*, incorporating green clauses) but also a broader commitment to personal responsibility and institutional reforms. A dynamic and collective approach was considered more effective than relying solely on rigid contractual clauses (*see in more detail Chapter III.J.*).
- **Develop Innovative Legal Strategies for Complex Climate Change Disputes**
  The second World Café table on climate change explored the challenges of addressing causation and quantum in climate change disputes. Participants in the two discussion rounds at this table highlighted that climate change disputes are becoming increasingly prevalent due to expanding environmental regulations and the transition to greener economies, which can unintentionally cause harm and trigger legal conflicts. These disputes pose complex challenges in proving causation and accurately assessing damages. Practitioners must adopt flexible and innovative legal strategies to effectively navigate these evolving issues (*see in more detail Chapter III.K.*).

The comprehensive reports on these discussions, thoughtfully compiled by the moderators following the World Café session can be found in the chapter below. They provide in-depth insights into the key findings and reflect the diverse perspectives and valuable contributions of all participants. These detailed analyses offer a solid foundation for further reflection and future developments in dispute resolution practice.

III. World Café Reports

A. Is Arbitration Generally Suitable to Resolve ESG Disputes?

Antje Baumann/Sofia Kovačević

1. Introduction

As the global focus on sustainability, human rights, and responsible governance intensifies, companies are increasingly facing disputes related to ESG criteria. These disputes often arise between businesses, investors, communities, and other stakeholders. One key question in that conjecture is whether arbitration can effectively address ESG disputes.

This report draws on insights from a roundtable discussion involving legal practitioners and industry experts during which the evolving nature of ESG disputes was explored and the suitability of international arbitration as a tool for their resolution was evaluated.

The primary objective of the roundtable discussion was to offer practical recommendations for enhancing the effectiveness of international arbitration in resolving ESG disputes ensuring that it not only serves the interests of the parties involved but also aligns with the broader public interest by promoting sustainable and responsible business policies and practices.

2. Understanding ESG Disputes

Environmental, Social, and Governance ("ESG") considerations have moved to the forefront of the business and regulatory landscape. However, the term "ESG" is not a "*new kid on the block*". It is a 20-year-old term that was first used in the "Who Cares Wins"[2]) report published under the guidance of then UN Secretary General Kofi Annan and UN Global Compact in collaboration with the Swiss government aimed at supporting the growth of sustainable capital flows by influencing, supporting, and enabling capital market stakeholders to better integrate the ESG factors into capital allocation and portfolio management processes.

In recent years, ESG is gaining traction and the companies will no longer have to demonstrate just their financial performance, instead they will have to demonstrate that their businesses have socially responsible and environmentally sensitive behavior contributing to sustainable development. Thus, the increase in ESG-related obligations will inevitably lead to an overall increase in potential

[2]) https://documents1.worldbank.org/curated/fr/444801491483640669/pdf/113850-BRI-IFC-Breif-whocares-PUBLIC.pdf, unless otherwise stated all online sources were last accessed on January 17, 2025.

disputes. For that reason, the roundtable discussion focused on exploring the definition of ESG disputes aimed at providing more guidance for the interpretation of ESG claims in international arbitration. Although the discussion during the roundtable demonstrated that there is no overarching definition of ESG disputes and that the exact elements are yet to be defined in the future and specified through practice, the moderators jointly with the participants categorized two types of claims in relation to the ESG obligations suitable to be resolved through international arbitration: a) claims based on or in the context of commercial contracts, and b) claims based on international trade and investment treaties, both to be addressed further below.

a) Types of ESG Claims: Claims based on Commercial Contracts

Although the ESG considerations are not seen as financial performance indicators, they remain at the top of the agenda for many companies which will have to align their corporate policies with ESG objectives. One of the mechanisms for managing ESG risks is including the ESG clauses in commercial contracts. Such clauses are either a product of the companies' own ESG objectives and policies or of the mandatory ESG due diligence rules aimed to force companies to take a more proactive approach with regards to their ESG risk management. An example of the latter is the Directive on Corporate Sustainability Due Diligence (Directive 2024/1760), entered into force on 25 July 2024,[3]) which introduced mandatory human rights and environmental due diligence requirements for large EU and non-EU companies operating in the EU.[4])

As a consequence of the evolving legal landscape, ESG clauses are becoming increasingly common in all types of commercial contracts. Most notable examples are supply chain agreements, sales agreements, loan facilities, construction project agreements, joint venture agreements, and M&A agreements. However, the ESG obligations can also be found in the long-term

---

[3]) The Directive on Corporate Sustainability Due Diligence (Directive 2024/1760) entered into force on July 25, 2024 which was after the Vienna Arbitration Days Conference that took place on June 7–8, 2024. For that reason, the implications of the Directive on Corporate Sustainability Due Diligence were not discussed at the roundtable.

[4]) Recital 16 of the Directive on Corporate Sustainability Due Diligence (Directive 2024/1760) stipulates that the aim of the Directive is to ensure that EU and non-EU companies *"contribute to sustainable development and the sustainability transition of economies and societies through the identification, and where necessary, prioritisation, prevention and mitigation, bringing to an end, minimisation and remediation of actual or potential adverse human rights and environmental impacts connected with companies' own operations, operations of their subsidiaries and of their business partners in the chains of activities of the companies, and ensuring that those affected by a failure to respect this duty have access to justice and legal remedies"*.

investment contracts in the energy, mining and infrastructure sectors. ESG clauses create a binding and contractual obligation(s) for the parties. Thus, their increased inclusion in the commercial contracts coupled with a fact that ESG clauses are usually drafted in a very broad manner to include complex standards will inevitably lead to disputes. Many of these commercial contracts will provide for international arbitration. In other words, once the dispute arises in relation to the ESG obligation(s) embedded in these commercial contracts containing an arbitration clause, the parties will be obliged to initiate arbitration and resolve their dispute before an arbitral tribunal.

It is noteworthy that, during the roundtable discussion, participants were initially asked about their experience with ESG disputes in their respective practices. At the outset, majority of participants indicated that they had not encountered such disputes. However, as the discussion progressed and the definition of ESG disputes was further elaborated – particularly in relation to claims arising from commercial contracts – several participants subsequently acknowledged that they may have indeed faced ESG-related disputes in their practices. This observation underscores the complexity and breadth of ESG standards, suggesting that even experienced practitioners may require additional time to fully comprehend these evolving concepts.

b) Types of ESG Claims: Claims based on International Trade and Investment Treaties

The landscape of investor state dispute settlement (ISDS) mechanisms is still largely dominated by the old-generation international investment agreements (IIA). Notwithstanding the fact that ESG considerations were not explicitly included in most of the old generation of IIAs, there is a growing number of arbitrations that were initiated due to matters such as lack of environmental permits, green incentives, corruption, etc. Conversely, IIAs signed since 2020 feature many reformed provisions aimed at safeguarding the State's right to regulate in order to support the countries' implementation of legitimate measures and their efforts towards achieving the sustainable development goals which are referenced in the treaty preamble.[5]) These reformed provisions usually provide for the ESG standards in a very broad manner[6]) and interpretation and application of these provisions may also give rise to disputes in the future.

---

[5]) IIA Issue Note; Trends in the Investment Treaty Regime and a Reform Toolbox for the Energy Transition, August 2023, 4–5.

[6]) For example, the Italian Model BIT 2022 stipulates in its preamble the importance of strengthening the investment relations in accordance with "*objective of sustainable development in the economic, social and environmental dimensions, and of promoting investment between them, mindful of the needs of the business communities of each Party, in particular small and medium-sized enterprises, and of high levels of environmental and labour protection through relevant internationally recognised standards and international agreements, to which both Parties are party.*"

The growing emphasis on ESG standards is gradually transforming the initial purpose of IIAs, which was primarily to provide foreign investors with protection and avenues for redress against host states. The shift toward expanding states' regulatory rights to achieve sustainability objectives may lead to scenarios where states are more likely to bring claims or counterclaims against investors. This was unanimously recognized by the participants at the roundtable.

3. Evaluating Arbitration as a Tool for Resolving ESG Disputes

Upon examining various types of ESG disputes, participants engaged in a deeper discussion concerning the suitability of international arbitration for resolving ESG claims. The moderators facilitated a brief debate evaluating the advantages and challenges of international arbitration as a mechanism for addressing ESG-related disputes.

a) Advantages of Arbitration in ESG Disputes

In an era where businesses are increasingly held accountable for their ESG practices, the need for efficient dispute resolution mechanisms has become more pressing. Although ESG disputes may be resolved through litigation, arbitration, or other forms of alternative dispute resolution, it seems that the traditional court systems might not be the best avenue for handling ESG claims due to the length of the proceedings, expenses and lack of specialized expertise. On the other hand, arbitration offers a tailored approach that can address these challenges more effectively.

Arbitration offers several advantages which makes it a well-suited avenue for resolving ESG claims, which were also unanimously recognized by the participants at the roundtable. In the first place, ***flexibility*** was recognized as one of the key benefits of arbitration in resolving ESG disputes. Compared to litigation, arbitration allows the parties to tailor the process to the specific needs of their ESG disputes by agreeing on the procedural rules, applicable law, and the language of the proceedings. Arbitration provides a ***neutral forum*** allowing the parties to select and appoint independent ***arbitrators with specialized knowledge and expertise*** in ESG-related matters. Arbitrators with specialized knowledge in ESG-related matters such as, *e.g.*, environmental law, corporate governance, or human rights will ensure that the nuances of ESG issues are properly understood and considered, which is often a challenge in traditional courts. Participants further emphasized neutrality as an important factor in resolving the ESG claims involving multinational corporations, particularly when one of the parties feels that local courts may not be impartial. Finally, the participants at the roundtable identified the ***enforceability of the arbitral awards*** through the worldwide coverage of the Convention on the Recognition and Enforcement of Foreign Arbitral Award (New York Convention) to be a significant advantage in the globalized context of ESG disputes, where companies may operate in multiple jurisdictions.

Arbitration presents a viable alternative for resolving ESG disputes, offering advantages such as flexibility, neutrality, expertise and worldwide enforceability. It is a popular alternative to litigation, and it has begun to emerge as a promising avenue for resolving ESG claims. However, its success will depend on how well it can evolve to meet the unique demands of ESG issues, including transparency and inclusivity of all affected stakeholders, some of the challenges which were pinned down during the roundtable discussion.

b) Challenges of Arbitration in ESG Disputes

While arbitration offers several advantages, there are also challenges that may limit its effectiveness in resolving ESG disputes. One such challenge is the ***lack of public accountability***. ESG-related matters often involve issues of public interest, *e.g.*, environmental protection, human rights violations, or governance failures that have substantial social impact. In this context, while the confidential nature of arbitration might be beneficial for businesses, it conflicts with public interest in ESG matters. For that reason, critics argue that such matters should be resolved in public courts to ensure transparency, accountability, and public scrutiny. Another challenge that speaks in favor of litigating ESG claims is the ***absence of precedent.*** Namely, the participants recognized that the transparent resolution of the ESG claims before the traditional courts would create case law which is necessary for improving certainty in the ESG dispute resolution, especially in the area where consistent legal standards and public guidance are needed to promote responsible business practices.

A further reason why arbitration is challenged as a means of resolving ESG disputes is its ***accessibility and dependence on parties' consent***. During the discussion, the participants acknowledged that arbitration ultimately depends on party consent. However, ESG disputes frequently impact communities or groups that are not direct parties to the arbitration agreement. In other words, it is challenging to ensure that the rights of the third parties, impacted by the ESG claims, are addressed within the traditional arbitration framework, which primarily focuses on resolving disputes between the named parties. As a further challenge, the participants indicated that even in situations where an ESG dispute impacts only the parties to the arbitration agreement, there is an ***unequal bargaining power***. This might concern the ESG disputes between large corporations and local communities or workers where a disproportionate difference in financial resources might exist between the parties, enabling big corporations to use their resources to potentially influence the selection of arbitrators or shape the arbitration process in their favor.

Finally, some of the participants raised the argument that ***arbitration lacks the coercive powers*** that national courts possess, and which are necessary for enforcing the ESG claims which relate to the wider public interest.

c) Need for Specific Rules or Reform

Finally, together with the participants, the moderators discussed whether ESG arbitration requires a specific set of "ESG Arbitration Rules". This question was negated because the arbitral procedure as such does not differ depending on whether ESG-related issues or other legal issues are at stake.

The only exception that was discussed concerned the publication of awards. For the reasons outlined above – *i.e.*, development of case-law and public accountability – the publication of awards is of particular importance when it comes to ESG-related disputes. For this reason, a reform of existing rules of arbitral institutions would be helpful. The participants discussed in this conjecture whether an option could be to provide not for a mandatory publication of the complete award but only of such sections of an award which are of interest for the public and for the emergence of the necessary case law. It was, furthermore, noted that a distinction between "real" ESG cases and such cases which only have an ESG-angle might be necessary when it comes to the need for a reform.

4. Concluding Remarks

The overall aim of the roundtable discussion was to jointly explore the tools available for facilitating the resolution of ESG-related disputes through international arbitration while also providing recommendations. To achieve this objective, the moderators led a discussion that examined the main characteristics of ESG disputes and addressed both the advantages and criticisms of international arbitration as a mechanism for resolving ESG-related disputes.

The roundtable discussion emphasized that while arbitration holds significant promise for resolving ESG disputes due to its flexibility, neutrality, specialized expertise of the arbitrators, and the enforceability of its awards under the New York Convention, its effectiveness will depend on its ability to evolve. To maximize the potential of arbitration in resolving ESG disputes, arbitration institutions and practitioners must work towards adapting arbitration to accommodate the unique demands of ESG-related matters, ensuring that it serves not just the interests of the disputing parties but also the broader public interest inherent in ESG matters.

B. Special Features of ESG Arbitrations: What are They, and What Makes Them so "Special"?

Friederike Schäfer/Marina Stanisavljević

1. Introduction

Concern for adverse environmental, social, and governance ("**ESG**") impact is exponentially growing. Corporate ESG policies, compliance, and investor due diligence are being scrutinized more than ever. ESG standards are seeping into commercial deals, financing arrangements, investment contracts, investment treaties, and indeed, international arbitration.

However, concern for ESG compliance and impact is not new. International arbitration disputes relating to ESG are not new. Investment tribunals have been dealing with issues of environmental damage and human rights for decades. Treaties concerning human rights have been around since at least the middle of last century. Is the term "ESG arbitration" just a new label for a phenomenon already observed for many decades or are there new elements? What do we even mean by ESG arbitrations?

The discussion revolved around these themes, as well as the specific features of ESG arbitrations, their procedural, legal, and factual particularities, while also exploring the question: are the features of ESG truly special, and if so, is international arbitration equipped to resolve them?

2. Discussion

a) Features of ESG Arbitrations

aa) What are ESG Arbitrations?

Participants agreed that "ESG arbitrations" include both (i) disputes involving direct breaches of ESG obligations or standards, and (ii) disputes that relate to, or have a component, involving ESG.

As for (i), participants considered the source of ESG obligations. They identified that ESG obligations may arise from private contracts, national laws and regulations, or international law. Of the three, participants focused on contractual ESG obligations, and drew the following conclusions:

1. International commercial contracts often have ESG-related clauses, but not necessarily specific ESG obligations. An example would be a general representation and warranty in a contract by one party that it has complied with all applicable environmental laws.
2. Contracts that do contain specific ESG obligations are either by reference to national or international law, or standalone obligations. The latter raised several issues: what do specific ESG clauses in contracts

look like, would they come in form of representations and warranties, reporting obligations, termination rights in case of violation, or in another form; how broadly should they be drafted; and how does their interpretation vary with time (as national laws on ESG evolve and ESG standards continue to be defined and re-defined and are even sometimes defined by the promisor itself, *e.g.*, where the obligation relates to compliance with a self-commitment to monitor the supply-chain or the like).

As for (ii), participants reflected on previous arbitrations and concluded that many involved ESG matters. *E.g.*, investment treaty disputes in energy transition projects, FIDIC contracts where use of materials was damaging to the environment, financing projects concerning lender ESG compliance, long-term development projects in the health sciences/pharmaceutical sector (supply-chain compliance with ESG), and post M&A disputes involving breaches of seller warranties concerning ESG.

When it came to the content of ESG obligations, various areas were mentioned including: the use of environmentally harmful materials, ground contamination, deforestation, greenwashing, unsafe work conditions, emission reduction (net zero) and child labor.

bb) Types of Claims in ESG Arbitrations

The types of claims that may arise are varied and not limited to any particular category. Participants explored potential claims for specific performance (the breaching party be ordered to comply with its ESG obligations), damages for delays in projects, reputational damages, and claims for loss of profit.

Reputational damages sparked an interesting discussion, with the majority agreeing that such a claim would most likely not suffice on its own and would be pursued together with other damage claims. Some participants flagged the idea of the involvement of third parties, such as NGOs, where the primary goal of the dispute would be to expose the non-compliance of large corporations. It was noted that the contractual and confidential nature of commercial arbitration may deter such involvement.

b) Issues Arising in ESG Arbitrations

aa) Interpreting ESG Clauses

One of the main points of discussion was how tribunals should interpret vague or broad ESG clauses. For example, where a contract provides that a party shall ensure "good work conditions", use "sustainable materials" or adopt "environmentally friendly practices". Does this create a playground for arbitrators? And if not a playground, does it create an unworkable problem? Most participants agreed it does not, and that interpreting vague contractual clauses is the bread and butter of judicial work. The question of interpretation would boil down to how well the parties could substantiate the meaning of "sustainable", "environmentally friendly" or "good" through supporting evidence (including expert testimony).

A further issue is that many ESG standards stemming from national (or international) law are too wide to create concrete legal obligations. They are seen as soft law, or aspirational standards. National ESG policies are often just that – policies. How much weight should an international tribunal give to aspirational standards and policies when interpreting hard law obligations?

bb) Ambiguous or Conflicting ESG Laws

Tribunals may also have to deal with conflicting ESG standards and laws, either between different national jurisdictions, or between national and international law. The point of geographical disparity was also raised: ESG standards are far more advanced and regulated in certain parts of the world (*e.g.*, in the EU) than in others. Participants concluded that this may not be a question of conflicting ESG standards (*i.e.*, it is not about good work conditions versus bad work conditions) but rather the absence of clear ESG obligations in some States that are still developing or implementing their ESG policies. Depending on the specific contract and configuration of statutory ESG obligations such questions may have to be solved by following conflict of laws rules, always bearing in mind the specific nature of ESG elements and the parties' expectations.

cc) Fact-finding, Causation, Damage

Participants briefly touched upon the topic of fact-finding, concluding that this was more a question of expertise than fact. The use of expert testimony was seen as the most effective way to help bridge the gap in ESG arbitrations and help meet the criteria for establishing breach, causation, and damage.

c) Are These Issues "Special"? Are Arbitrators Equipped to Resolve ESG Disputes?

The discussion concluded that the "specialty" of ESG disputes was more in the substance (*i.e.*, the value that we assign to ESG issues as a society), than in the process. For every issue raised during the discussion, participants eventually concluded that it was not a novel legal issue – *e.g.*, interpretation of legal obligations, the role of evidence, the role of experts, causal links, fears of due process, etc.

Participants also agreed that complex questions of causation and damage are not necessarily more complex because they relate to ESG. Arbitral tribunals deal with a variety of topics that concern highly sensitive global matters. They have well-developed legal principles available to them, a vast amount of international case law, and legal systems that may serve as reference. These are sufficient tools to help tribunals navigate ESG matters, to the extent they differ from topics that have come up in the past.

3. Conclusion

ESG arbitrations are not a novelty. The novelty is rather in the market's focus on compliance with ESG as a distinguishing factor in competition, and the acceptance of ESG standards as state-of-the-art.

Issues may arise on the definition of ESG obligations in commercial and investment contracts, national and international laws. These definitions may be affected when contractual provisions conflict with national or international laws, or where national laws are not yet in compliance with international ESG standards.

Although ESG arbitrations may raise complex questions, such as the scope of obligation, causation, fact-finding and damages, tribunals routinely deal with such issues in non-ESG cases. There is no reason why tribunals cannot continue to apply the same logic in ESG arbitrations. The discussion concluded that arbitration is well-equipped to handle and resolve disputes concerning, or arising out of, ESG issues.

C. ESG Defenses in ISDS – Reflections on New Commitments and Implications

Violeta Saranciuc/Anne-Karin Grill

1. Introduction

In the era of environmental, social and governance ("ESG") reforms, States face increasing pressure to enact and enforce regulations addressing ESG-related issues, such as climate change, human and labor rights, ethical practices for businesses and anti-corruption policies. In the past, regulatory activity often gave rise to compensation claims by foreign investors who argued that host State conduct affected their investments or was expropriatory. States, on the other hand, defended against such claims by invoking their sovereign right to regulate in the public interest. The increased focus on ESG commitments will likely further accentuate the tension between sovereign and private interests, contouring a new wave of ESG-based defenses.

The participants of the 'World Café' roundtable discussion co-moderated by the authors, convened on the occasion of Vienna Arbitration Days 2024, explored the interplay between host States' ESG commitments and those related to the protection of foreign investments and shared views about the future of the ISDS system in light of increasing ESG relevance. This report combines the results of two very lively rounds of discussions.

2. Where ESG Meets ISDS

The discussions elicited several possible scenarios in which ESG may intersect with investment arbitration, including instances of ESG commitments becoming the subject matter of compensation claims brought by investors, ESG non-compliance leading to allegations of illegality of the investment, ESG non-compliance (by investors or by host States) being taken into account in the assessment of liability or evaluation of damages, ESG counterclaims, etc.

One of the focal points of the discussions was the extent to which ESG-related public policy objectives can justify host States' regulatory conduct when it interferes with the rights of foreign investors. This question most often arises when ESG measures implemented by host States form the immediate subject matter of the international investors' compensation claims. The practical experience shared by some of the discussion participants related to investment arbitration cases in which host States invoked their regulatory autonomy in the area of environmental protection as a defense against investor claims. These practical accounts prompted the conclusion that the treatment of host States' regulatory conduct depends on the particular wording of each international investment agreement ("IIA") and on the specific facts of each individual case. Therefore, no generalization can be made with regard to the treatment of host States' regulatory activity in the field of ESG.

Many IIAs include provisions recognizing in explicit terms a right to regulate. This reflects the latest efforts on the part of State parties to prioritize their regulatory autonomy in matters of public interest when negotiating investment treaties. However, few of the new-generation IIAs have already entered into force and given rise to claims. Prior existing IIAs are either silent about host States' right to regulate or recognize it at least implicitly, with sometimes broad or inconclusive statements about welfare objectives in the recitals, and, only in rare instances, in the operative part of the treaty, limiting or restricting the scope of protection in the event of *bona fide* measures taken by host States that are in the public interest.

As part of the 'World Café' roundtable discussions, participants recalled that there is considerable diversity in the way international tribunals analyze claims against measures designed to protect the public interest, such as, but not limited to ESG measures. The approaches vary significantly and can range from accepting only a limited right to regulate without any prejudice to host States' obligations towards foreign investors to broad regulatory autonomy in matters of public interest.

Most often, host States' regulatory conduct was called into question in expropriation claims[7]) and/or in claims based on breaches of the fair and

[7]) *See, e.g., Técnicas Medioambientales Tecmed, S.A. v. United Mexican States*, ICSID Case No. ARB(AF)/00/2, Award, May 29, 2003, para. 121; *Quiborax S.A., Non-Metallic Minerals S.A. v. Plurinational State of Bolivia*, ICSID Case No. ARB/06/2, Award, September 16, 2015, paras. 202, 219.

equitable treatment standard ("FET").[8]) International tribunals analyzed regulatory measures as pertaining to the sovereign[9]) or police[10]) powers of states, sometimes even where the applicable treaty contained no explicit provision or allusion to the right to regulate.[11]) When analyzing the legitimacy of host States' regulatory conduct, international tribunals often emphasized that the right to regulate is not unlimited and is subject to certain conditions, such as good faith, transparency, non-discrimination and proportionality.[12])

International tribunals sometimes resorted to interpretation principles provided in the Vienna Convention on the Law of Treaties ("VCLT") to uphold regulatory measures of host States where the relevant IIA did not expressly provide for a right to regulate in the public interest or a carve-out provision for the specific ESG-related issues.[13]) Thus, IIAs that are silent about host States' ESG obligations (*i.e.*, the majority of the treaties currently in force) were interpreted pursuant to the principle of systemic integration and thus in light of other applicable rules of international law, including rules of customary international law, such as the doctrine of police powers. On the other hand, it was suggested that treaty interpretation by systemic integration may lead to host State's obligations undertaken in non-investment-related treaties being considered as part of the applicable law. Illustrative examples are the Paris Agreement on Climate Change as well as human rights treaties and other international treaties dealing with various specific ESG aspects.[14])

---

[8]) *Saluka Investments BV v. The Czech Republic*, PCA Case No. 2001-04, Partial Award, March 17, 2006, para. 260; *AES Summit Generation Limited and AES-Tisza Erömü Kft. v. Republic of Hungary (II)*, ICSID Case No. ARB/07/22, Award, September 23, 2010, para. 9.3.29.

[9]) *AES Summit Generation Limited and AES-Tisza Erömü Kft. v. Republic of Hungary (II)*, ICSID Case No. ARB/07/22, Award, September 23, 2010, para. 9.3.29.

[10]) *Saluka Investments BV v. The Czech Republic*, PCA Case No. 2001-04, Partial Award, March 17, 2006, para. 260.

[11]) *See, for instance, Gold Reserve Inc. v. Bolivarian Republic of Venezuela (I)*, ICSID Case No. ARB(AF)/09/1, Award, September 22, 2014, para. 595 with reference to Canada – Venezuela BIT (1996); *Saluka Investments BV v. The Czech Republic*, PCA Case No. 2001-04, Partial Award, March 17, 2006, para. 260 with reference to Czech and Slovak Republic – Netherlands BIT (1991).

[12]) *AES Summit Generation Limited and AES-Tisza Erömü Kft. v. Republic of Hungary (II)*, ICSID Case No. ARB/07/22, Award, September 23, 2010, para. 10.3.6; *Saluka Investments BV v. The Czech Republic*, PCA Case No. 2001-04, Partial Award, March 17, 2006, para. 303.

[13]) *Philip Morris Brand SARL, Philip Morris Products S.A. and Abal Hermanos S.A. v. Oriental Republic of Uruguay*, ICSID Case No. ARB/10/7, Award, July 8, 2016, para. 290; *Marfin Investment Group Holdings S.A., Alexandros Bakatselos and others v. Republic of Cyprus*, ICSID Case No. ARB/13/27, Award (Redacted), July 26, 2018, para. 827.

[14]) *See*, for instance, *Philip Morris Brand SARL, Philip Morris Products S.A. and Abal Hermanos S.A. v. Oriental Republic of Uruguay*, ICSID Case No. ARB/10/7, Award, July 8, 2016, para. 304, where the arbitral tribunal referred to Uruguay's obligations

The 'World Café' roundtable discussions also turned around the interplay between host States' commitments towards ESG objectives and the protection of foreign investments. It was highlighted by discussion participants that Host States sometimes challenge the legality of the investment at the jurisdictional stage, alleging that the investment does not qualify for protection on grounds of corruption.[15]) Investors' unlawful conduct, potentially also in respect of established ESG obligations, was brought up as a contributory fault in the assessment of damages.[16]) However, ESG pleas may play out against Host States when their conduct amounts to disregard of their own ESG commitments.

Specifically, one discussion participant pointed out that upholding public welfare objectives should not be achieved at the cost of affecting foreign investments, especially when Host States exercise regulatory power with the objective of overcoming issues caused by their own negligence or otherwise in an abusive manner.

3. Criticism and Reform of ISDS in light of ESG Objectives

During the two discussion rounds, the participants also considered the pertinence of the criticism of ISDS in the context of the ESG agenda and the potential effects of the reforms aimed at addressing such criticism.

It was recalled that in a report dated 13 July 2023, prepared by the Special Rapporteur appointed by the United Nations Human Rights Council ("UNHRC")[17]) on the issue of human rights obligations relating to the enjoyment of a safe, clean, healthy and sustainable environment, ISDS was described as a major obstacle to the urgent actions that States would need to take in order to address the planetary environmental and human rights

assumed under World Health Organization Framework Convention on Tobacco Control dated May 21, 2003.

[15]) *See Metal-Tech Ltd. v. Republic of Uzbekistan*, ICSID Case No. ARB/10/3, Award, October 4, 2013, where the arbitral tribunal denied jurisdiction on the grounds of corruption, and *Unión Fenosa Gas, S.A. v. Arab Republic of Egypt*, ICSID Case No. ARB/14/4, Award, August 31, 2018, para. 7.116, where the arbitral tribunal confirmed its jurisdiction finding that the allegations of corruptions had not been proved.

[16]) *See Yukos Universal Limited (Isle of Man) v. The Russian Federation*, PCA Case No. 2005-04/AA227, Final Award, July 18, 2014, para. 1637; however, in *South American Silver Limited v. The Plurinational State of Bolivia*, PCA Case No. 2013-15, Award, November 22, 2018, para. 875, the arbitral tribunal rejected the contributory fault argument, finding that the treaty violation by the host state was unrelated to the conduct of the investor.

[17]) The Human Rights Council is an intergovernmental body within the United Nations system responsible for strengthening the promotion and protection of human rights around the globe and for addressing situations of human rights violations and making recommendations on them.

crises.[18]) In the words of the Special Rapporteur: "*Foreign investors have weaponized a secretive international arbitration process, known as investor-State dispute settlement (ISDS), that is embedded in thousands of international investment agreements (IIAs), mostly bilateral investment treaties. Claims under the ISDS process are used to challenge climate and environmental actions taken by States and to demand billions of dollars in compensation. These cases are decided not by independent judges but by arbitration lawyers, many of whom work for law firms and represent investors. This unjust, undemocratic and dysfunctional process has sparked a legitimacy crisis in the international investment regime.*"[19])

Reflecting on the criticism of ISDS, the discussion participants exchanged views on whether the concerns regarding the regime's legitimacy and the perceived clash of investor interests with host States' ESG obligations are justified and what could be done to improve the system and its image in the eyes of the public.

Some discussion participants pointed out that the use of international arbitration in the settlement of disputes between international investors and host States should not be in and of itself a matter of concern, even if some concrete reforms could improve the level of confidence in the system. However, it was also suggested that, while such may be the perception among arbitration practitioners, outside this professional circle, international arbitration is often met with distrust, especially in jurisdictions where this dispute resolution mechanism is insufficiently known and used.

Participants broadly agreed that there is room for improvement in the ISDS system. However, a distinction would be necessary between substantive and procedural aspects. It was felt that the root cause of the criticism against ISDS lies in the substantive treatment of investments, which is regulated in IIAs.

As a general observation, it was pointed out that the most plausible reason for discontent is the lack of consistency and predictability in the interpretation and application of key concepts related to the protection of foreign investments and the States' regulatory autonomy. However, the variety of interpretations and outcomes in investment cases concerned with States' ESG measures reflects the diverse and broadly worded IIAs negotiated by States in line with

[18]) Report of the Special Rapporteur on the issue of human rights obligations relating to the enjoyment of a safe, clean, healthy and sustainable environment, *David R. Boyd*, in accordance with Human Rights Council resolution 46/7 (A/78/168): Paying polluters: the catastrophic consequences of investor-State dispute settlement for climate and environment action and human rights, 2.

[19]) Report of the Special Rapporteur on the issue of human rights obligations relating to the enjoyment of a safe, clean, healthy and sustainable environment, *David R. Boyd*, in accordance with Human Rights Council resolution 46/7 (A/78/168): Paying polluters: the catastrophic consequences of investor-State dispute settlement for climate and environment action and human rights, 2.

their economic objectives when importing and exporting capital. Thus, the primary cause of concern is how investment protection treaties are shaped by State parties.

The discussion also turned to the ongoing reform efforts led by UNCITRAL Working Group III in the field of ISDS and participants considered the possible effects of this reform.

To recall, in 2017, UNCITRAL Working Group III undertook work on the possible reform of ISDS aiming to address the concerns related to the legitimacy and efficiency of the system. In that context, UNCITRAL Working Group III is considering three alternative reform options aimed at revamping the ISDS system: (i) creation of a stand-alone review or appellate mechanism; (ii) a standing multilateral investment court with full-time judges; and (iii) a reform of the existing procedures for selection and appointment of arbitrators and adjudicators.[20]) Given the fundamental differences between these options and the difficulties in achieving consensus, UNCITRAL Working Group III is moving the potential reform solutions forward in parallel and has further identified concrete reform elements, particularly: (i) the establishment of an advisory centre; (ii) a code of conduct for adjudicators (the Code of Conduct for Arbitrators in ISDS was adopted in 2023, when also a separate code of conduct for judges was adopted in principle); (iii) the regulation of third-party funding; (iv) dispute prevention and mitigation and means of alternative dispute resolution; (v) treaty interpretation by States parties; (vi) security for costs; (vii) means to address frivolous claims; (viii) multiple proceedings and counterclaims; (ix) reflective loss and shareholder claims; (x) appellate and multilateral court mechanisms; (xi) the selection and appointment of ISDS tribunal members; and (xii) a multilateral instrument on ISDS reform.[21])

As pointed out by one of the discussion participants, the mandate given to UNCITRAL Working Group III is focused on the procedural aspects of dispute settlement rather than on substantive provisions.[22]) This prompted other participants to consider whether the root cause of the problem would be adequately addressed in the framework of UNCITRAL Working Group III.

One of the reform elements curated by UNCITRAL Working Group III refers to so-called cross-cutting issues of procedural reforms, which include substantive provisions that interact with the procedural aspects of ISDS. In this context, an issue that was considered in the framework of UNCITRAL

---

[20]) United Nations Commission on International Trade Law Working Group III (Investor-State Dispute Settlement Reform) Resumed thirty-eighth session Vienna, January 20–24, 2020 (A/CN.9/1004/Add.1), para. 14.

[21]) United Nations Commission on International Trade Law Working Group III (Investor-State Dispute Settlement Reform) Forty-second session New York, online, February 14–18, 2022 (A/CN.9/WG.III/WP.211*), para. 6.

[22]) *See* Report of Working Group III (Investor-State Dispute Settlement Reform) on the work of its thirty-fourth session (Vienna, November, 27 – December 1, 2017) (A/CN.9/930/Rev.1), para. 119.

Working Group III is the perceived regulatory chill attributed to ISDS, in view of "*costs associated with the ISDS proceedings and high amount of damages awarded by tribunals*", seen as "*some of the elements that could undermine the states' ability to regulate*".[23]) On the basis of the identified procedural and cross-cutting issues, the Secretariat of UNCITRAL Working Group III prepared a set of draft provisions (the "Draft Provisions") for potential inclusion in IIAs, investment contracts or domestic legislation.[24]) However, it remains to be determined how the Draft Provisions would be implemented by States.[25])

Against this backdrop, the roundtable participants exchanged views on the proposed content of the Draft Provisions concerning States' right to regulate in ESG related matters, which directly relates to the substantive part of the roundtable discussion. The relevant provision (as at the date of the 'World Café') roundtable discussions read as follows:

> *"Provision 12: Right to regulate. 1. Nothing in the Agreement shall be construed as preventing the Contracting Parties from exercising their right to regulate in the public interest and to adopt, maintain and enforce any measure that they consider appropriate to ensure that investments are made in a manner sensitive to the protection of public health, public safety or the environment, the promotion and protection of cultural diversity, or […]. 2. When assessing the alleged breach by a Contracting Party of its obligation under the Agreement, the Tribunal shall give a high level of deference that international law accords to Contracting Parties with regard to the development and implementation of domestic policies, the right to regulate in the public interest and the right to adopt, maintain and enforce measures sensitive to the protection of public health, public safety or the environment, the promotion and protection of cultural diversity, or […]. 3. No claim may be submitted for resolution pursuant to Draft Provisions 3 or 4, if the measure alleged to constitute a breach of the Agreement was adopted by the Contracting State to protect public health, public safety or the environment (including compliance with the Paris Agreement or any principle or commitment contained in articles 3 and 4 of the United Nations Framework Convention on Climate Change), the promotion and protection of cultural diversity, or […]."*[26])

---

[23]) *See* Report of Working Group III (Investor-State Dispute Settlement Reform) on the work of its thirty-seventh session (New York, April 1–5, 2019) (A/CN.9/970), paras. 36–37.

[24]) *See* United Nations Commission on International Trade Law* Working Group III (Investor-State Dispute Settlement Reform) Forty-sixth session Vienna, October 9–13, 2023 (A/CN.9/WG.III/WP.231*), para. 2.

[25]) United Nations Commission on International Trade Law Working Group III (Investor-State Dispute Settlement Reform) Forty-ninth session Vienna, September 23–27, 2024 (A/CN.9/WG.III/WP.244), para. 8.

[26]) Since Vienna Arbitration Days 2024, a revised form of the Draft Provisions was presented at the UNCITRAL Working Group III (Investor-State Dispute Settlement

Some participants raised the concern that all three options proposed in draft Provision 12 are broad and unconditional carve-outs for States' ESG-related regulatory measures, noting that neither of the options indicate any limits to the right to regulate, as previously recognized in investment cases, such as consistency, non-discrimination, transparency, non-arbitrariness of the regulatory measure, etc. The wording could be construed as giving States *carte blanche* to exercise regulatory power, leaving room for abusive conduct, although the intention of the drafters was likely the opposite. Out of the three options, the second one was felt to be more in line with the scope of the right to regulate as accepted in customary international law, since it would give international tribunals a margin of appreciation.

It should also be noted that the model provision on the right to regulate contemplated in the framework of UNCITRAL Working Group III is not an isolated recent example of model clauses recognizing States' ample regulatory powers in the field of ESG.[27]) However, some of the new-generation IIAs seem to favor a more balanced approach, leaving a protection margin for international investors against States' unreasonable conduct.[28])

Reform) Forty-ninth session Vienna, September 23–27, 2024 A/CN.9/WG.III/WP.244, in which Draft Provision 19 reads as follows: "*Right to regulate: Nothing in the Agreement shall be construed as preventing the Contracting Parties from exercising their right to regulate and to adopt, maintain and enforce any measure that they consider appropriate to ensure that investments are made in a manner sensitive to the protection of public health, public safety, human rights, essentials security interests or the environment, the promotion and protection of cultural diversity, or [...]. When assessing the alleged breach by a Contracting Party of its obligation under the Agreement, the Tribunal shall give a high level of deference that international law accords to Contracting Parties with regard to [the development of domestic policies as well as implementation of international commitments (including compliance with the Paris Agreement or any principle or commitment contained in articles 3 and 4 of the United Nations Framework Convention on Climate Change),] the right to regulate and the right to adopt, maintain and enforce measures sensitive to the protection of public health, public safety, human rights, essential security interests or the environment, the promotion and protection of cultural diversity, or [...]. No claim may be submitted if the measure alleged to constitute a breach of the Agreement was adopted by the Contracting State to protect public health, public safety, human rights, essential security interests or the environment, to promote and protect cultural diversity, or [...].*".

[27]) For such examples, *see* Report on use of ESG contractual obligations and related disputes by the ESG Subcommittee of the IBA Arbitration Committee (2023) – Annex B.

[28]) In Austria – Kyrgyzstan BIT (2016), Art. 7 (4) carves out from the protection against expropriation ESG regulatory measures that are "*non-discriminatory*" and are not "*so severe in the light of their purpose that they cannot be reasonably viewed as having been adopted and applied in good faith*"; *see also* Morocco Model BIT, cited in the Report on use of ESG contractual obligations and related disputes by the ESG Subcommittee of the IBA Arbitration Committee (2023) – Annex B, 64, which establishes a general exception for actions taken by States "*in good faith, on a non-discriminatory basis and of general application*" in Art. 21 and a similar provision in Art. 6.4.

It remains to be seen if the draft provision on the right to regulate currently contemplated in the framework of UNCITRAL Working Group III and other similar models will catch traction. In one of the roundtable sessions it was pointed out that the Draft Provisions are still in the early stages of discussion and are likely to undergo further revisions. Additionally, it should be noted that certain concerns have been raised in UNCITRAL Working Group III as to whether a definition of the right to regulate would fall within the mandate of the working group, considering its primary focus on procedural reforms.[29])

4. Conclusions

It goes without saying that in the evolving ESG landscape States need regulatory leeway to prioritize public policy interests related to core ESG objectives. International law has to provide appropriate tools allowing them to tackle climate change, violations of human rights, corruption issues and other such sensitive matters, without fearing financial repercussions in the form of compensation claims pursued by international investors. On the other hand, such tools should not encourage unaccountable conduct by States. As difficult as it may appear to reach such a goal, striking a balance between foreign investment protection and States' regulatory freedom is the right way forward.

D. Mediation and Environmental, Social and Governance (ESG) Related Disputes – Finding Common Ground

Arnela Maglić/Amelie Huber-Starlinger

1. Introduction

The Vienna Arbitration Days ("VAD") 2024 touched upon multiple issues of significant importance in the resolution of disputes, including challenges related to the resolution of Environmental, Social, and Governance ("ESG") disputes.

Already on the first day of the VAD 2024 multiple speakers recognized the importance of mediation as a means to resolve ESG disputes. On the second day of the conference, during the "World Café" sessions, the authors of this article had a vivid and engaging table discussion with several participants[30]) of the conference. This report is based on the mentioned table discussion titled "ESG: Finding common ground – mediating ESG disputes".

---

[29]) *See, e.g.,* Comments made by the European Union and its Member States on Draft provisions on procedural and cross-cutting issues (A/CN.9/WG.III/WP.231*), 14.

[30]) *Sara Darnot, Viktoria Simone Fritz, Lukas Jäger, Saara Jokela, Naim Krasniqi, Arbenita Rrmoku, Stella-Jo Turner, Besim Zllashi.*

The session focused on understanding the nuances of ESG disputes and exploring the critical role mediation can play. The discussion also highlighted the growing need for tailored dispute resolution mechanisms in this area, especially as ESG obligations become more embedded in both corporate policies and legal frameworks globally.

2. What are ESG Disputes?

ESG is a framework of criteria designed to evaluate the sustainability and ethical impact of an investment or business. [31]) The first component of ESG is "E for Environment" focuses on issues such as pollution, global warming, and clean energy, all critical amid the current climate change crisis – one of the defining issues of our time.[32]) The second component "S for Social" pertains to companies' responsibility to positively impact stakeholders like customers, employees, suppliers, and local communities by addressing issues such as workforce health, safety, and diversity. The third component "G for Governance" aims at fostering transparency and accountability through practices like anti-corruption measures, data protection, and corporate accountability to support sustainable growth.[33])

ESG was initially enacted in soft law instruments, such as the United Nations' (UN) Guiding Principles on Business and Human Rights.[34]) In recent years, ESG considerations are decreed in hard law intended to be binding on the parties, and those subject to the law.[35]) Stricter legal requirements heighten compliance obligations, scrutiny, and the risk of potential liabilities for non-compliance. Therefore, this shift from soft law to hard law will most likely increase the number of ESG disputes.

---

[31]) *Dirk De Meulemeester*, in *ESG and International Arbitration: Beyond the Acronyms*, (2023), 1.

[32]) *Gauthier Vannieuwenhuyse, Exploring the Suitability of Arbitration for Settling ESG and Human Rights Disputes, Journal of International Arbitration*, 40 JIA 1, 1–28 (2023).

[33]) *Gauthier Vannieuwenhuyse, Exploring the Suitability of Arbitration for Settling ESG and Human Rights Disputes, Journal of International Arbitration*, 40 JIA 1, 1–28 (2023).

[34]) The United Nations Human Rights Council endorsed the Guiding Principles on Business and Human Rights in its resolution 17/4 of June 16, 2011. The Guiding Principles on Business and Human Rights is a normative framework for socially and environmentally responsible business conduct.

[35]) *E.g.*, the Norwegian Transparency Act and the Dutch Child Labour Due Diligence Law entered into force in 2022, as well as the German Act on Corporate Due Diligence in Supply chains which entered into force in 2023. The most prominent development, however, is the European Union's Corporate Sustainability Due Diligence Directive ("CSDDD") which entered into force on July 25, 2024. CSDDD *inter alia* includes an obligation to obtain contractual assurances from supply chain partners on ESG issues.

Unlike "traditional" commercial disputes, ESG disputes are characterized by their overlapping legal, ethical and social dimensions, as well as multiple stakeholders with diverging interests. ESG disputes often involve allegations of environmental harm, such as breaches of climate commitments or pollution liabilities, as well as social concerns like labor rights violations or disputes over community impacts. At the Vienna Arbitration Days 2024, the participants of the World Café Table highlighted how ESG disputes often stem from the increasing societal demand for corporate accountability for its ESG impact.

3. What is the Most Suitable Dispute Resolution Method for Resolving ESG Disputes?

National and international legal frameworks provide for different dispute resolutions mechanisms. Next to informal negotiations between the disputing parties themselves, they provide for example for court proceedings, arbitration, conciliation and mediation. All these have their pros and cons. It depends on the circumstances of the particular case. Therefore, there is no clear-cut answer to this question.

The majority of the World Café participants, however, agreed that any dispute resolution method in relation to ESG disputes must strike a balance between transparency and confidentiality, neutrality and expertise, and promote collaboration, ideally resulting in impact-driven outcomes.

In comparison to all other dispute resolution methods mentioned, mediation stands out as a strong candidate for this role. It facilitates aligning resolutions with broader ESG objectives while fostering cooperative and effective solutions.

4. What is Mediation?

Mediation is an alternative dispute resolution method where an impartial third party ("the mediator") helps the parties to a dispute to find a mutually acceptable solution.[36])

As a dispute resolution method mediation combines the advantages of "informal" negotiations between the disputing parties and "formal" legal

---

[36]) This can be described at the lowest common dominator. Taking a look at various national and international legislations and legal instruments it becomes apparent that they provide for a variety of different definitions of the same dispute resolution method with highlighting different aspects of the proceedings; *e.g.*, Article 2 (3) of the United Nations Convention on International Settlement Agreements Resulting from Mediation (Singapore Convention) defines mediation as "a process, irrespective of the expression used or the basis upon which the process is carried out, whereby parties attempt to reach an amicable settlement of their dispute with the assistance of a third person or persons ('the mediator') lacking the authority to impose a solution upon the parties to the dispute".

proceedings like arbitration or court proceedings. As in *inter partes* negotiations, parties talk and negotiate in mediation. But at the same time and as "formal" court/arbitral proceedings, mediation is a "formal" proceeding with a clear beginning and clear ending led by a mediator. The Mediator is an impartial and neutral third party who does not take sides or decides the case like a judge or arbitrator, but facilitates the communication and negotiation between the parties to help them to reach a mutually acceptable agreement. In order to do so the mediator designs the process, guides the conversation, helps identify issues and encourages solutions that both sides can agree upon.[37])

Mediation is a very flexible process, in which each and every procedural step is tailored to the specific circumstances of the case including the needs of the parties, the dispute, the parties' representatives etc. Therefore, the exact process and progression of mediation cannot be universally described. No mediation resembles exactly another. However, most mediations (in particular international commercial mediations) follow an international standard with more or less significant deviations therefrom. Mediations can be divided in three phases:[38]) 1. the time prior to the mediation day, 2. the mediation day and 3. the time after the mediation day.

a) Phase 1

is the time prior to the mediation day used to deal with preliminary issues, *e.g.,* determination who should participate, agreeing on a schedule, determination how to handle documents, submissions and other notifications, agreeing to a confidentiality clause and determination when and how to file a mediation statement.[39])

b) Phase 2

is the actual mediation day,[40]) *i.e.,* the day or days on which the parties and the mediator meet to discuss the issues in dispute and to try to reach a settlement agreement.

---

[37]) Different mediation styles exist, *e.g.,* facilitative, evaluative or transformative mediation. A mediator's mediation style highly influences how the mediator shapes the mediation process and what methods the mediator uses. This includes if and, if yes, to what extent a mediator encourages solutions or even provides the parties with possible solutions to their dispute. A detailed presentation of the different mediation styles would exceed the scope and the extent of this article.

[38]) *Haugeneder/Huber-Starlinger/Netal, Konfliktmanagement,* in *Koller/Balog/Martinetz/Pichler,* Das grosse Handbuch Wirtschaftsrecht (2024) 764 *et seq.*

[39]) Mediation statements (also called position papers) are short summary of a party of the issues to be resolved in the mediation addressed to a) the other party and the mediator and/or b) the mediator only.

[40]) Although mediation day is generally used in the singular, a mediation may stretch over days, weeks or even months before a dispute can be resolved.

c) Phase 3

is the time after the mediation day. In this phase the parties have to fulfil their respective obligations agreed to in the mediated settlement agreement.

Despite the above and even if a specific mediation does not follow the phases set out above, each and every mediation process is guided by certain principles, which affect the way the mediation is designed. This ranges from cost- to time-efficiency, confidentiality, sustainable and creative solutions etc. Some of those principles guiding the mediation process were specifically highlighted by the participants of the World Café Table as benefitting the resolution of ESG disputes the most (*see* the next Section III.D.5).

5. What is the Benefit of Mediating ESG Disputes?

As noted in Section III.D.4 above, mediation offers a palette of distinct advantages for resolving ESG disputes. ESG disputes are often not cantered solely on regulatory or financial considerations, but their scope includes environmental, ethical and social concerns. Mediation, with its focus on collaboration and flexibility, provides a platform for creative and sustainable solutions benefitting all parties involved and supporting the effective and "best practice" implementation of ESG goals.

Key mediation principles benefiting the resolution of ESG disputes, as highlighted by the World Café Table participants, include:

a) Flexibility and Customization with a Future Oriented Focus

The World Café participants concluded that one of the most significant advantages of mediating ESG disputes lies in the inherent flexibility of mediation. In mediation, the parties have the opportunity to create a "bespoke" solution that mirrors their distinctive priorities and values. This approach has to be seen in contrast to litigation or arbitration. These dispute resolution methods focus typically on legal remedies and may not provide for the same level of flexibility to address broader ESG concerns. Furthermore, arbitrators and judges render a ruling over a dispute that arose in the past based on the law as it was applicable at a certain time. The arbitrator's/judge's view is therefore backwards. In comparison thereto, mediations are in general future oriented and not limited to legal arguments and reasoning. Although the cause of the dispute and its legal analysis will play a role in mediation, the parties are not limited to it. Parties have the possibility to generate creative solutions that take legal as well as financial aspects and future developments into account.

For example, if mediated, a dispute between a company and a local community over allegations of environmental damage is more likely to lead to an agreement that includes not only financial compensation but also a commitment to environmental restoration. Similarly, supply chain disputes may result in agreements that promote the adoption of more sustainable and improved practices for future business operations rather than merely imposing a penalty for non-compliance.

b) Preserving Relationships and Promoting Future Cooperation

The World Café Table highlighted how mediation can be particularly valuable in preserving relationships and promoting future cooperation. ESG disputes often involve stakeholders who need/want to continue interacting in the future (*e.g.*, companies, communities, NGOs etc.). The adversarial nature of litigation and arbitration may lead to long-lasting damage to relationships. In contrast, mediation encourages a more cooperative approach. Since ESG disputes often arise in contexts where ongoing relationships are essential such as between corporations and local communities, between companies and their suppliers, or between investors and companies, the cooperative approach mediation fosters would allow these relationships to further develop in a constructive and productive way.

c) Confidentiality in Service of a Safe Dialogue

In ESG disputes, confidentiality is often a critical factor (*e.g.*, because of reputational risks). This is of particular importance to corporations facing issues relating to environmental or social impacts, as public exposure of their shortcomings in, for example, internal ESG policies could lead to a significant reputational damage. However, the World Café participants concluded that mediation creates a safer environment for an open dialogue and negotiations. Parties have the opportunity to engage in discussions trying to resolve issues in private while still ensuring that all necessary stakeholders are involved and that the agreed-upon resolution is in the best interest of everyone involved. This safe dialogue would encourage conversations to go beyond immediate compensation or penalties. The parties can also take into account how their actions will align with broader societal and environmental goals. This approach is especially relevant in ESG disputes, which involve issues with long-term implications such as climate change, community welfare, or sustainable supply chains. Even in matters of public interest confidentiality of mediation can be a benefit, because after reaching an agreement the parties can jointly decide how it is communicated to the public.

Given the numerous benefits of mediating ESG disputes, the American Bar Association incorporated mediation as a key step in its model contract clauses ("MCCs"), designed for U.S. buyer companies to use in contracts with their suppliers.[41]) These clauses aim to enhance the protection of human rights

---

[41]) American Bar Association MCCs 2.0 Clauses 8.4, 8.5, 8.6; https://www.americanbar.org/groups/business_law/resources/business-law-today/2021-may/balancing-

across the supply chain and establish a multi-tiered dispute resolution process that includes informal good-faith negotiations, mediation, and a choice between arbitration or litigation.

d) ESG Disputes are Often Value Driven and Involve Multiple Parties

Although legal arguments play an important role in mediations, other aspects can be looked at as well. The latter include financial issues and even values and beliefs of the parties participating in the mediation. Mediation provides the framework to address such values and to align mediated settlement agreements with those values and beliefs. It is, in fact, the function of the mediator to assist all parties in identifying and communicating their differing interests.

6. Should Mediation be Voluntary or Mandatory when Facing an ESG Dispute?

The question whether mediations shall be voluntary or mandatory isn't easy to answer. Mandatory mediation is commonly understood as mediation, which the parties are required to attempt, whether by contract, law or court order, before they can proceed with litigation or arbitration. In comparison thereto, voluntary mediation is commonly understood as a mediation, which the parties are not required to attempt before they can proceed with litigation or arbitration. Expert circles[42]) discuss whether a practical distinction between voluntary and mandatory exists. Even if the parties are required to attempt to settle their case through mediation, they are not bound to agree to a settlement, as no one can force a party to agree to a specific settlement agreement.

However, as long as this question is not finally answered, the question whether to have mediations voluntary or mandatory, remains a key consideration in the design of dispute resolution systems and clauses. A clear-cut answer is impossible. Each approach has its advantages and disadvantages, depending on the context, the parties involved and the nature of the dispute.

Arguments in favor of voluntary mediations raised by the participants at the World Café Table were:

a) Likelihood to engage in conversations: The likelihood that parties engage in meaningful and productive conversation including a mutually satisfying outcome is much higher if they choose to participate at the time the dispute already exists.

---

buyer-and-supplier-responsibilities/ (last accessed December 4, 2024).

[42]) Like the Vienna International Arbitral Centre – Mediation Advisory Board, 360° ADR – Midweek Talk – "Contractual mediation cluases and Arb-Med-Arb" with *Julia Jung* broadcasted on April 14, 2021.

b) Preserving the relationship: The participants observed that in voluntary mediation preserving the relationship was of more importance to the parties than the monetary demands in the dispute. This included the parties' willingness to resolve the issue in order to keep the relationship, which was often higher than in mandatory mediation.

c) Upholding the value of choice and autonomy: Mediation is based on the presumption that the parties are best suited to decide which outcome suits them and their company the best. Voluntary mediation upholds the value of choice and autonomy. It reiterates the freedom to choose the dispute resolution process that works best for the parties.

On the other hand voluntary mediation risks that a party refuses to participate. This can prevent the mediation to take place at all. Sometimes it increases power imbalances between the parties and leaves the parties without an effective option for resolving the issue mutually.

Arguments in favor of mandatory mediation raised by the participants at the World Café Table were:

a) Expedite the resolution process: Mandatory mediation, if successful, can lead to settlements with minimal effort and thereby saves time and resources. By addressing the issues early on, it can prevent further conflicts and negative consequences of not settling at an early stage of the dispute.

b) Overcome the parties' reluctance to mediate: In some cases, parties may not want to mediate because of personal, emotional or strategic reasons. Making mediation mandatory ensures that parties engage in the process, potentially leading to resolutions that they would not have pursued voluntarily. It is an easy and comfortable entry door into mediation without the risk for any party to lose face. This is one of the most powerful advantages of mandatory mediation.

On the other hand, being forced into mediation may lead to a lack of cooperation and thereby to a less productive mediation. A full or partial failure of the mediation may be the consequence.

As indicated above the participants of the World Café were not clearly in favor or against mandatory mediation or voluntary mediation respectively. However, what should be noted is that those who had already participated in mediation where in favor of mandatory mediation.

7. Types of ESG Disputes in which Mediation is of Particular Importance?

Not all ESG disputes are capable of being resolved by mediation. Some ESG disputes lack mediability due to their nature, severity, or the relevant legal frameworks.[43]) The World Café discussion did not focus on the question of which ESG disputes can be mediated but rather centered on the appropriateness of mediating certain types of ESG disputes.

The World Café participants agreed that next to ISDS disputes,[44]) contractual ESG disputes which arise from contractual obligations related to ESG issues, are most appropriate for mediation.

ESG contractual clauses primarily aim to allocate liability risks arising during contract performance, traditionally placing responsibility on suppliers to ensure compliance with specified ESG requirements in their products and operations.[45]) In addition to allocating liability, ESG contractual clauses set expectations for achieving ESG goals, directing resources toward compliance and positive impact. By formalizing these commitments, such clauses help foster positive outcomes such as reduced emissions, diversity, and improved community relations.[46]) The rise of ESG-related contractual obligations is a continuing trend which is expected to be particularly impacted by the EU Corporate Sustainability Due Diligence Directive ("CSDDD"), which requires companies to implement environmental and human rights due diligences throughout their supply chains. Although the directive originates in the EU, its impact will be global, as companies operating in the EU, regardless of their headquarters, must designate an authorized EU representative and comply with its provisions.[47]) As ESG-related contract clauses continue to proliferate, the likelihood of disputes arising from these obligations is anticipated to grow, highlighting the critical role mediation can play in facilitating effective and collaborative resolutions to such conflicts, as described in Section III.D.5 above.

8. The Future of Mediation in ESG Disputes

It is expected that ESG issues gain greater prominence in business and investment decisions. Due to the increase of ESG-related issues disputes involving environmental protection, social responsibility, and corporate governance are likely to increase.

As a consequence thereof it is equally expected that mediation as a dispute resolution method will evolve significantly. Some participants were of the view that mediation is definitely more suited to solve ESG disputes than any other

---

43) The question of which disputes can be settled through mediation is to be addressed on a jurisdiction-by-jurisdiction basis. The Authors will provide a general overview without focusing on any specific jurisdiction.

44) Due to time constrains of the Conference, the World Café discussion did not focus of the issue of mediability of ESG related ISDS disputes.

45) *Lisa Bingham* & *Emily Hay*, Supply chain disputes and ESG contractual clauses, in ESG and International Arbitration: Beyond the Acronyms, 53–96 (2023).

46) *Ibid.*

47) *Ibid.*

dispute resolution method. However, several ESG related factors will influence how mediation develops including regulatory changes, increased demand for corporate responsibility, and the growing recognition of the value of resolving complex, multi-stakeholder conflicts outside of traditional litigation. In comparison to the latter, mediation is a time- and cost- efficient dispute resolution mechanism which allows the parties to preserve relationships and find creative solutions. Mediated settlements range from a mere monetary settlement to agreements that go beyond legal remedies providing, *e.g.*, for sustainability initiatives or community investments. The interests and needs of involved in an ESG dispute (*e.g.*, communities, companies, governments, NGOs) can be best worked up and aligned in mediation. Furthermore, and in case different jurisdictions are affected, mediation can find solutions to address complexities of regulatory frameworks as well as jurisdictional and cultural differences. Mediation provides a less confrontational way for companies to demonstrate their commitment to resolving ESG-related disputes and enhancing their ESG practices.

The mediation market will have to adjust to this development. Mediators are well advised to invest in ESG related trainings enabling them to handle the nuances of such disputes effectively. This specific knowledge required ranges from climate change and human rights to corporate governance. The participants specifically mentioned that the mediator should be firm in detecting and handling cultural differences.

As soon as the number of mediations in this area grows, the more likely it is to be used by consumers, investors and other stakeholders. As a side effect, mediation in the area of ESG disputes will become self-perpetuating. Businesses will look to mediation to demonstrate their commitment to responsible corporate behavior as it may play an essential role in fostering cooperation, reducing the risks of protracted legal battles and supporting the achievement of sustainable, socially responsible and ethical outcomes. Mediation could be integrated into compliance processes to address any discrepancies between a company's practices and its ESG commitments. Furthermore, the beauty of mediation lies not only in solving the dispute at hand, but also in the possibility to commit to future actions, apologies, commitments and new business.

E. Arbitration Transformed – Leveraging AI Tools for Smarter Dispute Resolution

Nata Ghibradze/Ondrej Cech

1. Introduction

Artificial intelligence (AI) may be understood as a set of technologies enabling a computer or a machine to perform tasks commonly associated with human intelligence, such as the ability to reason, analyze data, solve problems, generalize, and learn from past experiences.[48])

The rise in AI usage across various fields has sparked discussions about its potential application in arbitration. Below, the authors outline some general limitations which affect all forms of AI usage, before addressing AI's possible uses in arbitration. These sections are followed by a summary of the discussion during Vienna Arbitration Days 2024, which revealed that for now, AI use seems to be quite limited among arbitration practitioners.

2. AI's Limitations

Although AI is potentially useful, it still has some important weaknesses and limitations which prudent practitioners should be wary of. Below, the authors address: AI hallucinations; privacy and confidentiality obligations threatened by AI use; and the lack of transparency in AI. This is by no means an exhaustive list of AI's limitations, but rather serves as a short list of the issues the authors felt most relevant to legal practice, as addressed during the discussions.

a) Hallucinations

A *"hallucination"* is the term for when an *"AI model generates false, misleading, or illogical information, but presents it as if it were a fact."*[49]) For example, if a user were to ask OpenAI's ChatGPT to summarize an important decision from the German Federal Court of Justice, ChatGPT might quickly summarize that case, or it could hallucinate an answer with no basis in reality. This is especially problematic because the user will have no way of immediately distinguishing between an accurate answer and a hallucination.

The reason hallucinations occur in the first place is beyond the scope of this article but suffice to say that hallucinations happen frequently in AI tools. Recent studies indicate that different AI tools hallucinate answers to anywhere between 3% and 27% of queries.[50]) Whether a user means to use AI for sum-

---

[48]) Copeland, *Artificial intelligence,* in Encyclopedia Britannica (2024), available at <https://www.britannica.com/technology/artificial-intelligence>; *see* Google Cloud, *What is Artificial Intelligence (AI)?*, Google Cloud (retrieved December 10, 2024), available at <https://cloud.google.com/learn/what-is-artificial-intelligence>.

[49]) *Ellen Glover, What Are AI Hallucinations?*, Built In (March 14, 2024), available at <https://builtin.com/artificial-intelligence/ai-hallucination>.

[50]) *Connie Guglielmo, AI Chatbots Are Here to Stay. Learn How They Can Work for You*, CNET (January 16, 2024), available at <https://www.cnet.com/tech/computing/features/ai-chatbots-are-here-to-stay-learn-how-they-can-work-for-you/>; *Yochai Konig, AI hallucination examples: When artificial intelligence gets it wrong*, ada (retrieved December 9, 2024), available at <https://www.ada.cx/blog/ai-hallucination-examples-when-artificial-intelligence-gets-it-wrong/>.

marizing case law, compiling evidence, drafting arguments, or translating documents, the risk of hallucination is always present.

This means that users must be vigilant when using AI tools. Users can identify hallucinations if either the user knows the expected answer already or the user goes to check the answer themselves. For example, asking an AI tool to summarize a case may be useful where the user is already familiar with that case, or where they plan to read it themselves anyway. But this need to verify answers obviously greatly reduces AI's utility, especially if users were turning to AI tools in order to increase efficiency.

b) Privacy and Confidentiality Obligations

One of the most salient concerns on AI for legal practitioners is how use of that AI tool fits into their privacy and confidentiality obligations. Lawyers in almost every country in the world have an obligation to protect client confidentiality.[51]) Lawyers using AI tools run the risk of breaching their professional obligations, although there are solutions to mitigate these risks.

There are numerous confidentiality risks for legal practitioners using AI tools. For example, AI tools may store, retrieve, or retain client information in ways that compromise client confidentiality, by passing client data through third-party servers outside the law firm's control.[52]) Additionally, this storage may be vulnerable to cybersecurity risks, making client information accessible to hackers that illegally access the AI system.[53]) Further, since AI systems often use input data from users to further train the AI, client data may be used to train the AI model and could potentially be used to answer other users' queries.[54]) And finally, some jurisdictions are debating whether providing client data to an AI company necessarily voids solicitor-client privilege, as the lawyer has thereby provided privileged information to a third party.[55]) Each of these issues is a serious threat to a lawyer's professional obligations, and any one of these issues may make it challenging for lawyers to use AI tools.

One potential solution to these issues is employing in-house AI tools where client data is stored exclusively on local servers, or which otherwise

[51]) *See* IBA Presidential Task Force on Lawyer-Client Confidentiality, *IBA Statement in Defence of the Principle of Lawyer-Client Confidentiality*, IBA, at (January 10, 2022), available at <https://www.ibanet.org/document?id=%2FIBA-Statement-in-Defence-of-the-Principle-of-Lawyer-Client-Confidentiality>.

[52]) *Jennifer L. Villier, Ethical Implications of Generative Artificial Intelligence on the Practice of Law*, WealthCounsel (September 13, 2024), available at <https://info.wealthcounsel.com/blog/ethical-implications-of-generative-ai>.

[53]) *Id.*

[54]) *Richard De Maio, Ethics and AI: What Lawyers Need to Know*, The Legal Brief (September 16, 2024), available at <https://cmmllp.com/ethics-ai-law-lawyers/>.

[55]) *See id.*

protect client data from access by third parties.[56]) And practitioners are of course free to use AI tools insofar as such use does not involve providing any client information to third parties.

c) Lack of Transparency

One of the drawbacks for AI is the lack of transparency in how it operates, which creates obstacles to legal oversight.

AI is sometimes referred to as a *"black box"*, in that internal workings, decision-making workflows, and contributing factors remain unknown to human users.[57]) A user can see what went in and what came out, but has no insight into what happened in between. The AI tool will arrive at conclusions or decisions without providing any explanation as to how they were reached.[58])

This opacity is a major concern in areas that might require human oversight. For example, in 2019, the Canadian government used an AI system in place of a human mediator to mediate a dispute between two parties.[59]) This may be fine for mediation, but if parties were ever bound by a decision from an AI judge or arbitrator, it would be impossible to effectively appeal that decision, as the reasoning behind it would be unknowable. Wherever a legal process may require human oversight, practitioners must not put those processes under the *"black box"* of AI machinations.

3. AI's Uses in Arbitration

Despite the limitations outlined above, there are several avenues of legal practice in which AI can be greatly beneficial. Below, the authors discuss: evidence and document production; legal research; and translation. There are numerous other avenues which the authors were forced to set aside for the sake of brevity – honorable mentions include drafting, contract review, AI arbitrators or mediators, transcription, and selecting professionals such as arbitrators or experts.

a) Evidence and Document Production

The document production phase of arbitration hinges on each parties' ability to find and produce relevant documents. AI could make this process quicker, cheaper, and potentially more accurate but at the same time, less transparent.

---

[56]) *See* Villier, *Ethical Implications of Generative Artificial Intelligence on the Practice of Law*, *supra*.

[57]) *Rahul Awati & Kinza Yasar*, *What is black box AI?*, TechTarget (October 2024), available at <https://www.techtarget.com/whatis/definition/black-box-AI>.

[58]) *Id.*

[59]) *Nick Hilborne*, *Robot mediator settles first ever court case*, ADR Institute of Canda (February 19, 2019), available at <https://adric.ca/robot-mediator-settles-first-ever-court-case/>.

AI based systems could be an alternative to a keyword search which often produces many irrelevant documents and prolongs the subsequent manual review.[60]) Keyword searches may also omit relevant documents simply because the documents contain typos, non-textual data,[61]) or non-English characters.[62]) AI alternatives could be more accurate and faster, which creates cost savings. This is particularly true for complex cases, which sometimes require parties to review thousands of documents.[63]) In fact, some AI systems designed for this purpose have already been introduced.[64])

On the other hand, ensuring parties' compliance with document production orders could become more challenging with the adoption of AI. Under the current framework, tribunals can impose certain requirements on how document searches must be conducted, for example ordering parties to use specific search terms or other means of searching for documents.[65]) This oversight can also work retrospectively, for instance in *Tidewater*, wherein the tribunal accepted a request for disclosure of a party's discovery process to ensure that its search was conducted reasonably.[66])

The use of AI systems could significantly reduce the ability of tribunals to oversee the discovery process. As discussed above, AI is effectively a "*black box*"; the system's internal processes are opaque and complex, making it impossible for humans to deduce how the system reached its conclusion.[67]) As a result, neither the tribunal nor the parties would fully understand how the system selected the relevant documents. This may render it impossible for a tribunal to oversee the parties' compliance with the document production orders.

---

[60]) *See Esmé Shirlow, E-Discovery in Investment Treaty Arbitration: Practice, Procedures, Challenges and Opportunities,* in Journal of International Dispute Settlement, Vol. 11, Issue 4, Oxford University Press (2020), at 549 *et seqq.*

[61]) *Robert Hardaway* et al., *E-Discovery's Threat to Civil Litigation: Reevaluating Rule 26 for the Digital Age,* in Rutgers Law Review Vol. 63 (2011), at 28.

[62]) *Ronal Yu & Paul Taylor, Hong Kong's New Electronic Discovery Procedures,* in Digital Evidence & Electronic Signature Law Review Vol. 11 (2014).

[63]) *Shirlow, E-Discovery in Investment Treaty Arbitration, supra.*

[64]) *Martin Magal* et al., *Artificial Intelligence in Arbitration: Evidentiary Issues and Prospects,* in Global Arbitration Review (2023).

[65]) *Shirlow, E-Discovery in Investment Treaty Arbitration, supra; see also* Art 3 (3) (a) IBA Rules on the Taking of Evidence in International Arbitration (2011).

[66]) *Tidewater v Venezuela,* ICSID Case No. ARB/10/5, Procedural Order No. 1 (2011), at para. 21.

[67]) *Warren J. von Eschenbach, Transparency and the Black Box Problem: Why We Do Not Trust AI,* in Philosophy and Technology, 34 (2021), at 1608, available at <https://doi.org/10.1007/s13347-021-00477-0>.

b) Legal Research

AI can also improve legal research. There are commercially available AI tools which can assist with legal searches and summarizing texts.[68]) These AI tools promise not only increased speed and efficiency, but also improved results.

Some legal research platforms have already incorporated these capabilities to some extent, offering AI-powered search feature or AI-generated summaries of case law.[69]) This technology could be helpful not only for lawyers but could make law simpler and more accessible to other stakeholders.[70]) Taking this a step further, some AI systems have even been developed to predict the likely outcome of a given case, providing additional insights to support informed settlement discussions among the parties.[71])

However, as discussed above, there is still the risk of hallucinations. Readers are no doubt familiar with stories of American litigators sanctioned for relying on cases which did not exist, because the AI tool drafting their pleadings hallucinated fictional cases.[72]) Practitioners should be wary of blindly citing AI-produced legal research.

c) Translation

AI tools are a promising means for translating legal documents. These AI tools are faster and cheaper than human translators.[73]) However, they are also imperfect, and practitioners should be cautious.

---

[68]) *See Akash Takyar, AI for legal research: Applications, architecture, benefits, tools and development*, LeewayHertz (retrieved December 9, 2024), available at <https://www.leewayhertz.com/ai-for-legal-research/#Optimizing-legal-research-workflows-with-generative-AI>.

[69]) *See, e.g.*, Jus Mundi, Kluwer Arbitration.

[70]) *Cristina Ioana Florescu*, *The Interaction Between AI (Artificial Intelligence) and IA (International Arbitration): Technology as the New Partner of Arbitration*, in Revista Română de Arbitraj, Vol. 18, Issue 1, Wolters Kluwer România (2024).

[71]) IBA Alternative and New Law Business Structures Committee, *Guidelines and Regulations to Provide Insights on Public Policies to Ensure Artificial Intelligence's Beneficial Use as a Professional Tool* (2020), at 106.

[72]) *See, e.g., Michael A. Delaney, Fake News In Court: Attorney Sanctioned for Citing Fictitious Case Law Generated by AI*, New Hampshire Bar News (April 17, 2024), available at <https://www.mclane.com/insights/fake-news-in-court-attorney-sanctioned-for-citing-fictitious-case-law-generated-by-ai/>; *see, e.g., Robert J. Ambrogi, Not Again! Two More Cases, Just this Week, of Hallucinated Citations in Court Filings Leading to Sanctions*, LawSites (February 22, 2024), available at <https://www.lawnext.com/2024/02/not-again-two-more-cases-just-this-week-of-hallucinated-citations-in-court-filings-leading-to-sanctions.html>.

[73]) XTM Content Team, *The Pros and Cons of Artificial Intelligence in Translations*, XTM (retrieved December 9, 2024), available at <https://xtm.cloud/blog/the-pros-and-cons-of-artificial-intelligence-in-translations/>.

Numerous AI tools are already available for translating large volumes of foreign language documents.[74]) One prominent example is DeepL, which uses AI technology to consistently improve its translation capabilities across numerous languages.[75])

AI is often more efficient than human translators. AI-powered translation tools can process and translate large volumes of legal documents quickly.[76]) What would normally take a human translator a few hours or even days might take AI mere seconds.[77]) This increase in speed also leads to substantial cost savings. Better still, international arbitration will sometimes involve translations between numerous languages, and having one AI tool which can translate among a wide range of languages, including between less common pairings, is far less costly than having numerous human translators that can each only translate between two languages respectively.[78])

However, AI translation tools also have their drawbacks. By way of illustration, in *Occidental Petroleum v Ecuador*, Prof. *Brigitte Stern* in her dissenting opinion spoke of *"serious problems of translation"* of two judgments that in her view led to a misunderstanding of the applicable law.[79]) Although *Occidental* was not likely the result of AI hallucination, cases like this one may become common in the future, if practitioners come to carelessly rely on AI translators in their practice. It is important to remember that even where using an AI translation tool might save time and money, it is still better to review the results before relying on the translation.

4. Discussion

In the discussion hosted by the authors, the arbitration practitioners in attendance shared their experience with using AI systems in their practice. It quickly became apparent that, at present, the arbitration profession is still in

---

[74]) *See, e.g., Kevin Goedecke, Top 5 AI PDF Translator Tools in 2024 that are Free,* SlideSpeak (July 17, 2024), available at <https://slidespeak.co/blog/2024/07/17/top-5-ai-pdf-translator-tools-free-2024/>.

[75]) *Alexander Pinker, DeepL Revolutionizes Translations with New AI Technology,* MediaList (July 21, 2024), available at <https://medialist.info/en/2024/07/21/deepl-revolutionizes-translations-with-new-ai-technology/>.

[76]) XTM, *The Pros and Cons of Artificial Intelligence in Translations, supra.*

[77]) Murf Resources, *AI Translation vs. Human Translation: What Works Best?,* Murf Resources (April 12, 2024), available at <https://murf.ai/resources/ai-vs-human-translation/#mcetoc_1hr90kdni42>.

[78]) Loie Favre, *AI translation vs human translation: the brief guide*, Smartcat (November 2, 2023), available at <https://www.smartcat.com/blog/ai-vs-human-translation/>.

[79]) *Occidental Petroleum Corporation and Occidental Exploration and Production Company v. The Republic of Ecuador*, ICSID Case No. ARB/06/11 (2012), (dissenting opinion) at para. 68 *et seqq.*, available at <https://www.italaw.com/sites/default/files/case-documents/italaw1096.pdf>.

the early experimenting phase with respect to AI tools. Most, if not all, practitioners present had had some experience with AI tools but very few use AI tools on a regular basis. A notable exception to this approach was AI-powered translations, which some of the practitioners were using quite often. Nevertheless, others pointed out that their firm policy prohibits any use of AI tools, including translation, for fear of confidentiality breaches. Many practitioners fear that uploading confidential documents to AI tools could expose sensitive information to third parties or make it vulnerable to cyberattacks.

Only one of the practitioners present was able to share that they use AI tools regularly for drafting simpler communication with clients. This brought about a discussion on how generic such communication can be and that this could indeed be a field in which some form of automation could be helpful without significant risks to accuracy or confidentiality.

In conclusion, while the current use of AI in arbitration remains largely limited to experiments and translations, it demonstrates the potential for broader applications in the future, for example, in the area of evidence and legal research. At the same time, several challenges will need to be overcome before AI systems can be adopted for broader use.

F. Do We Need Rules to Adress AI in Arbitration?

Torsten Lörcher/Nicol Schneider

1. Introduction

Even a brief research on the topic of "*AI and arbitration*" shows that the question of *whether* AI should be used in arbitral proceedings has long been outdated. The crucial questions are rather: "*How can and shall we use AI in arbitration?*" and "*Is there a need for regulation and if yes where?*"

In the last couple of years numerous tools have emerged which all have the potential to facilitate the work of counsels, arbitrators and experts. Parallelly, more and more voices raised concern about the use of AI in arbitral proceedings identifying risks with regards to their confidentiality, transparency and objectivity.[80]) In addition, there is no doubt that the potential of AI has not yet

[80]) Just to name a few: *Crenguta Leaua* & *Corina Tanase, Artificial Intelligence and Arbitration: Some Considerations on the Eve of a Global Regulation,* 17 Rom. Arb. J. 31; *Mohammad Ali Solhchi* & *Faraz Baghbanno, Artificial Intelligence and Its Role in the Development of the Future of Arbitration,* 2 INT'L J.L. CHANGING WORLD 56 (2023); *Jurgis Bartkus, AI v. Arbitrator: How Can the Exclusion of Evidence Increase the Appointments of the Arbitrators?,* 2023 Access to Just. E. Eur. 111 (February 2023); *Jordan Bakst, Matthew Harden, Tyler Jankauskas, Micaela McMurrough* & *Mark Morril, Artificial Intelligence and Arbitration: A US Perspective,* 16 Disp. Resol. Int'l 7 (May 2022); *Paul*

been fully explored, consequently, nor has the extent of its effects on arbitral proceedings. As of now, navigating through this labyrinth seems – to put it simply – quite difficult.

Unsurprisingly, there are currently hardly any regulations that provide a framework for the use of AI in arbitral proceedings. In February 2024 the Silicon Valley Arbitration and Mediation Center presented the first edition of "*Guidelines on the Use of Artificial Intelligence in Arbitration*". However, according to the guidelines, these only serve to "*assist participants in arbitrations with navigating the potential applications of AI*".[81]) They therefore do not provide for a binding or detailed set of rules.

Against this background, the 2024 VAD World Café session co-lead by the authors examined the following set of questions: Are regulations needed at all? If so, how binding should they be? Are mere guidelines sufficient to draw users' attention to the risks of AI or is a stricter framework in the form of procedural rules or even in the *lex arbitri* needed?

2. The Common Ground

The discussions during the World Café sessions clearly showed the challenges involved in answering the questions raised by the use of AI in arbitration. Interestingly, however, both discussion groups quickly established a similar "*common ground*":

On the one hand, there was agreement that the use of AI is a path that everyone should follow if want to avoid lagging behind their competitors in the coming years. Both discussion groups therefore took the view that the use of AI in arbitration is certainly something that should be pursued.

On the other hand, the participants also showed a certain skepticism regarding this progress and, in particular, the known risks associated with the use of AI. They agreed that it is at least currently unthinkable to completely dispense with the "*human factor*" in arbitration and that there is a need for some regulation.

In an attempt to find a path between these poles, two criteria emerged that could at least point the way when answering the question *how* such regulation should look like:

Bennett Marrow, Mansi Karol & *Steven Kuyan, Artificial Intelligence and Arbitration: The Computer as an Arbitrator – Are We There Yet?,* 74 Disp. Resol. J. 6 (2020); *Gizem Halis Kasap, Can Artificial Intelligence ("AI") Replace Human Arbitrators?* Technological Concerns and Legal Implications, 2021 J. Disp. Resol. 209 (Spring 2021); *Sean Shih* & *Eric Chin-Ru Chang, The Application of AI in Arbitration: How Far Away Are We from AI Arbitrators?,* 17 Contemp. Asia Arb. J. 69 (May 2024); *Lee-Ford Tritt, The Use of AI Based Technologies in Arbitrating Trust Disputes,* 58 Wake Forest L. Rev. 1203 (2023).

[81]) Silicon Valley Arbitration & Mediation Center, Guidelines on the Use of Artificial Intelligence in Arbitration (1st ed. 2024), https://svamc.org/wp-content/uploads/SVAMC-AI-Guidelines-First-Edition.pdf.

1) *Who is using AI*: The need for rules might be dependent on the question of who is using AI to facilitate their work. While it is arguable that the use of AI by counsels in arbitral proceedings is subject to their discretion and ultimately their accountability (similar to the involvement of external experts), the use of AI by arbitrators may raise more complex issues and hence trigger a stronger need for regulation (similar to the involvement of tribunal secretaries).
2) *To what extent does AI replace the "human factor" in the proceedings*: The use of AI can range from AI-assisted arbitration to AI-based arbitration. A merely supportive use of AI probably requires less regulation than if AI is used to draft pleadings, expert opinions or even awards.

With these two factors in mind, a number of scenarios were discussed during the sessions. The authors have taken the liberty of sorting the results first into two categories ("*Use of AI by counsel*" vs "*Use of AI by the tribunal*") and within each category into a traffic-light-like system (following the example of the IBA Guidelines on Conflicts of Interest in International Arbitration).[82]) Within this system, the ***Green*** section describes scenarios in which the participants saw no need for regulation; the ***Orange*** section, on the other hand, lists scenarios in which participants subjected the use of AI to certain conditions. Lastly, the ***Red*** category describes scenarios in which participants identified a very strong need for regulation.

3. Use of AI by counsel

Green: The participants saw no need for regulation in the case where a counsel might use AI when drafting submissions. There was consensus that in such a case it would be the counsel's responsibility to assess whether they wanted to accept the risks of using AI in this context. This situation was described as very comparable to that when a counsel entrusts his tasks to an associate, which also is not an aspect regulated by any "*arbitration rules*". Finally, if there was an actual need for regulation in this area, the participants considered it as a question that should be answered by the respective (national) codes of professional conduct rather than by rules governing arbitral proceedings.

Furthermore, the participants saw no issue with the scenario in which AI is used to draft witness statements. This, however, under the assumption that the basis for the generated witness statement are documents or other information provided by the witness and that the witness is given the opportunity to edit the text of the witness statement as it sees fit. In this context, parallels were drawn with the assistance provided by counsel to witnesses in

[82]) Int'l Bar Ass'n, Guidelines on Conflicts of Interest in International Arbitration (2024), https://www.ibanet.org/document?id=Guidelines-on-Conflicts-of-Interest-in-International-Arbitration-2024.

preparing their witness statements, which is an established (and unregulated) practice in arbitration proceedings.

Lastly, no need for regulation was seen in the context of the use of AI in the selection of arbitrators. This applies to the search for arbitrators appointed by the parties as well as to the search for a presiding arbitrator. Although the participants acknowledged the risk that such a generated selection process would lack reasoning and exchange and therefore might increase discrimination and bias, the participants ultimately agreed that such a risk probably also exists with regard to a non-AI-supported selection process and therefore needs no further regulation.

Orange: The discussion surrounding the question of whether regulation is needed when AI is used instead of an expert in arbitration proceedings was more cautious. The main motivation behind this scenario being, in particular, the cost savings associated with not using an expensive expert. Interestingly, it was not the concern that an AI-generated expert opinion would be wrong that triggered the perceived need for regulation. According to the participants, wrong expert opinions and mistakes are also something that is human at its core. Rather, the need to create rules arose from the concern that the analysis and the sources of such an "AI-expert" could probably not be verified. Hence, the participants tended to allow the possibility of having AI perform an analysis only on the condition that the AI tool used offers a certain degree of transparency and review options. Some participants also tended to allow non-verifiable analyses to be admitted, but only on condition that the parties had agreed to it in full knowledge of this "weakness".

Similar considerations led the participants to favor regulatory intervention in the context of the use of AI in document production. Complex and large proceedings in arbitration already regularly require technical support for document searches that can no longer be handled manually. In this respect, many participants also saw it as the next logical step to enable searches using AI. However, there was consensus that this should only be available to a certain extent, namely using a tool that would prevent AI from creating documents itself (so-called "*hallucinations*"). Furthermore, according to the participants, regulations should ensure that the sources for the documents produced in this way were traceable. This seemed particularly important as it was the participants' view that AI must be prevented from obtaining access to documents that shall not be available to the opposing party in the arbitral proceedings and could therefore be considered to have been obtained illegally.

Red: Participants saw a strong need for regulation in scenarios where the use of AI could result in an immense imbalance and inequality of arms between the parties. In this regard, however, the discussion did not focus on scenarios in which a party would us an AI tool to facilitate its work (*e.g.*, to draft a submission), but rather on the more general situation in which the use of AI would be envisaged by the parties and the arbitral tribunal in order to increase the efficiency of the proceedings (*e.g.*, for the purposes of producing certain documents). The outcome of the discussion was that if an AI tool is to play such a "role" in arbitration proceedings, this can only take place on the condition that both parties have sufficient experience with and access to said AI tool. Otherwise, there is a risk of significant disadvantage to one party, which must be avoided at all costs.

4. Use of AI by the Tribunal

Green: When discussing possible conditions for an arbitral tribunal using AI, the participants quickly acknowledged that an arbitral tribunal should be allowed to use AI in order to enhance the efficiency of arbitral proceedings. In this respect, the participants considered it to be particularly unproblematic if an arbitral tribunal wished to use AI tools to perform organizational tasks, such as setting up meetings, drafting a procedural calendar or planning the logistics of a hearing. Hence, the consensus was that there was no need for specific regulations in that regard.

Orange: The participants were more critical of the scenario in which the arbitral tribunal would use AI for tasks that went beyond mere organizational issues, but did not necessarily concern a core duty of an arbitrator. Examples mentioned were the drafting of procedural orders, drafting of parts of the arbitral award such as the procedural history or the summary of the parties' arguments. The participants drew a parallel between these tasks and the support provided by a tribunal secretary. Consequently, the discussion came to the conclusion that an arbitral tribunal in general should be allowed to outsource these tasks to AI as it would be the case with a tribunal secretary. However, the condition being that the arbitral tribunal would disclose such use of the AI-tools in detail and would be only allowed to use the tools with the consent of all parties involved.

Red: The participants unanimously agreed that the use of AI shall be strictly prohibited when it comes to using AI to generate the decision and (if technically even possible) the reasoning of an arbitral award. Thus, the participants took the view that it is not allowed to use of AI for such tasks. This position was based on the consideration that the personal evaluation of evidence, and the subsequent reasoning of a decision in particular, still requires the "*human factor*". According to the participants, aspects such as personal perceptions during the examination of witnesses or simply life experience form a pivotal factor in any proceeding that should not be dispensed with for reasons of efficiency and cost.

5. Conclusion

In conclusion, the discussions surrounding the use of AI in arbitration highlight the nuanced and evolving nature of this issue. While there is a strong consensus on the potential benefits of AI in enhancing efficiency and supporting arbitrators and counsel, concerns about confidentiality, transparency, and fairness cannot be overlooked. The proposed regulatory framework should therefore be flexible and context-dependent, distinguishing between AI use by counsel and the tribunal, as well as considering the extent to which AI replaces the "*human factor*" in arbitration.

G. Ethical and Other Challenges of using AI Arbitration: AI – Friend or Foe?

Milica Savić/Ilma Kasumagić

1. General Overview

Artificial Intelligence has been a transformative force across the globe and its impact has been equally as striking in law. AI is observed as a powerful ally, enhancing efficiency, reducing costs, and improving the accuracy of legal processes. AI tools can go through vast amounts of data quickly, identifying patterns and precedents that might take human counsel significantly longer to uncover.

However, concerns have been raised about the technology's influence on confidentiality, potential biases, lack of transparency, and the ethical implications of its use. For instance, AI systems are only as good as the data on which they are trained; if that data reflects historical biases, the outputs may perpetuate these biases, raising questions about fairness in arbitration.

Ultimately, the debate over AI's role in arbitration revolves around finding a balance: leveraging its capabilities while mitigating risks and a similar debate was held during our World Café round table discussion. Although there were some points of agreement, there was a striking ambivalence in receptiveness towards AI between seasoned practitioners and practitioners at the beginning of their career, but it proved to be a great mixture of participants that contributed to the quality of the discussion.

2. Experience So Far

a) Using AI for Drafting and Evidence Analysis

Discussion showed that many law firms have begun experimenting with AI technologies to draft documents and analyze evidence. For example, natural language processing tools can assist in generating pleadings or summarizing witness statements by extracting relevant information from numerous documents.

Experience shows significant reductions in the time spent on preliminary research and document drafting, allowing legal teams to focus on strategic elements of their cases. However, challenges remain. Integrating AI into existing workflows requires training and adaptation, and some practitioners are hesitant to rely heavily on technology due to fears of losing the nuanced understanding that comes from traditional legal training.

b) Criteria for Use of AI

When considering the use of AI, there was consensus on the necessity to evaluate the criteria for its appropriateness in different roles and in different stages of arbitration. An additional topic was whether there should be any diversity in establishing these criteria for counsel and arbitrators.

There was general consensus that using AI as an assisting tool should not be a problem, however, the main question that came up during the discussion was whether the use of AI in any stage of arbitration should be disclosed. Naturally, practitioners that mainly do counsel work were not as concerned with using AI as an assisting tool in drafting, compiling evidence, extracting certain pieces of information from the vastness of the case file, but were more reserved when it came to arbitrators using AI. There was also a strong opinion that arbitrators need to disclose the volume, manner and outcome of their use of AI during the process, either during the procedural stages of the process or during deliberations, and particularly when drafting the award.

However, regardless of the role within arbitration, participants must assess the technology's potential impact on the integrity of the process itself. For counsel, the emphasis may be on using AI to enhance their argumentation; for arbitrators, the focus might be on ensuring that AI tools do not inadvertently introduce bias or undermine the quality of the traditional concept of deliberations. Establishing clear ethical guidelines for both roles will be crucial as AI continues to evolve, and there has been much discussion on the need to introduce such guidelines sooner rather than later.

c) Guidelines – Balancing Innovation and Fundamental Principles

Coincidentally, just before this year's World Café discussion, the Silicon Valley Arbitration & Mediation Center (SVAMC) has established guidelines to govern the use of AI in arbitration, aiming for a fair, secure, and balanced approach. These guidelines complement existing national regulations and are divided into three parts addressing all participants, parties and their representatives, and arbitrators. According to the Guidelines, Artificial Intelligence is defined as any computer system that "perform[s] tasks commonly associated with human cognition, such as understanding natural language, recognizing complex semantic patterns and generating human-like outputs." The drafters intended to cover all current and future variations of Artificial

Intelligence. Some of the most relevant guidelines are summarized below, as those were the topics that raised most concern among all participants to the discussion.

aa) Safeguarding Confidentiality (Guideline 2):

- All participants must ensure that AI tools used comply with confidentiality obligations.
- Confidential information should not be submitted to AI tools without vetting, and only AI tools that adequately safeguard such information should be used.
- Participants are encouraged to assess data use and retention policies and to redact or anonymize materials when appropriate.

bb) Disclosure (Guideline 3):

- There is no general requirement to disclose the use of AI tools; disclosure should be determined on a case-by-case basis considering due process and applicable privileges.
- If disclosure is deemed appropriate, details such as the tool's name, settings, how it was used, and the prompts and outputs may be provided.

cc) Duty of Competence (Guideline 4):

- Party representatives must adhere to ethical standards when using AI tools, ensuring that the output is factually and legally accurate.
- They are responsible for reviewing and correcting any inaccuracies generated by AI, acknowledging the potential for "hallucinations" (misleading but plausible-sounding outputs).

dd) Non-Delegation of Decision-Making Responsibilities (Guideline 6):

- Arbitrators cannot delegate their decision-making responsibilities to AI tools.
- They must maintain independent analysis and review AI outputs, ensuring the human element crucial to fairness and integrity is pre-served.

It remains to be seen in practice how these guidelines are implemented in SVAMC cases and how other institutions will tackle this very relevant issue.

3. Using AI in Different Stages of Arbitration: Pros and Cons

The following conclusions were reached on using AI in different stages in arbitration:

a) Initial Case Review and Preparing Strategy

Pros: AI can provide comprehensive data analytics, helping counsel identify key legal precedents and assess case strengths and weaknesses. Predictive analytics can also offer insights into likely outcomes based on historical data.

Cons: Overreliance on AI may lead to missing nuanced details that a human review might catch. AI's analytical frameworks may not account for unique aspects of specific cases.

b) Arbitrator Appointments

Pros: AI tools can analyze arbitrators' qualifications, past performance, positions from available publications on certain legal issues, improving the appointment process's efficiency.

Cons: The complexity of AI decision-making processes raises concerns about fairness. Institutions should consider disclosing their use of AI in arbitrator selections to enhance transparency and have parties make informed assessments of such AI generated output.

c) Pleadings

Pros: AI can streamline the drafting process, ensuring consistency and reducing typographical and formatting errors. Tools can suggest language and phrasing based on successful past pleadings.

Cons: The risk of "hallucinations" – where AI generates plausible but inaccurate or misleading content – remains a significant concern, necessitating careful human oversight.

d) Witness Statements

Pros: AI can help organize and synthesize witness information efficiently, providing a clearer picture of testimonies and potential discrepancies.

Cons: Authenticity concerns arise if AI-generated content is mistaken for genuine human testimony. This may undermine trust in the integrity of witness statements and potentially cause issues during cross-examination.

e) Disclosure

Pros: AI tools can efficiently manage large volumes of documents, facilitating the identification and retrieval of relevant evidence generated through document production, which can increase efficiency in handling this type of voluminous data.

Cons: The potential for bias in AI-driven data selection poses risks, especially if critical information is overlooked or misrepresented.

f) Merits Hearing

Pros: AI can aid in real-time data analysis during hearings, providing arbitrators and counsel with immediate access to relevant segments from previous days of the hearing such as counsel arguments, objections, witness and expert witness testimony on any relevant matter.

Cons: Overreliance on AI may detract from the human elements of persuasion and deliberation that are essential in arbitration.

g) Drafting Awards

Pros: AI can assist in drafting awards by ensuring legal consistency and providing templates based on successful past awards.

Cons: Concerns about the interpretation of complex legal principles arise, as AI may lack the depth of understanding required to address intricate legal issues adequately. Lack of clear guidelines on this matter causes concern. SVAMC may be used as a step in the right direction in terms of transparency and predictability of AI use.

4. The Ambivalence in Generational Perception of AI Tools

One of the topics that was not planned for the World Café discussion, but emerged quite a relevant one is the difference in perception of AI and its relevance and effectiveness in the legal work. Younger practitioners often embrace AI for its potential to enhance efficiency and streamline workflows, viewing it as an integral part of modern legal practice. In contrast, more seasoned professionals may express skepticism, concerned about the reliability of AI outputs and the potential erosion of traditional legal skills. This divide reflects broader apprehensions about technology's role in the legal field. Balancing these perspectives is crucial as we integrate AI into our practices while maintaining the integrity of our work.

a) Seasoned Practitioners Perspectives

Senior lawyers approach AI with caution and mainly express concerns about the reliability of AI-generated content. They question the accuracy of AI outputs, citing instances of "hallucinations" or misleading information. The ethical implications of using AI tools in legal practice weigh heavily on their minds. Concerns about confidentiality, data security, and the potential for biased outputs prompt many to approach AI with skepticism. They also raised concerns on the appropriateness of legal training when relying heavily on AI generated tools and the capacity of younger generations to develop critical and supervision skills without traditional means of research, drafting and strategizing.

b) Junior Practitioner's Perspectives

In contrast, interns and younger associates tend to embrace AI tools like ChatGPT with enthusiasm. Their familiarity with technology and digital tools and general openness to innovation shapes their perceptions. Interns often view AI as a means to enhance their productivity. They appreciate how AI can automate mundane tasks, allowing them to focus on more complex legal analysis and strategy. This generational comfort with technology translates into a willingness to experiment with AI in drafting documents, conducting research, and managing case information. By interacting with AI, they can explore legal concepts, test arguments, and receive instant feedback on their writing. They perceive that this interactive learning experience can supplement traditional mentorship and training.

c) Bridging the Gap

To address this ambivalence and foster a more cohesive approach to AI in the legal field, it is essential for law firms and arbitration institutions to facilitate intergenerational dialogue. Providing training sessions that emphasize both the capabilities and limitations of AI tools can help align the perspectives of senior lawyers and interns. Workshops can focus on best practices for integrating AI into legal workflows while reinforcing the importance of critical thinking and ethical considerations. Promoting collaborative projects that involve both senior lawyers and interns can foster a culture of innovation. By working together on tasks that utilize AI, both groups can gain insights into each other's perspectives, creating a more unified approach to technology adoption in legal practice.

5. Conclusion

The integration of AI into arbitration presents both opportunities and challenges that require careful navigation. While AI can enhance efficiency, reduce costs, and streamline processes, concerns about confidentiality, bias, and ethical implications remain paramount. The recent guidelines established by SVAMC provide a useful framework for ensuring responsible AI use, emphasizing the importance of safeguarding confidential information, maintaining transparency, and upholding the integrity of the arbitration process. The generational divide in perceptions of AI further complicates the landscape, with younger practitioners enthusiastic about its potential while seasoned professionals express skepticism regarding its reliability and ethical implications. Bridging this gap through intergenerational dialogue, training, and collaborative projects will be essential for fostering a cohesive approach to AI adoption in legal practice. Ultimately, balancing innovation with fundamental legal principles will be critical as the profession embraces the transformative power of AI while preserving the core values of fairness and justice in arbitration.

H. EU Sanctions Against the Russian Federation and Commercial Arbitration

*Marija Dobrić/Kamalia Mehtiyeva**

1. Introduction

Since the Russian Federation's invasion of Ukraine in 2022, the EU has expanded the sanctions regime of EU Council Regulations 269/2014 and 833/2014, which were imposed in 2014 in response to the annexation of Crimea and Sevastopol.[83]) This sanctions regime against Russia has had a significant effect on contractual relationships between EU and Russian operators. As a result, there has been a drastic increase in sanctions-related disputes, many of which are settled in commercial arbitration.

EU restrictive measures (sanctions) also have an impact on arbitration and pose particular challenges for parties and practitioners. In this context, the round table participants discussed (amongst others) the following topics: (*i*) Relevance of EU Sanctions in Arbitration (*ii*) Impact of EU Sanctions on Substantive Issues and (*iii*) Impact of EU Sanctions on Procedural Rights and Procedure. The discussions are summarized in Sections 2 – 4 below.

The authors are particularly grateful for the participants'[84]) insightful contributions during the round table discussion.[85])

2. Relevance of EU Sanctions in Arbitration

a) Introduction

Even if EU sanctions do not explicitly target arbitration, they may have a significant impact both on the substantive aspect of disputes and the conduct of proceedings. Arbitrators, counsel, and arbitral institutions should be mindful of when and how EU sanctions may affect disputes. This requires, above all, that practitioners and institutions keep up to date with new developments such as the EU sanctions packages and case law on EU sanctions.

However, this is not as simple as it sounds. Particularly in commercial arbitration, parties and practitioners often have little arbitral case law to rely on, as only a relatively small number of arbitral awards are published. In this

---

*) The authors would like to thank *Gregor Kobierski* for his valuable assistance with research for this contribution.

[83]) Council Regulation 269/2014, 2014 O.J. (L 78) 6; Council Regulation 833/2014, 2014 O.J. (L 229) 1.

[84]) Among others, *Therry Augsburger, Manuela Grosu, Franz J. Heidinger, Anna Kozmenko, Justin Friedrich Krahé, Matthias Krivdic, Christopher Lytras* (sorted alphabetically).

[85]) Where not explicitly referenced, the opinions expressed are those of the authors.

regard, national decisions can be helpful in identifying the impact of EU sanctions on disputes and proceedings before state courts and can assist practitioners in drawing parallels with arbitral proceedings. The EU Commission's Consolidated FAQs on the implementation and interpretation of EU Council Regulation 833/2014 and 269/2014, which are updated regularly, provide helpful guidance on the interpretation and application of the EU sanction regulations.[86]) However, the EU Commission's Consolidated FAQs are not binding. The Court of Justice of the European Union ("**CJEU**") is the only authoritative court to interpret EU sanctions.[87]) However, the CJEU has not yet rendered many decisions interpreting EU sanction regulations.

In recent years, a considerable amount of scholarly work and guidelines have been published which may also assist in navigating sanctions-related arbitrations. To give an example, in September 2023, the International Association of Lawyers has adopted a guide titled "Economic Sanctions and Arbitration: A Practical Guide for Parties, Counsel and Arbitrators" ("**Guide**") with the purpose of providing "*an introduction to issues that users of international commercial arbitration may encounter when economic sanctions affect a person, place or asset involved in a matter*" and to provide guidance in identifying relevant issues during disputes.[88]) It is noteworthy that the Guide does not distinguish between economic sanctions adopted by the EU, states or international organizations but rather provides a broad overview of how these sanctions might affect arbitration. In line with the Guide, the authors find that EU sanctions may impact arbitral proceedings particularly where a party is directly or indirectly targeted by sanctions or where a party is a national of a sanctioned state or where the seat of arbitration lies in the EU.[89])

---

[86]) EU Commission, *Commission Consolidated FAQs on the implementation of Council Regulation No 833/2014 and Council Regulation No 269/2014* (last updated on December 20, 2024).

[87]) Article 19 (1) Treaty on European Union: "*The Court of Justice of the European Union* [CJEU] *shall include the Court of Justice* [ECJ], *the General Court and specialised courts. It shall ensure that in the interpretation and application of the Treaties the law is observed.*"

[88]) UIA, *Economic Sanctions and Arbitration: A Practical Guide for Parties, Counsel and Arbitrators* 6 mn 1, 7 mn 6 (2023), https://www.uianet.org/sites/default/files/uia_-_economic_sanctions_and_arbitration_guide_en.pdf (accessed on October 31, 2024). *See also* Global Investigations Review, *The Guide to Sanctions – Fifth Edition. Crucial sanctions challenges in civil litigation and arbitration* (2024).

[89]) UIA, *Economic Sanctions and Arbitration: A Practical Guide for Parties, Counsel and Arbitrators* 17 mn 35 (2023), https://www.uianet.org/sites/default/files/uia_-_economic_sanctions_and_arbitration_guide_en.pdf (accessed on October 31, 2024). *See also* Global Investigations Review, *The Guide to Sanctions – Fifth Edition. Crucial sanctions challenges in civil litigation and arbitration* (2024).

b) Relevance of EU Sanctions on the Merits

During the round table discussion, the authors focused on the question of when arbitral tribunals have to apply EU sanctions to the merits of a case.

As a starting point, if the parties have chosen the law of an EU Member State as the applicable law to the contract, the arbitral tribunal will have to examine the applicability of the EU regulations to the facts of the case.[90]) In the absence of a choice of law, an arbitral tribunal will generally have a wide margin of discretion in determining the applicable law, by applying the law it deems appropriate either directly or by virtue of the conflict of law rules it deems applicable.[91])

However, it is important to note that the EU regulations on restrictive measures may also apply irrespective of a given choice of law. In this regard, it must be stressed that arbitrators must render enforceable awards and must make every effort to reduce the risk of the awards to be set aside. Thus, arbitral tribunals should be careful in assessing whether to apply or not to apply EU sanctions if the seat of arbitration is in the EU.[92]) For example, the Austrian Supreme Court has held that fundamental principles of EU law are part of the Austrian public policy and has set aside awards in the past that violated such principles of EU law.[93]) At least from the perspective of Austrian law, it is likely that a breach of EU sanctions will also be considered a breach of national Austrian public policy.[94]) Similar considerations appear to have been taken by national courts in France.[95])

---

[90]) In this regard, Article 13 of EU Council Regulation 833/2014 and Article 17 of EU Council Regulation 269/2014 provide that the regulations apply (a) within the territory of the EU, (b) on board any aircraft or any vessel under the jurisdiction of an EU Member State, (c) to any person inside or outside the territory of the EU who is a national of an EU Member State, (d) to any legal person, entity or body, inside or outside the territory of the EU, which is incorporated or constituted under the law of an EU Member State, (e) to any legal person, entity, or body in respect of any business done in whole or in part within the EU. Different from Article 13 (a) of EU Council Regulation 833/2014, Article 17 (a) of EU Council Regulation 269/2014 provides that the regulation applies within the territory of the EU includes its airspace.

[91]) *See, e.g., Tamás Szabados, EU Economic Sanctions in Arbitration*, 35(4) Journal of International Arbitration 439, 450 (2018).

[92]) UIA, *Economic Sanctions and Arbitration: A Practical Guide for Parties, Counsel and Arbitrators* 17 mn 36 (2023), https://www.uianet.org/sites/default/files/uia_-_economic_sanctions_and_arbitration_guide_en.pdf (accessed on October 31, 2024).

[93]) *See* OGH, Feb 18, 2015, docket no. 2 Ob 22/14w (Austria); OGH, Mar 1, 2017, docket no. 5 Ob 72/16y (Austria); *Elisabeth Lovrek & Gottfried Musger, Aufhebungsklage*, in *Dietmar Czernich & Astrid Deixler-Hübner & Martin Schauer*, HANDBUCH SCHIEDSRECHT 579 *et seq.* mn 16.84 (2018) for further details.

[94]) *See also Tamás Szabados, EU Economic Sanctions in Arbitration*, 35(4) Journal of International Arbitration 439, 459 (2018).

[95]) *Nadia Darwazeh & Sophie Grémaud, 2024 PAW: Sanctions and Arbitration: Lessons Learned and Possible Strategies*, Kluwer Arbitration Blog (2024).

Irrespective of the seat of arbitration, should assets be located in the EU, the arbitral tribunal is again well advised not to simply ignore EU sanctions, as there is a risk that enforcement courts in EU Member States will refuse recognition and enforcement of an award on similar public policy considerations (Art V (2) (b) New York Convention 1958).[96]) Conversely, however, there is also a risk that an award giving effect to EU sanctions will be considered as a violation of Russian public policy by Russian enforcement courts.[97])

c) Arbitral Seat Outside of the EU?

The round table participants further discussed (*i*) whether the choice of a non-EU arbitral seat might release the tribunal from the application of EU sanctions and (*ii*) whether in such case, arbitral tribunals would have the power to move the seat based on a request of one of the parties only. Firstly, in view of the considerations made above, a transfer of the seat to a sanction-neutral state may not necessarily release a tribunal from applying EU sanctions to the merits of a case. Secondly, as regards the question of whether a tribunal may move the seat without mutual party consent, the participants were aware that this could be the case only in extreme circumstances. For instance, the Secretariat's Guide to ICC Arbitration provides that "[i]*f the parties have agreed on the place of arbitration, as a general rule it can be changed only by a subsequent agreement of the parties.* […] *In extreme cases where the place of arbitration initially agreed upon can no longer function as such, and assuming that at least one party refuses to agree on a different place, it is conceivable that a party could apply to the arbitral tribunal to change the place of arbitration.*"[98]) The necessary prerequisites for a change of seat without mutual consent will hardly be met only because the parties agreed on a place of arbitration in the EU.

Conversely, arbitral tribunals may not have to apply EU sanctions to the contract if the place of arbitration is in a third state and none of the parties has assets in the EU. It is arguable that a non-EU court competent for setting aside and/or enforcement proceedings would likely conclude that non-compliance with EU sanctions is not contrary to the public policy of the third state.

---

[96]) *See Tamás Szabados, EU Economic Sanctions in Arbitration,* 35(4) Journal of International Arbitration 439, 459 (2018) on European public policy.

[97]) *Marija Dobrić & Ingeborg Edel, Security for Costs Against (Non-Sanctioned) Russian Claimants? – An Overview Under the Vienna Rules*, Kluwer Arbitration Blog (2024); *see, for instance,* Stavropol Arbitrazh Court, Nov 11, 2022, docket no. A63-7553/2022 (Russia) regarding a broad interpretation of public policy.

[98]) *Jason Fry, Simon Greenberg & Francesca Mazza, The Secretariat's Guide to ICC Arbitration* mn 3-690 *et seq.* (2012). *See in more detail Diego Rueda & Diego Perez, Do Tribunals Have the Power to Relocate the Arbitral Seat?* (2024), https://riskandcompliance.freshfields.com/post/102jaun/do-tribunals-have-the-power-to-relocate-the-arbitral-seat (accessed on October 31, 2024).

3. Impact on Substantive Issues

Additionally, the authors discussed with the round table participants the impact of EU sanctions on the types of disputes and the substantive difficulties when it comes to arbitrating commercial disputes in the context of sanctions.

a) Typical Sanctions-Related Commercial Disputes?

The round table participants discussed that EU sanctions against Russia have a major impact on the contractual relationships between EU and Russian operators resulting in a wide range of commercial disputes. In this regard, the participants also shared that they experienced an influx of sanctions-related disputes in their daily practice.

In the context of EU sanctions, the participants acknowledged that disputes between EU and Russian operators often result from non-performance of the contract by the EU operator relying namely on *force majeure*. For instance, in case of supply agreements, the contract will likely not be performed by the EU operator if the goods to be exported by the EU operator to Russia were added to the list of sanctioned goods after conclusion of the contract or if the Russian contractor is targeted by the EU restrictive measures.

There are particularly two reasons why such cases are increasingly brought before courts and tribunals. To begin with, it is fair to say that the invasion of Ukraine was not foreseeable and that affected contracts were not drafted with the expansion of EU sanctions in mind.[99]) As a result, usually contracts between EU and Russian parties do not explicitly regulate the outcome if the contract subsequently becomes impossible to perform. In this context, it will also have to be borne in mind that generally none of the parties will be at fault for the non-performance of the contract. On top of that, the complexity and vague content of the EU sanctions are also increasingly leading to disputes not being settled amicably but being brought before courts and tribunals (*see also* below Sec. 3b)).

Having said this, arbitral tribunals will often have to deal with the question of whether a contract affected by EU sanctions could have been terminated unilaterally. Some contracts provide for a specific *force majeure* clause that grants a right of termination in case the performance of the contract is impeded. In the absence of specific contractual provisions, it must be analyzed whether national laws recognize the concept of *force majeure* or other concepts (*e.g.*, in Austria: *Wegfall der Geschäftsgrundlage*).[100]) Depending on the applicable national law, contracts may potentially also become void if they contravene

---

[99]) *See, e.g.*, Global Investigations Review, *The Guide to Sanctions – Fifth Edition. Crucial sanctions challenges in civil litigation and arbitration* (2024).

[100]) *Valerie Hohenberg & Theresia Franziska Welser, ESG, private enforcement and strategic litigation in times of war* (2022), https://www.wolftheiss.com/insights/esg-private-enforcement-and-strategic-litigation-in-times-of-war/ (accessed on October 31, 2024).

EU sanctions. In all likelihood, EU operators will try to use EU sanctions as a defense to claim that they have not breached their contractual obligations.

In this context, EU operators may try to rely on the so-called no claims clause of Article 11 (1) EU Council Regulation 833/2014 to argue that their Russian counterparty is not entitled to claim damages in relation to the non-fulfilment of the contract, if performance by the EU operator has been affected, directly or indirectly, in whole or part, by said EU regulation. Whether the no claims clause also prohibits the return of advance payments to Russian parties is debated in literature.[101]) The broad wording of Article 11 (1) ("[n]*o claims in connection with any contract or transaction the performance of which has been affected* [...]") and the past case law of the CJEU, which interprets EU sanction regulations generally broadly, could suggest that Article 11 prohibits the return of advance payments. National bodies of Germany and Malta officially acknowledge that the no claims clause of Article 11 EU Council Regulation 833/2014 prohibits the repayment of an advance payment received prior to the imposition of the EU sanctions if the performance of the contract is no longer possible.[102]) Currently, a request for a preliminary ruling is pending before the CJEU on this question (C-802/24, Reibel). It will remain to be seen how the CJEU will interpret Article 11 (1).

b) Substantive Difficulties in Arbitrating Sanctions-Related Disputes?

From a substantive view, the round table participants noted that difficulties in dealing with sanctions-related disputes arise from the fact that the EU sanction regulations are often formulated too vaguely. In particular, the scope of the prohibitions put in place by the EU sanction regulations is often not clear and EU operators will often struggle to identify whether a certain behavior is still in compliance with restrictive measures or not. Moreover, scholars also criticize that the rules are sometimes hard to grasp and thus limit effective enforcement.[103]) Other difficulties in arbitrating sanctions-related disputes pertain to the frequently changing sanction regime. Arbitrators and counsel

---

[101]) *See, for instance, Martin Vogt & Katrin Arend, Sanktionen und Embargos der EU,* in *Bärbel Sachs & Christian Pelz,* AUSSENWIRTSCHAFTSRECHT 1247 mn 260 (3rd ed. 2024); *Bärbel Sachs, Sanktionen und Embargos der EU,* in *Bärbel Sachs & Christian Pelz,* AUSSENWIRTSCHAFTSRECHT 1289 mn 341 (3rd ed. 2024); *Christian Pelz, Exportkontrolle und Sanktionen im Bereich der Automobilwirtschaft,* RAW 41 (2024).

[102]) *See* German Federal Ministry for Economic Affairs and Climate Action, *FAQs about sanctions against Russia* (2023), https://www.bmwk.de/Redaktion/EN/FAQ/sanctions-against-russia/faq-russland-sanktionen.html (accessed on September 11, 2024); SMB, *Guidance Note on Article 11 of Council Regulation (EU) No. 833/2014 relating to refund of advance payments* (2024), https://smb.gov.mt/wp-content/uploads/2024/02/Guidance-on-article-11-8332014.pdf (accessed on October 31, 2024).

[103]) *Daniel Wiedmann & Daniel Hoppen, Die Russlandsanktionen der EU: Die Sanktionspakete 8 bis 13 und weitere Entwicklungen,* RIW 401 (2024).

must adapt to the newly introduced sanctions packages and regularly review whether new changes were implemented.

Although the EU Commission's Consolidated FAQs and the statements issued by national authorities help parties, counsel and arbitrators to interpret the EU sanctions, the ultimate competence for interpretation of EU sanctions lies, as discussed previously, with the CJEU. However, if an arbitral tribunal seated in the EU is in doubt about the interpretation of an EU regulation and no case law of the CJEU exists to that effect, it may not directly refer the question to the CJEU through a preliminary ruling request. This is because arbitral tribunals are not considered as courts of an EU Member State.[104])

In this context, the question arises whether questions of EU law may be referred by an arbitral tribunal indirectly via judicial assistance. In the *Nordsee* decision, the CJEU has held that an indirect referral by a requested state court is generally permissible under EU law.[105]) From an Austrian perspective, the prevailing opinion holds that requesting judicial assistance by an arbitral tribunal also includes a request for a preliminary ruling by the CJEU and is not limited to assistance by the state court when taking evidence.[106]) However, to the best knowledge of the authors, there has not yet been a case where such an indirect ruling request has been made in Austria via judicial assistance.

4. Impact on Procedural Rights and Procedure

The round table participants also discussed procedural issues which could arise in relation to sanctions-related arbitrations. In particular, the participants discussed, on the one hand, whether Russian parties encounter obstacles to access to justice in arbitration, and, on the other hand, whether EU parties having a Russian counterparty encounter difficulties in asserting and enforcing their claims through arbitration due to the reform of the Russian procedural code in 2020. Regarding the latter, requesting (*i*) anti-suit injunctions in foreign courts or (*ii*) security for costs from the competent tribunal might mitigate these hurdles for EU parties.

a) Access to Justice for Russian Parties

First, the participants discussed whether Russian parties face difficulties when it comes to legal representation in arbitration. In this regard, the participants agreed that while the implemented legal framework would suggest

---

[104]) *Ulrich Ehricke, Art 267 AEUV*, in *Rudolf Streinz*, EUV/AEUV mn 33 (3rd ed. 2018).

[105]) *See* CJEU, *Nordsee*, Mar 23, 1982, docket no. C-102/81, mn 14 *et seqq*.

[106]) *See, e.g.*, *Lisa Beisteiner*, in *Gerold Zeiler, Austrian Arbitration Law* 158 *et seqq*. mn 13 (2016); *see also Helmut Heiss & Leander D. Loacker, Auslegung von europäischem Gemeinschaftsrecht*, in *Christoph Liebscher & Paul Oberhammer & Walter H. Rechberger*, SCHIEDSVERFAHRENSRECHT II 233 *et seqq*. (2016); *Katharina Plavec, § 602 ZPO*, in *Georg E. Kodek & Paul Oberhammer*, ZPO-ON mn 6 (2023).

that this is not the case, EU sanctions may have factual implications on the right to representation of Russian entities.

In this regard, it is important to note that Article 5n (2) of EU Council Regulation 833/2014[107]) prohibits "*to provide, directly or indirectly,* [...] *legal advisory services* [...] *to: (a) the Government of Russia; or (b) legal persons, entities or bodies established in Russia.*" However, Article 5n (5) and (6) EU Council Regulation 833/2014 exclude from this ban the provision of services that are strictly necessary for the exercise of the right of defense in judicial proceedings and the right to an effective legal remedy and the provision of services which are strictly necessary to ensure access to judicial, administrative or arbitral proceedings in an EU Member State, as well as for the recognition or enforcement of a judgment or an arbitral award rendered in an EU Member State. The provision of services must, however, be consistent with the objectives of EU Council Regulation 833/2014 and EU Council Regulation 269/2014.

In recent cases, the General Court upheld the prohibition to provide legal advice to the Russian Government and to entities established in Russia.[108]) The General Court, however, also expressly clarified that this prohibition does not prohibit legal advisory services linked with judicial proceedings and does not apply to natural persons; consequently, the ban does not breach the fundamental right of access to legal advice from a lawyer under the Charter of Fundamental Rights of the EU.[109])

Having said this, Russian parties may nevertheless be unable to factually find legal representation, which may exacerbate their ability to bring an arbitral claim.[110]) Law firms and lawyers may be hesitant to take up legal representation for the Russian Government or sanctioned parties after the start of the war in Ukraine. Moreover, the round table participants discussed that legal counsel will often only work on the basis of a retainer. Russian parties, however, may have difficulties to provide immediate payment of legal fees for representation

---

[107]) Council Regulation 2022/1904, 2022 O.J. (LI 259) 3 amending Council Regulation 833/2014, 2014 O.J. (L 229) 1.

[108]) General Court, Oct 2, 2024, docket no. T-797/22; General Court, Oct 2, 2024, docket no. T-798/22; General Court, Oct 2, 2024, docket no. T-828/22. CJEU Communications Directorate Press and Information Unit (2024), https://curia.europa.eu/jcms/upload/docs/application/pdf/2024-10/cp240155en.pdf (accessed on October 31, 2024). *See also recently*, CJEU, *Jemerak*, Sep 5, 2024, docket no. C-109/23.

[109]) General Court, Oct 2, 2024, docket no. T-797/22; *see also* General Court, Oct 2, 2024, docket no. T-798/22; General Court, Oct 2, 2024, docket no. T-828/22. CJEU, Communications Directorate Press and Information Unit (2024), https://curia.europa.eu/jcms/upload/docs/application/pdf/2024-10/cp240155en.pdf (accessed on October 31, 2024).

[110]) *Stephanie Tsang, Sanctions in Current Geopolitical Climate: Challenges to International Arbitration in the Context of the Russia-Ukraine War* (2024), https://arbitrationblog.kluwerarbitration.com/2024/04/04/sanctions-in-current-geopolitical-climate-challenges-to-international-arbitration-in-the-context-of-the-russia-ukraine-war/ (accessed on October 31, 2024).

due to bank restrictions. In case of short deadlines, this may seriously affect the Russian party.

b) Implications of Russian Laws on Arbitration

Secondly, the round table participants discussed Russia's Federal Law No. 171-FZ ("**Federal Law**") dated 8 June 2020, in force since 18 June 2020 that amends the Russian Arbitrazh (Commercial) Procedure Code and has brought about several changes for sanctions-related arbitrations.[111)]

The Federal Law allows Russian courts to ascertain exclusive jurisdiction over disputes involving a sanctioned Russian party (or disputes arising out of foreign sanctions) and consequently to ignore a validly concluded forum-selection clause on the basis of a presumption that sanctioned entities do not enjoy equal fair trial protection in states that apply restrictive measures (so-called "unfriendly states").[112)] The recent Russian court practice suggests that a Russian sanctioned party will not have to prove that it actually encounters obstacles to its right to fair trial. Rather, Russian courts seem to presume that already the imposition of sanctions means an obstacle to the right to fair trial and that foreign arbitral tribunals and institutions are not impartial.[113)] For the same considerations, Russian courts may also issue anti-suit injunctions preventing a foreign party from pursuing arbitration or litigation outside of Russia. What is more, the breach of a Russian anti-suit injunction results in a substantial penalty, which may rise to the amount of the claim on the merits.[114)] Moreover, the competence of Russian courts to assume exclusive jurisdiction and issue anti-suit injunctions creates real risks for parallel proceedings and competing decisions on the same matter between the same parties.[115)]

While Russia is a party to the New York Convention 1958, the Federal Law has also increased the risk that Russian courts will more readily deny recognition and enforcement of arbitral awards rendered in EU states against sanctioned Russian entities based on Russian public policy. Russian courts will, however, require that the Russian sanctioned party has objected to foreign proceedings and has applied for an anti-suit injunction. The recent Russian court practice questioning the impartiality of foreign seated tribunals and institutions makes it likely that public policy considerations will also be applied by Russian courts to non-sanctioned Russian parties.[116)]

---

111) *See, e.g., Kamalia Mehtiyeva, Civil Procedure and International Sanctions,* 13(2) International Journal of Procedural Law 270, 274 *et seqq.* (2023).

112) *Ibid.* at 271 *et seqq.;* 275.

113) *Ibid.* at 279 *et seqq.; Marija Dobrić* & *Ingeborg Edel, Security for Costs Against (Non-Sanctioned) Russian Claimants? – An Overview Under the Vienna Rules,* Kluwer Arbitration Blog (2024).

114) *Kamalia Mehtiyeva, Civil Procedure and International Sanctions,* 13(2) International Journal of Procedural Law 270, 278 (2023).

115) *Ibid.* at 275.

116) *Marija Dobrić* & *Ingeborg Edel, Security for Costs Against (Non-Sanctioned)*

The authors find it also worthwhile to discuss how opponents of Russian parties may defend themselves against actions taken by Russian parties based on the Federal Law or against the above-displayed enforcement risks. In case Russian courts assume exclusive jurisdiction or render anti-suit injunctions despite of a validly concluded arbitration agreement, EU parties may try to obtain themselves an anti-suit injunction in another country (so-called anti-anti-suit injunction). While such an anti-anti-suit injunction will not be enforceable in Russia,[117]) it may still have negative consequences on the Russian party (*e.g.*, in the United Kingdom: risk of contempt of a foreign court).[118]) This could force a Russian party to comply with foreign anti-anti-suit injunctions. At least from the perspective of Austrian law, however, such anti-suit injunctions are prohibited, as they are interfering with the judicial competence of foreign courts.[119]) The issuance of anti-suit injunctions within the EU would very likely also be incompatible with the Brussels Ia-Regulation.[120])

Moreover, the risks of refusal of recognition and enforcement of arbitral awards in Russia may be mitigated by applying to the arbitral tribunal for security for costs. Several institutional rules provide for the possibility to request interim measures, which arguably also allows to request security for costs. Other institutional rules explicitly provide for a right to request security for costs. For instance, Article 33 (6) Vienna Rules provides that a party may request security for costs against the claimant or counter-claimant, "*if the requesting party shows cause that the recoverability of a potential claim for costs is, with a sufficient degree of probability, at risk.*" In this regard, the authors stress that the standard of proof of Article 33 (6) Vienna Rules is reduced.[121])

Russian Claimants? – An Overview Under the Vienna Rules, Kluwer Arbitration Blog (2024).

[117]) *Kamalia Mehtiyeva, Civil Procedure and International Sanctions*, 13(2) International Journal of Procedural Law 270, 273 (2023).

[118]) *Sarah Garvey* et al., *Anti-Suit Injunctions, Arbitration Clauses and (Pro) Active English Courts* (2024), https://www.mayerbrown.com/en/insights/publications/2024/09/anti-suit-injunctions-arbitration-clauses-and-pro-active-english-courts (accessed on October 31, 2024); *see, e.g., Herbert Smith Freehills, English High Court grants anti-suit and anti-anti-suit injunctions to restrain Russian proceedings brought by sanctioned entities* (2023), https://www.herbertsmithfreehills.com/notes/arbitration/2023-11/english-high-court-grants-anti-suit-and-anti-anti-suit-injunctions-to-restrain-russian-proceedings-brought-by-sanctioned-entities (accessed on October 31, 2024).

[119]) *See Martin Weber, Das staatliche Gericht im Schiedsverfahren*, in *Dietmar Czernich, Astrid Deixler-Hübner & Martin Schauer*, Handbuch Schiedsrecht 491 mn 14.20 (2018); *Christian W. Konrad, Die allgemeinen Bestimmungen der ZPO zum Schiedsverfahren*, in *Christoph Liebscher, Paul Oberhammer & Walter H. Rechberger*, Schiedsverfahrensrecht I 69 *et seqq.* mn 2/80 (2011).

[120]) CJEU, *Charles Taylor Adjusting Ltd*, Sep 7, 2023, docket no. C-590/21, mn 25; *Christian W. Konrad, Die allgemeinen Bestimmungen der ZPO zum Schiedsverfahren*, in *Christoph Liebscher, Paul Oberhammer & Walter H. Rechberger*, Schiedsverfahrensrecht I 69 *et seqq.* mn 2/80 (2011).

[121]) *Marija Dobrić & Ingeborg Edel, Security for Costs Against (Non-Sanctioned)*

The above displayed risks that Russian enforcement courts will not recognize and enforce arbitral awards rendered in EU states will thus likely suffice to grant security for costs.[122]) Furthermore, Article 33 (6) Vienna Rules will likely also allow to request security for costs against a non-sanctioned Russian claimant.[123]) Whether arbitral tribunals would grant security for costs under other institutional rules under these circumstances is questionable.

5. Conclusion

The EU sanctions against Russia have a big impact on commercial arbitration. This report does not aim to provide a conclusive analysis but aims to touch upon certain substantive and procedural questions that are frequently at issue. Importantly, the vivid discussion at the World Café round table showed yet again that EU sanctions are a complex but hot topic which concerns many of us practitioners.

I. Transparency in International Arbitration – How Good is it?

Isabelle Michou/Caroline Strohmeier[124])

1. Introduction

Transparency is a cornerstone of trust and legitimacy in any dispute resolution process, yet a concept that remains highly controversial in the context of international arbitration. For decades, practitioners, academics and stakeholders have dealt with a central question: How much transparency is enough? Striking the right balance is no small feat – it requires navigating the fine line between promoting fairness, predictability, consistency and accountability on one hand, and preserving the confidentiality that makes arbitration so appealing on the other.

This article dives into the heart of this ongoing debate. How transparent is international arbitration today and how should it – in the eyes of arbitration practitioners – evolve? Through insights gleaned from the World Café discussions, where the authors had the great pleasure to moderate a table with

---

Russian Claimants? – An Overview Under the Vienna Rules, Kluwer Arbitration Blog (2024).

[122]) *Ibid.*

[123]) *Ibid.*

[124]) Participants to the discussion at the World Café were (among others) *Michael Komuczky, Anja Cervenka, Mihaela Maravela, Alicia Quijano-Evans, Susanne Schwalb, Constanza Trofaier, Caroline Wenisch, Mark Campbell, Andrea Domac, Sofia Cozac, Jurgita Petkutė, Manuela Grosu* and *Stefani Funke Rodriguez.*

the subject of debates evolving around the different perceptions of transparency and its current and future role in international arbitration, this article explores the perspectives of practitioners across Europe, the tools and rules shaping transparency in arbitration and the challenges posed by "over-transparency".

Join us as we summarize the World Café discussions in chapters 2.–3. below, thereby trying to unpack the complexities of this essential yet contentious topic and ask the critical question: Is transparency in international arbitration as good as it could (or should) be?

2. Does Transparency Impact the Perception of Arbitration and how?

There is no doubt that transparency increasingly plays a role in shaping how arbitration is perceived by parties, practitioners, the public and other stakeholders. While transparency enhances arbitration's legitimacy and credibility – dispelling its image as a "behind closed doors" process – it also introduces risks that can diminish its benefits if not carefully managed. This chapter explores the dual-edged impact of transparency on arbitration and examines regional variations in its perception.

a) What are the Positive Effects of Transparency on Arbitration?

Transparency significantly enhances how arbitration is perceived, benefiting not only the immediate stakeholders but also the broader public and the global arbitration community. Key positive impacts include:

- **Enhanced legitimacy and credibility:** Transparency fosters trust in arbitration as a fair and neutral dispute resolution mechanism. Open access to proceedings, documents and arbitral awards reassures parties and the broader public that decisions are grounded in legal principles rather than opacity. This strengthens confidence not only in individual cases but also in arbitration as a whole.
- **Increased predictability and consistency:** Transparency contributes to the development of a more predictable and consistent body of arbitral jurisprudence. Access to case law and reasoning enables parties, counsel and arbitrators to identify patterns and principles in decision-making. This predictability enhances arbitration's appeal by reducing uncertainties and setting clearer expectations.
- **Promotion of accountability:** Transparency ensures that arbitrators and institutions are held to higher standards of accountability. It provides a check on arbitrators' impartiality and professionalism, encouraging adherence to ethical and procedural norms. It also ensures

greater efficiency by making sure that arbitrators do not unjustifiably delay issuing their award.

- **Educational value:** Transparency provides invaluable resources for academics, practitioners, and future arbitrators. Published awards and procedural decisions offer insights into arbitral practices, contributing to professional development and academic discourse.
- **Encouragement of settlements:** Knowing that arbitral decisions may be made public can encourage parties to resolve disputes amicably, avoiding the scrutiny and potential reputational risks of a fully transparent arbitration process.
- **Promotion of diversity:** Transparency in arbitrator selection and decision-making sheds light on representation in arbitration, encouraging greater regional, generational and gender diversity in the appointment of arbitrators. Publicly available data can highlight gaps and drive initiatives to address them, potentially leading to heightened inclusion.
- **Influence beyond the parties involved:** The effects of transparency extend beyond the immediate participants in a dispute, especially in investment arbitration cases. The public perception of arbitration can benefit from openness, particularly in cases involving public interest or significant policy implications.

By fostering openness and trust while reinforcing the legitimacy of the process, transparency plays a pivotal role in ensuring that arbitration remains a credible, efficient and evolving method of dispute resolution.

b) What are the Challenges and Pitfalls of "Over-Transparency" and how can These be Balanced?

While transparency is undeniably a cornerstone of trust and legitimacy in arbitration, excessive or poorly implemented transparency – often referred to as "over-transparency" – can pose significant challenges, particularly when it undermines confidentiality, efficiency, flexibility or party autonomy.

In the following, the key challenges and potential pitfalls commonly linked to over-transparency are explored:

- **Erosion of confidentiality:** One of arbitration's defining advantages, especially in commercial disputes, is its confidential – or at least its private – nature. Over-transparency threatens this benefit, potentially deterring parties from choosing arbitration as their dispute resolution method and shifting perceptions of arbitration as less secure than previously thought. Disclosing sensitive business information or trade secrets may also harm competitive positions, creating a chilling effect on parties' willingness to arbitrate.

- **Perceived loss of party autonomy and flexibility:** Arbitration is valued for its flexibility and party-driven nature. Transparency, by increasing predictability and formalizing processes, may inadvertently lead to a perception that arbitration is becoming rigid and less tailored to parties' needs, not least due to an unintended reliance on precedents. Such reduction of arbitration's hallmark flexibility and overemphasis on prior decisions may make parties and tribunals feel constrained, detracting from the adaptability of arbitration to unique disputes.
- **Increased procedural complexity, costs and delays:** Transparency obligations often add layers of procedural complexity, thereby increasing costs and delays. Excessive disclosure requirements can overburden arbitrators and counsel, which can harm arbitration's reputation as a faster and more cost-effective alternative to litigation.
- **Exploitation of disclosed information:** Parties may misuse disclosed information to gain tactical advantages, either by disrupting ongoing proceedings or by using such information in subsequent disputes. This risk can diminish trust in arbitration.
- **Media misrepresentation:** Media coverage of arbitration proceedings can oversimplify complex legal issues or procedural nuances, leading to distorted public perceptions. Non-expert interpretations may undermine trust in outcomes, especially in high-profile disputes.
- **Inconsistent standards and expectations:** Over-transparency often stems from unclear or inconsistent standards across jurisdictions and arbitral institutions. This lack of uniformity creates confusion for parties and tribunals, leading to uneven application of transparency measures. Regional variations in expectations regarding transparency further complicate the landscape. While such differences may justify tailored standards, they also highlight the importance of establishing clear and consistent guidelines.

c) Strategies for Balancing Transparency and Mitigating Concerns

To avoid the pitfalls of over-transparency while maintaining its benefits, the participants at the World Café emphasized the importance of thoughtful, balanced approaches. Key strategies to mitigate concerns associated with over-transparency include:

- **Context-specific transparency:** Transparency mechanisms should be tailored to the nature of a specific dispute. For example, investment arbitration involving public stakeholders may warrant greater openness, while commercial arbitration should prioritize confidentiality to protect parties' interests.

- **Balancing transparency with confidentiality:** Mechanisms must carefully weigh transparency against the need for confidentiality, particularly when handling sensitive business or proprietary information.
- **Clear and flexible standards:** Transparency frameworks should be guided by clear, consistent standards that reduce ambiguities while allowing parties to customize solutions to suit their needs. Examples include anonymization or redaction of sensitive data before publication.
- **Limited public access with safeguards:** Public access to arbitration-related information should be limited and controlled, using tools like redactions or summarized disclosures to strike a balance between openness and privacy.

By balancing transparency to align with arbitration's core values – confidentiality, efficiency and flexibility – stakeholders can foster trust and accountability without falling into the trap of over-transparency. This balanced approach ensures that arbitration remains an effective and attractive dispute resolution method while adapting to evolving expectations of openness and fairness.

d) Regional Differences in the Perception of Transparency in Arbitration

One of the most fascinating insights from the World Café discussions was the variation in how transparency is perceived across regions. While its importance was universally recognized, the rationale and emphasis placed on transparency differed significantly.

- **Eastern Europe:** Transparency in arbitration is highly valued in Eastern Europe as a means to build trust and confidence in the process and align with international standards. Given the region's historical and institutional contexts, transparency is seen as a way to counteract lingering skepticism and enhance the arbitral process' credibility.
- **Western Europe:** Western European countries generally view transparency and confidentiality as complementary values that can coexist. The emphasis is on striking a balance, ensuring openness while preserving the confidentiality that parties expect from arbitration. The perception of arbitration as a well-established and trusted mechanism may explain the region's more measured approach to transparency.

Transparency undeniably influences how arbitration is perceived, with its ability to enhance legitimacy and public confidence balanced against the risks of undermining confidentiality, efficiency, flexibility and autonomy. Regional differences further underscore the need for tailored approaches to transparency, reflecting local expectations while adhering to global best practices. By managing these nuances effectively, arbitration can maintain its appeal as a trusted and flexible dispute resolution mechanism across diverse contexts.

3. Does Arbitration Need More Transparency?

This question sparked a lively debate at the World Café, inviting the participants to share their experiences with transparency in arbitration and explore where there might still be room for growth. Building on these discussions, this chapter dives into whether practitioners find the current standards and rules on transparency sufficient or whether there's a growing appetite for more openness in the arbitral process.

a) Which Databases, Tools and Platforms on Transparency Currently Exist?

While not exhaustive, this chapter highlights key databases, tools and platforms that emerged during the World Café discussions as vital to enhancing transparency in international arbitration.

aa) The Role of Case Law Databases

The participants underscored the value of accessible case law databases, such as those provided by Jus Mundi, Kluwer or arbitral institutions.

At the same time, however, the participants voiced their dissatisfaction with the limited availability of arbitral case law, highlighting it as a critical area in need of improvement. The consensus was clear: Greater availability of arbitral case law is essential to ensure predictability, enhance consistency and provide much-needed legal certainty for parties and counsel.

bb) User-Friendly Resources from Arbitral Institutions

The participants, particularly in their roles as counsel, emphasized the importance of resources that arbitral institutions present in a clear and user-friendly format. Examples included tools for estimating arbitration costs and databases of arbitrators that allow filtering by specific criteria in order to facilitate the selection of the best suitable candidates as party-appointed arbitrators. While some institutions already offer such tools, the participants expressed a strong desire for expansion and improvements, particularly in usability and accessibility.

cc) Enhancing the Arbitrator Selection Process

A recurring topic of interest was the potential to advance the arbitrator selection process. Tools like Arbitrator Intelligence, founded by *Catherine A. Rogers*, were a focal point of discussion. Such platforms, designed to help users make informed and predictable decisions when selecting arbitrators, were recognized as highly valuable. The ability to assess arbitrators' experience and other relevant criteria is particularly critical in cross-border disputes or unfamiliar jurisdictions.

Regrettably, as *Catherine A. Rogers* herself noted, Arbitrator Intelligence has ceased operations.[125]) However, the continued demand for such tools underscores their importance. The participants expressed hope that innovative projects will rise to fill this gap, offering much-needed support in the arbitrator selection process.

These discussions reflect a collective ambition to leverage technology and innovation to make arbitration more transparent, predictable, and efficient.

b) In Which Fields of Arbitration is There a Need for Increased Transparency?

The discussions at the World Café made one thing clear: Almost every aspect of arbitration would benefit from increased transparency – albeit with a balanced approach to avoid the pitfalls of over-transparency (as outlined in chapter 2.c) above).

aa) Identifying Key Information and Stakeholders

Transparency begins with understanding what information should be made available and to whom. Stakeholders in arbitration – including parties, counsel, arbitrators, arbitral institutions and third-party funders – each have unique interests.

bb) What are Arbitration Practitioners Seeking?

The participants at the World Café emphasized that arbitration practitioners may need transparency at every stage of the process, from drafting dispute resolution clauses to enforcement of awards. Three specific areas stood out as particularly significant:

- **Access to information about arbitrators:** Practitioners are eager for comprehensive databases that include arbitrators' experience, such as the number of cases they have handled as sole arbitrator, chair or party-appointed arbitrator. Other desired information includes professional background, legal training, certifications, publications and prior counsel roles. Such data empowers counsel to select the most suitable arbitrator for their case while also allowing less prominent arbitrators to showcase their qualifications, which may – ultimately – even serve to enhance diversity of arbitrators.
- **Access to arbitral case law:** Availability of arbitral case law is critical for fostering predictability and consistency in decision-making, either by serving as precedents or at least as guidelines. Both counsel and

[125]) *Catherine A. Rogers, Arbitrator Intelligence is Dead! Long Live arbitrator intelligence!*, Kluwer Arbitration Blog (2024).

arbitrators benefit from consistent case law to build persuasive arguments and ensure alignment with established practices. Further, parties may benefit from receiving insights into the likelihood of success when comparing their case to similar ones.

- **Access to regional data:** Availability of information about certain jurisdictions, such as national case law at the seat of arbitration or enforcement location, can contribute to the ability of evaluating the arbitration-friendliness and average case duration, which may be relevant already at the stage of contract drafting when agreeing on the seat of arbitration.

cc) How can These Needs be met?

Satisfying these demands for transparency requires action on two fronts:

1) Enabling Access to Information:

- Arbitrators should be encouraged to share relevant details about their professional background, with peer evaluations serving as a valuable additional resource.
- Arbitral institutions and parties should commit to granting access to anonymized or summarized arbitral decisions.

2) Developing Effective Tools and Databases:

- Practical, user-friendly tools or databases must be developed to house and present this information.
- While existing tools and projects offer a foundation, most are still in early stages. The participants strongly advocated for a successor to Arbitrator Intelligence, as its innovative approach to gathering and sharing arbitrator data remains a highly valued concept among practitioners.

dd) Special Considerations for Investment Arbitration

The World Café discussion also highlighted a clear distinction between the transparency needs of commercial and investment arbitration. While acknowledging that the ICC was key to promoting greater transparency in commercial arbitration (with publication of composition of tribunals and its program to publish awards with parties' consent), the participants agreed that investment arbitration, given its broader public interest implications, is an area where there was a need for a higher level of transparency.

This sentiment is reflected in existing transparency-focused frameworks, such as:

- The **UNCITRAL Rules on Transparency in Treaty-Based Investor-State Arbitration**.

- The **ICSID Arbitration Rules**, which introduced substantial transparency enhancements in their 2022 amendments.[126])
- Specialized arbitration rules designed for investment disputes that include a higher transparency standard (as compared to commercial arbitration rules).

The public's role as a stakeholder in investment arbitration underscores the importance of greater openness, ensuring accountability and legitimacy in cases that often involve taxpayer resources or state policies.

By addressing these transparency needs, arbitration can further strengthen its position as a predictable and legitimate process that serves the interests of all stakeholders without compromising its core values.

c) Can (Increased) Disclosure by Arbitrators Contribute to Transparency in Arbitration and how?

Another important dimension of transparency in arbitration, extensively discussed during the World Café, is the role of disclosure duties by arbitrators. While it is evident that increased disclosure enhances transparency, the critical question remains: At what cost? This chapter explores the benefits and potential drawbacks of imposing greater disclosure duties, aiming to strike a balance between transparency and efficiency.

aa) What Should Arbitrators Disclose?

While disclosure duties primarily concern arbitrators, they can also extend to parties, such as in cases involving third-party funding. As highlighted in the discussions at the World Café, disclosure duties are a natural progression from the initial process of selecting arbitrators. Once a shortlist of potential candidates is identified, counsel must probe for relevant information to make an informed choice and detect any potential conflicts of interest.

While established guidelines (such as the IBA Guidelines on Conflicts of Interest in International Arbitration) address conflicts of interest, the scope of potential disclosure goes far beyond this. At the World Café, the participants emphasized the need for arbitrators to disclose details such as:

- **Availability:** How busy is the arbitrator, and can they commit sufficient time to the case?
- **Resources:** What access does the arbitrator have to legal sources, research tools or support teams?
- **Technology:** Does the arbitrator intend to use advanced tools or AI to assist in their work?

---

[126]) *Gary J. Shaw, The 2022 ICSID Rules: A Leap Towards Greater Transparency in ICSID Arbitration*, ICSID Review, published by Oxford University Press (2022).

- **Other factors:** Any additional elements that may affect their ability to serve impartially and efficiently.

Currently, the absence of mandatory obligations in many of these areas means parties and counsel rely heavily on the goodwill and honesty of potential arbitrators, likely creating an uneven landscape.

bb) Advantages of Enhanced Disclosure

Increased disclosure duties bring several important benefits:

- **Strengthened impartiality and independence:** Comprehensive disclosures build trust in the neutrality of arbitrators and the integrity of the arbitral process.
- **Prevention of post-award challenges:** By addressing potential issues upfront, parties can avoid costly and time-consuming challenges based on undisclosed information.
- **Streamlined arbitrator selection:** Detailed disclosures provide parties and counsel with a solid foundation for making informed choices, ensuring that the selected arbitrator is well-suited to the case.
- **Alignment with best practices:** Greater transparency reflects evolving norms in arbitration and fosters public confidence in the process as fair, accountable and professional.

Enhanced disclosures by arbitrators do not necessarily lead to increasing challenges, but help to increase trust and fairness in arbitration by giving parties the opportunity to make informed decisions on the choice of arbitrators. It also aligns the process with evolving standards, ensuring it remains credible, efficient and globally respected.

cc) (Potential) Downsides of Increased Disclosure

In addition to these general challenges over-transparency brings about, the following challenges are connected to heightened disclosure requirements:

- **Administrative burden:** Arbitrators may face increased workloads due to detailed disclosures, diverting focus from substantive issues.
- **Risk of errors and disputes:** Failing to disclose minor or irrelevant details inadvertently could lead to unnecessary disputes or even disqualifications, potentially creating a chilling effect on arbitrators' willingness to serve.
- **Exploitation of information:** Parties might misuse disclosed information to file frivolous challenges, disrupting proceedings or gaining tactical advantages. However, a notable counterpoint discussed was that such challenges could inadvertently promote diversity, as the pool of arbitrator candidates would need to expand.

- **Inconsistent standards:** Variability in disclosure requirements across jurisdictions and institutions can create confusion and uncertainty for arbitrators and parties alike.

dd) Striking the Right Balance

Finding an equilibrium between the advantages and challenges of disclosure duties is essential. To achieve this balance, the following rules shall be observed:

- **Focus on proportionality:** Disclosures should concentrate on material or relevant information that directly impacts impartiality, independence or case management.
- **Adopt clear standards:** Consistent guidelines and standards, such as those provided by the IBA Guidelines on Conflicts of Interest in International Arbitration, should serve as benchmarks to reduce ambiguity.
- **Encourage concise disclosures:** Arbitrators should provide comprehensive but focused disclosures to avoid excessive administrative burdens.

By tailoring disclosure requirements thoughtfully, arbitration can achieve the transparency necessary to enhance trust and legitimacy without sacrificing efficiency or deterring qualified arbitrators from serving.

4. Conclusion

Transparency is undeniably a driving force behind the legitimacy and trustworthiness of international arbitration. As this article has explored, it enhances fairness, predictability and accountability, addressing concerns of arbitration as a "closed-door" process. However, transparency must be balanced carefully to preserve arbitration's core values of confidentiality, efficiency and flexibility.

The discussions at the World Café underscored a collective ambition among arbitration practitioners to embrace transparency as a means of strengthening the process while acknowledging its potential challenges. From the need for robust tools like case law databases and arbitrator profiles to region-specific approaches that respect diverse expectations, transparency should evolve thoughtfully to meet the demands of a globalized arbitration landscape whilst ensuring that regional particularities are sufficiently considered.

Ultimately, transparency is not a one-size-fits-all solution. By fostering innovation, establishing clear standards and tailoring approaches to the unique contexts of disputes, arbitration can continue to adapt as a trusted and effective mechanism for resolving complex conflicts worldwide. The path forward lies in striking the right balance – one that ensures openness without undermining the very qualities that make arbitration so valuable.

The authors would like to express their sincere gratitude to all participants for their valuable contributions and insightful input, which greatly enriched the debate and fostered engaging discussions.

J. Green Arbitration Clauses: A Contractual Commitment to Good Behavior?

Philippa Charles/Brian Gabriel-Oiwoh[127])

1. Introduction

In recent years, the momentum for integrating environmentally sustainable practices has gained traction across various sectors, including the legal field. Arbitration, in particular, has seen the emergence of "green" elements, offering a progressive approach to dispute resolution through alignment with broader environmental sustainability goals. The global shift to virtual hearings and electronic document submissions during the COVID-19 pandemic, coupled with the introduction of the Greener Arbitration Pledge in 2019, seemed poised to cement such approach in arbitration. However, as the pandemic receded, there has been a noticeable return to traditional arbitration practices, including in-person hearings and the use of hard-copy bundles. This reversion underscores a critical observation: despite their clear benefits and initial momentum, the adoption of green arbitration clauses remains limited in practice – at least after the dispute has arisen, if not in the contracting phase. This raises important questions about the viability of such clauses and the obstacles hampering their broader implementation, which were considered, debated and discussed at the World Café during the Vienna Arbitration Days 2024.

2. Green Arbitration Clauses – A Noble Notion, But Not a Panacea

The Vienna Arbitration Days 2024 placed ESG considerations at the heart of discourse within the arbitration community. Naturally, green arbitration clauses emerged as one of several key topics of interest. A green arbitration clause represents a contractual commitment to integrating environmentally sustainable practices into the arbitration process, encompassing measures such as (i) electronic submissions/communications to reduce paper use, (ii) virtual

---

127) **Participants**: *Stefan Dobrijevic, Ferdinand Hartig, Lukas Jäger, Iris Koberg, Matthias Krivdic, Niamh Leinwather, Christopher Lytras, Judith Sawang, Sabine Supper* and *Anna Weinzierl.*

hearings to minimize travel and its associated carbon footprint, and (iii) selecting energy-efficient venues that align with sustainability goals. Incorporating such a clause into a commercial contract, so the theory goes, raises awareness and sets the tone for more sustainable practices during any dispute resolution proceedings. It also seeks to minimize disputes about the adoption of greener practices during the arbitration by committing the parties to environmentally responsible practices long before the dispute crystallizes. At that later point, the proposal of green approaches to the process may be resisted for tactical or strategic reasons unrelated to the merits of the proposal itself.

Despite their clear environmental benefits, the discussion among the World Café participants revealed that green arbitration clauses remain notably absent from most commercial contracts. Whereas electronic submissions and virtual hearings are increasingly observed in practice, none of the participants had yet encountered a contract explicitly containing a green arbitration clause or committing to an environmentally friendly dispute resolution process.

This reluctance stems from both practical and strategic concerns among parties and their legal advisors alike. To begin with, one aspect raised by some participants is the low priority that dispute resolution clauses generally have during contract negotiations. Notorious as "midnight clauses", arbitration provisions typically receive minimal attention in the rush of finalizing contracts. Needless to say, trying to introduce green elements in such clauses seems overly ambitious, if not unrealistic, at this juncture.

What is more, most participants at the World Café questioned the general viability of such clauses in a contract. During contract negotiations it is virtually impossible to anticipate the nature and complexity of future disputes, so that a firm commitment to green practices at such an early stage may often be unreasonable. In disputes involving the core of a high value construction project with complex technical or commercial issues, say, parties typically prefer traditional arbitration methods, including site visits and in-person hearings. Yet the same high value construction project may also give rise to a merely minor dispute (*e.g.*, involving the non-payment of a single invoice), which might indeed warrant an extensive usage of green elements like virtual hearings or even written submissions only. Such a Janus-faced predicament underscores the reasonableness of deferring the decision of how to structure the procedure of the arbitration process at a later juncture, *i.e.*, once the dispute has crystallized and the parties have a better understanding of its dimension.

Furthermore, parties prepared to adopt green elements into arbitration proceedings must inevitably observe and navigate potential technological, legal, and regulatory barriers. Technological obstacles may, for example, arise where jurisdictions or parties with limited technological infrastructure are involved. On the legal and regulatory side specifically, some jurisdictions mandate in-person hearings or require hard-copy document submissions, consequently stymying a wider use of green practices. Yet in this context it is worth noting that courts in arbitration-friendly jurisdictions, such as the Austrian

Supreme Court, have generally recognized the appropriateness of virtual hearings without any major due process or procedural fairness concerns.

Against this backdrop, the participants at the World Café generally agreed that the consideration and incorporation of green elements is most sensible once a dispute has arisen and after the dispute resolution process has commenced (*e.g.*, during the case management conference).

3. Divide (Responsibility) and Conquer (Over a Green Process)

Just about all of the participants at the World Café table agreed that an increase in green arbitration practices would be desirable. The participants specifically pondered on the question as to which stakeholders in the arbitration realm bear the major responsibility for this to become reality in the future.

Virtually all of the participants attributed the parties to bear the lion share of such responsibility. Consent is a cornerstone in arbitration. Within certain boundaries the parties are therefore free to design and structure the proceedings according to their specific needs and wishes. Recognizing the (above-mentioned) impracticality of committing to specific green arbitration measures before a dispute arises, many participants suggested that parties should at least enshrine within the contract to consider green processes once a dispute occurs. In doing so, the parties ensure that environmentally friendly practices remain a consideration, even when tensions rise during a dispute at a later stage. This would reduce the risk of an argument over the implementation of green policies at all in a dispute, while retaining the desired flexibility for the procedure to match the dispute which has arisen.

In addition, arbitrators also have a significant responsibility for a greener arbitration world given that most of the existing green arbitration guidelines are specifically directed towards them. One tool for arbitrators to promote green elements discussed among some of the participants revolved around the idea of adopting a "green badge", specifically signaling their firm commitment to conducting arbitrations preferably in an environmentally sustainable manner. The appointment of an arbitrator bearing such "green badge" would then be a tacit offer of the relevant party appointing them, to engage in a green arbitration setting.

Finally, also arbitral institutions the world over have a prominent role to play in promoting green arbitration. Institutional rules, say, could specifically reference the Green Arbitration Pledge and provide an opt-out mechanism. By selecting these rules in their contract, the parties would implicitly agree to a green arbitration framework, while still retaining the option to deviate from this agreement once the dispute actually arises. Another talking point revolved around the ideas of a reduction of administrative fees for cases that are being conducted in an environmentally friendly manner and of granting the arbitrators a certain discretion to factor in environmental considerations in their cost decisions. Another practical measure could be for institutions to provide a specific checklist that can be used by arbitrators in a case management conference to discuss environmental considerations with the parties.

4. Conclusion and Outlook

The discussions at the Vienna Arbitration Days 2024 revealed a growing recognition of the importance of green arbitration practices, but also highlighted the challenges in their widespread adoption. While the desire for sustainability is clear, practical hurdles, such as the unpredictability of future disputes and the entrenched nature of traditional arbitration methods, continue to limit the integration of green clauses into contracts. However, the consensus is that the arbitration community must share the responsibility of driving change. Parties, arbitrators, and institutions each have a role in promoting environmentally sustainable processes, whether through contractual flexibility, personal commitment, or institutional reforms.

Looking ahead, the potential for greener arbitration lies in incremental yet meaningful adjustments. Parties can prioritize environmental considerations at key procedural stages, arbitrators can signal their dedication through tools like the "green badge", and institutions can innovate by offering incentives and guidelines that facilitate eco-friendly practices. As the push for sustainability grows across industries, arbitration, too, has the opportunity to evolve, aligning its practices with broader environmental goals. The future of green arbitration may not lie in rigid contractual clauses, but in a dynamic, collective approach that fosters a more sustainable dispute resolution landscape. Arbitration has proven its resilience and reliability under "forced" environmentally friendly conditions during the pandemic. The continued use of those conditions will signal arbitration's adaptability to the challenges posed by climate change and the need to safeguard the planet, while preserving its effectiveness as a trusted dispute resolution mechanism.

K. Navigating Legal Challenges in a Changing World: Addressing Causation and Quantum in Climate Change Disputes

Katherine Khan/Peter Režnik

1. Introduction

It is widely recognized that climate change is one of the most pressing challenges of our time, with profound implications for the environment, economies, and societies worldwide. In 2015, the need for coordinated efforts led 194 countries within the United Nations Framework Convention on Climate Change ("UNFCCC") to adopt the Paris Agreement in order to establish a framework for international cooperation to limit global warming to below 2° C above pre-industrial levels, and an aspirational goal of 1.5° C.[128]) Despite the progress represented by this accord, finding reasonable and adequate balance between economic progress and environmental protection has proven difficult. For dispute settlement practitioners, this means that disputes relating to climate change and greener economies are here to stay.

The challenges presented by this pressing issue are exactly what motivated us to engage in this topic. We were fortunate to host a number of arbitration practitioners at our table, including counsel, arbitrators, clients, and expert witnesses, from many different jurisdictions. While the practical application of some of the topics is still evolving, the discussion nonetheless provided invaluable insights into climate change disputes and in particular into issues related to causation and quantum. We summarize the outcome of the discussion below.

2. Types of Climate Change Related Disputes

The starting point for our discussion was a 2019 Report published by the International Chamber of Commerce (ICC) with the results of its task force on the role of arbitration and ADR in the resolution of international disputes related to climate change (ICC Report).[129]) The authors of the ICC Report took a broad view of climate change-related disputes and categorized them into three categories: (i) disputes directly related to transition, mitigation, and adaptation efforts; (ii) disputes indirectly related to transition, mitigation, and adaptation efforts involving a climate or related environmental issue; and (iii) disputes brought up by submission agreements once the dispute has arisen.

a) First Category – Disputes Directly Related to Transition, Mitigation, and Adaptation Efforts

The first category of disputes comprises disputes arising out of contracts entered into by an investor, funder, or State entity, in accordance with or in order to implement energy or other systems transition, mitigation or adaptation efforts in line with Paris Agreement commitments. These contracts can either directly refer to the UNFCC commitments, but also encompass, more broadly, general investments in energy transition (such as contracts relating to funding

[128]) Paris Agreement, December 12, 2015, U.N. Doc. FCCC/CP/2015/10/Add.1.

[129]) International Chamber of Commerce, Resolving Climate Change-Related Disputes through Arbitration and ADR (November 2019). Available at: https://www.iccwbo.org/climate-change-disputes-report.

and commissioning or supply of renewable energy, as well as new infrastructure for the forestry and agricultural industries).[130])

Hypothetical examples of such disputes would include a contractor in a project for the construction of a wind farm that, once finalized, seeks a takeover certificate, an order preventing the drawing of performance guarantees, and payment of the balance of the contract. The counterparty would be the owner of the project, claiming that the contractor failed to meet technical specifications to achieve financing.[131])

In the field of investor-state dispute resolution (ISDS), a possible scenario could include an energy company that invests in a new power plant, only to face a newly issued permit with much stricter requirements than initially anticipated. Another scenario, and perhaps the most common in recent investment arbitrations, involves renewable energy project investors who, on the condition of receiving some incentives or subsidies from a state, invest in the state only to see the incentive regime fundamentally altered by the state in violation of existing treaty standards and protections.

b) Second Category – Disputes Indirectly Related to Transition, Mitigation, and Adaptation Efforts

The second category identified in the ICC Report and further discussed at our table relates to disputes that are only indirectly related to transitional economy and mitigation measures. These are contracts without a specific climate change-related purpose, but which incorporate a climate or environmental issue, or disputes where climate risks or policy changes may have materially impacted obligations, assets and their value.

Disputes can arise, for example, from insurance policies affected by climate events, as well as supply chain disputes due to extreme weather conditions. For example, in one author's home country of Slovenia, recent floods had directly affected several factories. From the companies' perspective, this event meant, on top of the damages and overall business disruption, that they were not able to fully comply with their deadlines and contractual obligations. Should disputes arise, the event and the presence or absence of fault (*force majeure*) might be relevant.

Another example discussed by the group was the construction of a harbor at a river delta. Different salinity levels of the water (which increase as sea levels rise) meant that different materials needed to be included in the project, causing further delays.[132]) An inquiry into the reasons for the delay would also need to be considered in the valuation of damages.

---

130) ICC Report, 9.

131) *Ibid.*

132) *Ibid.*, 10.

c) Third Category – Submission Agreements

The last category relates to disputes that are referred to arbitration through a submission agreement, which is entered into after the dispute has arisen. In practice, these cases are relatively rare given the inherent difficulty of getting parties to reach an agreement once a litigious tone has been set.

d) Current Scenarios and Future Trends

In identifying the types of disputes commonly arising around climate change, our discussion examined both current scenarios and emerging trends in terms of commercial and investment disputes.

First, and perhaps the most significant, are disputes that at least indirectly relate to the EU's push towards a climate-neutral economy by 2050.[133]) This political backdrop led the EU to abandon the Energy Charter Treaty after failed negotiations on the so-called modernization of the treaty to bring it "*into alignment with the principles of the Paris Agreement, the requirements of sustainable development and the fight against climate change.*"[134]) Regardless, investors are likely to continue bringing disputes under the treaty if violations occur.[135])

Notable cases cited during our discussion included, for example, *Vattenfall v. Germany (II)*,[136]) that arose from Germany's enactment of legislation to phase out nuclear power plants in the country. Participants mentioned, however, that not all changes in a country's regulatory framework of its energy policy will give rise to new claims, as these decisions are often highly case- and fact-specific.

We continued with discussions about the extent to which the ISDS system can adequately address a state's inaction concerning climate change. By way of example, participants considered whether the current ISDS legal framework provides relief in the hypothetical case of an agricultural investor whose fields were destroyed due to changes in regional rainfall which were attributable to climate change. In such cases, establishing causation remains difficult. The participants proposed suggestions to address this issue, such as drafting and adopting rules to allow plaintiffs to be able to prove collective contribution to climate change. These ideas, while legal in form, are obviously political in

[133]) European Commission, *The European Green Deal*, available at: https://commission.europa.eu/strategy-and-policy/priorities-2019-2024/european-green-deal_en.

[134]) European Union. Council Decision (EU) 2024/1638 of 30 May 2024 on the Withdrawal of the Union from the Energy Charter Treaty. Official Journal of the European Union, L 1638, June 5, 2024, https://data.europa.eu/eli/dec/2024/1638/oj.

[135]) The sunset clause contained in Article 47 (3) of the Energy Charter Treaty provides protection to investments for a period of twenty years from withdrawal.

[136]) *Vattenfall AB and others v. Federal Republic of Germany (II)* (ICSID Case No. ARB/12/12, Award, May 10, 2021).

nature, and thus require broader political engagement for a satisfactory solution.

Regarding the economic fields and industries where future climate-related disputes may arise, the field of insurance was cited as potentially the most prominent. As climate-related disasters become more common, insurance companies may increasingly face claims related to those disasters (to the extent that the insurance policy does not expressly exclude those risks), as well as a hypothetical subrogation against governments for their approach (or omission) in regard to climate change, provided that causation can be established. In a more abstract sense, it would not be inconceivable for insurers to increase premiums or refuse to operate in certain geographical areas due to the impact of climate change in those areas. An example would be the use of flood maps used by insurance companies for establishing higher premiums in flood-prone areas.

3. Causation and Quantum Issues

The second part of our discussion revolved around causation and related quantum issues. It was highlighted that, in general, when deciding disputes, tribunals usually progress through three steps. First, tribunals assess whether a wrongful act or breach has occurred. If it has, the following step is to ascertain whether the alleged injury was caused by that particular breach (causation). If causation is established, the final task is to determine the amount of compensation (valuation). Our discussion focused on the latter two aspects, and the conclusions are summarized below.

a) Causation-related Issues

The presence of a causal link between a breach (whether in relation to contractual obligations or to protections afforded by a treaty) and the resulting specific harm is required under most national laws and in general also under international law.[137])

In standard commercial disputes, the causal link between one's actions and the harm caused to another may be relatively straightforward in some cases (*e.g.*, an unjustified non-delivery of supplies breaches a distribution agreement and causes financial harm to the other party). However, determining causation in climate change-related disputes may prove more challenging.

Complexities that may occur in climate change disputes include, among others, concurrent causes, collective contribution (*i.e.*, when the claimed damages cannot be attributed solely to a single person or entity), and, additionally,

---

137) *See, e.g.*, the Draft articles on Responsibility of States for Internationally Wrongful Acts by the International Law Commission, Yearbook of the International Law Commission, 2001, vol. II, Part Two, https://legal.un.org/ilc/texts/instruments/english/commentaries/9_6_2001.pdf.

the evolving role of science. These factors can make it difficult to demonstrate an unbroken chain of causations and to apportion it correctly. In case of concurrent causes, questions about which cause contributed to the damage (and to what extent), as well as 'but for' scenarios, will likely be in dispute and complicate the establishment of a clear causal link.

As part of our discussions, it was highlighted that the issue of collective contribution (or collective causation) had already arisen in cases such as *Billy et al.* v. *Australia*.[138]) This case was brought before the United Nations Human Rights Commission by Australian nationals, islanders who had suffered due to Australia's failure to adequately protect their communities against adverse impacts of climate change. Australia argued that it was not possible to trace causal links between a state's contribution to climate change, its efforts to address climate change, and the alleged effects of climate change on the enjoyment of the claimants' rights.[139])

This case also highlights the issue of how omissions, in particular the failure to undertake mitigative actions, may, in certain circumstances, amount to a wrongful act under international law. Some participants reflected on the damages caused by recent floods in Germany and to what extent floods are purely a *force majeure* issue or if there is at least a smaller portion of the liability that can be attributed to the States' inaction.

The issue has also been dealt with by national Courts. In the US, for example,[140]) a Ninth Circuit decision reasoned that "*there is limited scientific capability in assessing, detecting, or measuring the relationship between a certain* [greenhouse gas] *emission source and localized climate change impacts in a given region.*"[141]), In turn, a recent decision by the UK Supreme Court ordered that downstream emissions of fossil fuel projects must be assessed before granting planning permissions.[142]) In said decision, Lord Leggat noted that climate change "*is a global problem precisely because there is no correlation between where* [greenhouse gases] *are released and where climate change is felt*".[143])

Some conclusive thoughts on the issue of the liability of States for their omissions were established. First, before establishing causation, one must establish the obligation and its extent. French courts, for example, have

[138]) United Nations Human Rights Committee, Views adopted by the Committee under article 5 (4) of the Optional Protocol, concerning communication No. 3624/2019, UN Doc CCPR/C/135/D/3624/2019 (September 23, 2022).

[139]) *Ibid.*, at 4.3.

[140]) For an overview of the issue under U.S. Law, please *see Causation in Environmental Law: Lessons from Toxic Torts*, Harvard Law Review, vol. 128, no. 8, 2015, available at https://harvardlawreview.org/print/vol-128/causation-in-environmental-law/.

[141]) Wash. Envtl. Council v. Bellon, 732 F.3d 1131 (9th Cir. 2013), 22.

[142]) R (Finch on behalf of the Weald Action Group & Others) v. Surrey County Council (& Others) [2024] UKSC 20, para. 79.

[143]) *Ibid.*, para. 97.

recognized the French State's failure to act in response to climate change for not to complying with the emission limits it had imposed on itself.[144]) Second, in most scenarios, a breach of that obligation must be established in the States' action (or inaction), unless the State is under a strict liability.

b) Use of Experts and Evolving Science

As established, while most of these issues are still incipient, the participants agreed that the role of industry and climate science experts is becoming increasingly important. It should be highlighted that the very discussion of the acceleration and impacts of climate change is only possible precisely due to the advancement of science. Thus, climate science will likely be at the core of climate change related disputes. This is particularly true in terms of causation. Examples may include examining environmental conditions before and after an alleged breach occurred, as well as the challenging task of assigning CO_2 emissions to a State (whether current or predicted).

In the context of ISDS, expert evidence will also be critical in establishing whether a State's regulatory actions addressing climate change were justified and non-arbitrary. Experts are expected to provide guidance on how scientific facts translate into legal consequences (*e.g.*, how the action can be linked to the occurence and extent of the damages).

Thus, apart from involving quantum experts (dealt with in detail later in our discussion and detailed below), climate change disputes are likely to require industry or science experts, given that, in most cases, the quantum expert will likely not have the expertise to determine specific industry or climate factors such as supply and demand, pricing, and access to capital, among other specificities.

c) Quantum-related Issues

Climate change-related disputes present unique challenges in several aspects, including quantum determination. The first point of reflection in our discussion on this topic was evaluating how appropriate traditional quantum valuation methods are for environmental, social, and governance (ESG) disputes and, if not, how they might need to be adapted.

aa) Unreasonable Conduct of Inaction and Unreasonable Conduct to Mitigate Damages

The participants further discussed the possibility of reducing the awarded quantum due to the contributory fault of the claiming party or to its failure to undertake mitigative measures. Arguments and findings of this nature have already been observed in practice.

Regarding contributory fault, a notable case cited during the discussions was *Bridas v Turkmenistan*. In that case, the tribunal reduced the awarded damages by USD 50 million because the claimant continued incurring the

[144]) Paris Administrative Court, *Notre Affaire à Tous and Others v. France*, Decision of February 3, 2021, Nos. 1904967, 1904968, 1904972, and 1904976/4.

operating costs of the oil field despite the fact that Turkmenistan had passed legislation restricting such activities. The Tribunal considered that the claimants should have foreseen that the lifting of these measures in the future was unlikely.[145])

In another example of an alleged failure to take mitigative measures, the respondent State in *Uniper v The Netherlands* argued that the claimants should have mitigated their losses by converting their coal power plants to run on biomass.[146]) Similar arguments and findings are likely to be raised in other climate change-related disputes.

bb) Valuation Considerations and Approaches

When it comes to valuation, critics of arbitration, particularly of investment arbitration, have long alleged that some damages awards can be excessive or speculative, especially in cases where the investment was not operational at the time the contested measures were taken. A relatively recent decision in *Rockhopper v Italy* was mentioned as a possible example of such a scenario.[147]) In this case, the tribunal's valuation accounted for future cash flows from a hydrocarbon project that had never left the exploration phase when Italy banned offshore drilling within 12 miles of its coastline. Regardless of the merits, one can expect that such criticism is likely to increase in the politically and socially sensitive topic of climate change disputes.

The discussion around damages is also reflected in the work of UNCITRAL Working Group III, whose mandate is to identify concerns and propose reforms to the ISDS system. The Working Group has considered a potential approach of limiting damages in ISDS to less than full compensation, an approach viewed with caution by many practitioners. This skepticism is due to the longstanding international law principle of full reparation, first established in the Chorzów factory case.[148])

It is well known that most traditional damages valuation approaches include market-based, costs-based, and income-based methods, with Discounted Cash Flow (DCF) being the most commonly used by arbitral tribunals.

---

[145]) *Bridas S.A.P.I.C.*, et al., *v. Government of Turkmenistan and Turkmenneft*, ICC Case No. 9058/FMS/KGA, Third Partial Award, para. 53.

[146]) As seen in the Claimants Memorial: *Uniper SE, Uniper Benelux Holding B.V., and Uniper Benelux N.V. v. Kingdom of the Netherlands*, ICSID Case No. ARB/21/22, Claimants' Memorial, May 20, 2022, para. 3.

[147]) *Rockhopper Exploration Plc, Rockhopper Italia S.p.A. and Rockhopper Mediterranean Ltd v. Italian Republic*, ICSID Case No. ARB/17/14, Final Award, August 23, 2022.

[148]) The relevant paragraph reads: "The essential principle contained in the actual notion of an illegal act – a principle which seems to be established by international practice and in particular by the decisions of arbitral tribunals – is that reparation must, as far as possible, wipe out all the consequences of the illegal act and reestablish the situation which would, in all probability, have existed if that act had not been committed." *Factory at Chorzów (Germany v. Poland)*, 1928 P.C.I.J. (ser. A) No. 17, at 47.

While the most adequate one will depend on the particularities of each case, it is also reasonable to expect variations in their application to climate change-related disputes. Regulatory risks, such as a host State's obligation to pursue mitigation measures under the Paris Agreement, can significantly influence this process. After considering all elements, a tribunal can choose a valuation method to award compensation with reasonable confidence, taking into account the specific circumstances defining a relevant market and any significant uncertainties that may prevent the use of DCF valuation.

When applying the widely used income-based approaches, for example, a possible solution which was discussed would be adjusting cash flow and/or discount rate estimates to incorporate the effects of both climate policy changes and other climate risks. Changes in government policies, such as taxes and subsidies, can directly affect the returns for an investor as well as the competitiveness of an entire industry. As a rule, and in case no apportionment of liability is needed, a possible approach would be to use the DCF method in ESG cases only for shorter evaluation periods, given that predicting cash flows and risks over extended periods may become increasingly speculative under rapidly evolving climate conditions. In that sense, it may be feasible to adjust cash flow and discount rate estimates in the income-based approach to incorporate the effects of climate policies and risks. When projecting cash flows, it is necessary to consider both direct impacts and the broader effects on industry competition under various climate policy scenarios.

Particularly in fossil fuel phase-out disputes, valuation might require consideration of the host State's obligations under the Paris Agreement, distinguishing it from compensation for other types of disputes. The selected valuation method will likely align with obligations arising from international climate mitigation measures, affecting how compensation is determined. For example, choosing a method that disregards these obligations may lead to unjust enrichment for the investor, undermining the host State's mitigation and adaptation capacity.

Addressing the more pragmatic aspects, when considering long-term climate change impacts, experts face challenges in quantifying damages due to the varying complexities of different types of disasters. In a hypothetical scenario, an expert might apply a two per cent adjustment for damages over a 50-year period to account for long-term climate-related effects. However, this approach becomes complicated when addressing different types of events. For example, the quantification of flood damage was said to be generally more straightforward due to its clear and immediate impacts. In contrast, assessing the damages from events like fires or health effects would involve greater complexity, as these damages are often less tangible and harder to link directly to specific causes, making accurate valuation more challenging.

In practice, within the context of climate change disputes, a quantum expert could typically begin by analyzing the financial statements of the affected company, using projected revenues as a baseline for valuation. One of the many difficulties encountered would be determining the appropriate period for calculating damages, given the long-term nature of climate-related impacts. Additionally, the expert would also need to account for mitigation efforts, assessing whether the claimant has taken sufficient steps to reduce the damages. Such considerations are inherently highly complex and would require extensive discussion in a dispute setting.

4. Conclusion

The main outcome of the discussions at our table was that climate change disputes already form part of the legal landscape, and their numbers are likely to grow as environmental regulations increase in scope and complexity. As states transition to greener economies, there is a risk that even well-intended regulations inadvertently cause harm and damages, leading to more disputes. States' actions, and in particular the lack thereof, could also be sources of further disputes. Such cases often raise challenging issues of causation, particularly in the broader context of proving that the specific harm can be directly attributed to the actions or omissions of a specific state. Additionally, determining the quantum of these disputes presents unique challenges, as traditional methods may not effectively account for the broad and often long-term nature of climate-related damages. Adaptations to those valuation methods may be necessary. Practitioners must remain flexible and adaptable, as many of these issues are still developing, requiring novel approaches to both legal reasoning and dispute resolution.

Chapter III

The Award and the Courts

Gerard Doolin

Software Project Contracts Conflict – Fit for Context ADR

Software Project Contracts Conflict – Fit for Context ADR

Gerard Doolin

I. We Have Come a Long Way in a Short Time

The design, build and implementation of software systems has been rapid, some 50 years of conceptualization, design and delivery evolution. In comparison, the first pyramid was designed and built in 2700 BC.

Both endeavors, electronic and physical construction, depend on quality of planning, technical alignment, and human delivery and management. However, it seems that successful outcomes in physical construction are better delivered in comparison to software system delivery outcomes.

This conundrum is evidenced by the modest global success rates of software systems project implementation (referred to herein as "*software projects*"). The Boston USA based consultants, *The Standish Group*, have published periodically from 1995 to 2022 the *Chaos Reports*, that over time have assessed a large pool of global software projects against sophisticated failure/success metrics. In their final report in 2022 they determined that about 35 % of software projects were deemed successful (being completed on time, on budget, and with satisfactory functionality implemented), 46 % challenged, and 19 % failed. *The Standish Group* have also developed in key subject areas, processes that, if executed well, promote supplier and customer good software project outcomes.

With the impact of the global pandemic accelerating remote workforce demand and coinciding with the endless acceleration of cloud delivered business and service models, there is an all-prevailing need for accelerated and successful digital transformation software projects.

There is no question that the software systems industry abounds with technical and business processes that focus on procurement improvement and/or optimization (including via software automation) and use of the rapidly evolving software development methods, all to de-risk software systems procurement, contracting and delivery (design, build and implementation).

The author believes, given the proven inherent delivery misalignment risk, there is a compelling need for optimal ADR processes that assist suppliers and customers to unlock, resolve and reset software projects, and, through their timely use, avoid software project and relationship cessation and resulting

Arbitration or Litigation focused on fault attribution and award of financial Damages.

In relation to this objective, this article sets out a research and design initiative that was undertaken 2018–2022 by the author in partnership with an ADR institution, the New Zealand International Arbitration Centre ("*NZIAC*")[1].

II. International Research and Design Collaboration

For over 20 years internationally (including for large multinational software systems consultants and implementers) in complex software and services enterprise engagement, the author has been a senior software project contractual legal advisor engaging directly with technical SMEs (*e.g.*, solution architects), project (*e.g.*, project managers) and commercial stakeholders (*e.g.*, CEO, CFO, COO) concerning the full software project cycle from procurement initiation to contracting to implementation to ongoing managed services.

In addition to these roles, the author is an accredited Mediator (via *CEDR*[2]) and a specialized software project contracts Mediator on the Mediation panel of NZIAC and the Mediators list of the Vienna International Arbitral Center.

In the author's advisory work, he has intervened in failing software projects to renegotiate or remediate the reset of emerging or conflicted software projects and contractual relationships. In these interventions the author has observed distinct relationship fatigue, escalating conflict, diminished confidence, and entangled causes of commercial and technical misalignment seeding emerging or actual contractual performance misalignment and/or fault. These circumstances together make renegotiation or remediation arduous and often too late to be effective.

A. International Survey and Report

Given this experience, and with the support of NZIAC, the author commenced an international research project with key industry or software project stakeholders (including CEOs, CIOs, software systems program or project managers, solution architects and other technical subject matter experts, sales leads, general and other inhouse counsel and external advisors) all with extensive supplier or customer side complex software project expe-

---

[1]) https://nziac.com/it-disputes/; all online sources last accessed on 15 January 2025.

[2]) https://www.cedr.com/event/mediator-skills-training/.

rience in key verticals such as finance, retail, utilities or government. These stakeholders' experiences were based in the Asia Pacific, United Kingdom, European Union, North American and Australia and New Zealand markets.

The stakeholders responded to a detailed quantitative and qualitative research survey focused on all software project phases from initiation to procurement to contracting to delivery to implementation and ongoing support.

The survey was focused on two key themes:

- What perspectives or understandings did a stakeholder have as to material causes of software project misalignment and/or emerging contract disputes and the behaviors observed in response?
- What was stakeholder involvement when a contract dispute crystallized? Both in relation to the applicable Dispute Resolution process used and their views on effectiveness of the Dispute Resolution process?

A detailed report resulted "Avoiding Conflict – Improved Dispute Resolution for IT Projects".[3]

B. Survey Findings

In relation to the first theme, the findings were:

- *Software project misalignment* usually occurs after contract signing and emerges in key delivery phases (*e.g.*, further requirements analysis or design or build and sometimes in testing).
- *Material causes or contributors* included:
  - Incomplete preparation of the customer business case due to budget constraints, insufficient time and coordinated effort by the customer software project sponsor and internal stakeholders to understand transformational scope (current to future state), user needs, optimal solution selection, and desired business objectives;
  - Inadequate preparatory discovery between customer and supplier in baselining mutual understandings whether known requirements or recognition of to be discovered transformation scope and related risk/potential costs;
  - Overambitious project scheduling;
  - Resourcing performance quality and capacity – planning and execution; and
  - Technical mis-scoping – including as to the limits of standard software and often failure to understand complexity.

[3]) https://nziac.com/avoiding-conflict-and-improving-dispute-resolution-for-it-projects/.

- *Development methodology* – use of the *Agile* method[4] was improving software project outcomes for smaller or medium sized software projects. However, for complex deployments, the *Waterfall* method[5] or a hybrid of *Agile* and *Waterfall* methods is preferred.
- *Change control* – its use often leads to disagreement as to what is in scope for an agreed change and what is not (*i.e.*, new scope).
- *Governance* - strong consensus that quality of governance engagement (motivated, informed about the context and deliverables) and experience level (communicative, leading, resolving, guiding and constant measuring and ensuring satisfactory iterative outcomes) are critical to software project success. It was also noted that software project misalignment is compounded by failure to escalate issues, or, when escalated, based on inadequate or misleading information exchanges.
- *Contracting* – Stakeholders found that software project delivery-based understandings can deviate from rigid contracted understandings and their contractual expression. This can leave little scope to deal with new or unforeseen circumstances, noting change control is problematic at times. There was a consensus that project contract terms should enable some flexibility to address evolving project journey.

In relation to the second theme, the findings were:

- *Lack of awareness* – there is often a lack of awareness that a software project misalignment or contract dispute is emerging. Once known, the parties often show positional and conflict orientated behaviors.
- *Renegotiation and Mediation preferred* – Software project misalignment is mutually recognized, and a contract dispute emerges, re-Negotiation or Mediation is preferred. These deliver satisfactory outcomes but need to be used as early as possible when trust and respect (absent power leveraging) are still present. Furthermore, an advisor or a Mediator needs to exhibit strong analytical and facilitative skills to unlock entrenched positions.
- *Determinative processes* – Arbitration or Litigation were not viewed favorably given they involved fault attribution, are resource and cost intensive, and generally put the relationship and project at risk (if not already at an end).

---

[4]) Agile method means generally building workable software in increments in short intensive sprints.

[5]) Waterfall method means generally detailed specification of the project delivery from the outset with the goal of delivering all workable software at the end against pre agreed acceptance testing criteria.

III. Context, Contract, Conflict and (ADR) Choice

In relation to the role of ADR processes the findings highlighted the interrelationship between context, contract, conflict and (ADR) choice.

A. Context

The findings highlight that in software project endeavor there is a material risk of decisions, behaviors, and actions and unknown factors, which may lead to software project misalignment and an emerging contract dispute. This is despite best efforts to document mutual contract understandings as to requirements, financials, delivery performance scope and risk allocation.

B. Contract

There is a structural approach to software projects that generally applies. It comprises two categories.

First, the capture, usually set out in a schedule or statement of work to a framework master services terms, of specific technical and performance-based understandings concerning the software system implementation. These focus on the software solution, development and implementation processes, specific party performance dependencies, mutually agreed baselined or performance assumptions, performance criteria, and specific acknowledgement of performance or outcome risks and limitations. In the author's experience, when prepared by lawyers or counsel, who have a deeper understanding of the specific software system technical context, the parties will commence the software project with reasonably aligned contractual understandings.

The second category, the framework master services terms (the *"Framework"*), in the author's view, can in negotiation and finalization lead to a disproportionate and rigid contractual relationship with respect to key terms. The Framework usually will clearly set out terms focused on performance failure or fault and consequences for the breaching party. These terms often define specific or general failure or default events and enable a party to serve notices to remedy in a defined time and/ or to terminate. There will be related terms that address financial Damages recovery, whether by liquidated Damages (negotiated pre-determined amounts) when a material project deliverable is not achieved by an agreed date or other recoverable losses and expenses (subject to exclusions and financial limitations). There will also be terms as to the formal Damages recovery process whether via an Arbitrator's award or judicial determination or by enforcement of a contractual indemnity (a promise to pay on demand).

The Framework will also set out how a contract dispute is managed. Usually, once a party formally initiates a Dispute process, the first phase is often further expedited Negotiation by the parties. However, if this remains deadlocked, the parties often provide for a Mediation process (without specifying any specific industry knowledge and experience on the Mediator's part). If Mediation does not resolve the dispute, then the next Dispute Resolution process is determinative (Arbitration or Litigation). This is usually a costly complex journey (including conflict based, costs, lost time, personnel impacts (including on morale), potential brand damage etc.) where a judge or Arbitrator ultimately determines fault and awards Damages.

C. Conflict and (ADR) Choice

In the author's view, in the software project context of emerging contract disputes and therefore conflict in varying forms, the fault and remedies terms of a Framework are a somewhat binary construct that do not consider the exploration, greyness and therefore consequent risks between parties as to understandings and expectations. This risk profile, it seems statistically proven, exists notwithstanding focused alignment efforts in procurement and contracting.

In order to provide parties with a post contract execution choice how to manage and resolve software project misalignment and emerging contract Disputes, the author and NZIAC determined that what was needed was a sequence of tailored conflict avoidance or Dispute Resolution processes. These processes aim to maximize the opportunity to reset software projects and relationships for better outcomes and avoid parties defaulting too readily to fault-based claims or proceedings and pursuing determinative financial recovery outcomes.

At the same time, we recognize there will be software projects, where due to capital and time invested, depth of misalignment and contractual fault and loss of confidence or trust, which are simply not recoverable via non-determinative ADR. For these circumstances, recourse immediately to the exercise of a fault-based termination right and pursuit of claims and remedies via Litigation or Arbitration will occur.

IV. Contract Modules

NZIAC and the author, following the Report's publication and based on further industry stakeholder consultation in relation to the findings, undertook a design process to create ADR processes that could be incorporated into software project implementation contracts (whether *Agile* or *Waterfall*[6]).

---

[6]) *See supra* Notes 4 and 5.

A. Design Approach – Key Software Project Factors

As outlined in the prior paragraph, these key aspects of a software project informed the design process:

- Software project costs (*e.g.*, personnel and governance) for a customer accumulate from the moment it considers change and begins to engage with potential software systems suppliers.
- A supplier similarly once engaged incurs evolving personnel costs.
- Procurement and contracting phases for complex software projects are cost and time intensive.
- Usually by the delivery phases in a software project when misalignment occurs or an emerging contract dispute emerges, relationships are well advanced, and sunken costs have been incurred.
- At this moment, often key stakeholders have multiple demands in their respective organizations. With a range of accountability pressures and varying understandings levels of cause within and across the organizations, the ability to stand back, unlock, resolve and reset can be challenging.

Given the above design factors, the contract terms needed to be expressed in a practical manner that resonates with software systems project risk mitigation managers (*e.g.*, project or program managers [in *coordination* with their inhouse counsel, where necessary]) and their use of periodic software project governance forums to review, manage risk, and problem solve. The key goal being that such stakeholders promptly and systematically resolve delivery and engagement problems via structured ADR processes.

B. Designed Content

In summary, the designed content centers on:

- A conflict avoidance and Dispute Resolution service model based on easily adoptable "best-for-project" Contract Modules[7].
- The Contract Modules core elements are:
  - Recommended (editable) *Agile* project governance terms plus conflict avoidance and Dispute Resolution terms (editable only due to local law requirements); and

---

7) https://nziac.com/it-disputes/contract-modules/.

  - Recommended (editable) *Waterfall* project governance terms plus conflict avoidance or Dispute Resolution terms (editable only due to local law requirements).
- The conflict avoidance and Dispute Resolution processes comprise:
  - *Risk Event Notification* – A positive contractual obligation to surface and promptly notify a party of a material software project delivery risk event. This notification then triggers accelerated and concerted efforts (*e.g.*, project manager and escalated as needed to executive level) to self-solve via Negotiation the risk event (including reaching agreement on actions, costs, on-going monitoring and reporting);
  - *Mediation* – A right to seek facilitation assistance from an industry knowledgeable and experienced accredited Mediator. It is expected that matters to be referred to Mediation will be commercial interests based (*e.g.*, financial and resourcing allocations) and less technically based issues;
  - *Adjudication* – The right to refer an issue, expected to be a complex technical issue relating to the software system and its implementation (*e.g.*, a complex design and integration deliverable) and/ or a requirement for a monetary assessment, to an Adjudicator for Adjudication, who has sufficient knowledge and experience in software project contracts, to make a ruling; and
  - *Arbitration* – in the event the issue and resulting dispute cannot be resolved then parties can seek fault determination and financial compensation via Arbitration.

C. Liquidated Damages or Service Level Credits/ Rebates – Temporary Relief

To incentivize recourse to the ADR processes, the Contract Modules set out an agreed temporary relief from any sanctions, *e.g.*, liquidated damages, accruing from the date a deliverables milestone is missed. This is conditional based on timely progression through the ADR processes.

D. Choice of ADR Processes

Before setting out in more detail the reasons for each ADR process chosen, there was deliberation by the author and NZIAC on what would be the best fit. There is a role for Dispute Review Boards that can be scaled (as necessary) comprising external persons with sufficient knowledge of software project implementation to provide some form of periodic supervisory and advisory support. However, we resolved to use Mediation and Adjudication. The author, based on his experience in software projects, has observed that the early and emerging or potential contract disputes that come to a relationship impasse involve specific technical and or commercial subject matters for which the parties hold different positions. Often at this stage the parties do not want to move to claims and an adversarial Dispute Resolution process. Therefore, offering the parties objective external facilitation support and or providing a technical ruling promptly ideally enable a solution and software project resumption and progression. It has been well established by the aforementioned *Standish Group* that latency in decision making in software projects is very determinative of good outcomes.

E. Why Mediation?

The author believes that software project contract conflict and emerging contract disputes are well suited to Mediation. It provides for a without prejudice issue re-exploration and solutioning through the engagement of a neutral.

Material software procurement and implementation life cycles are multi-faceted multi-stakeholder journeys. Between organizations stakeholders there arises layered fatigue (including, from the author's experience in misaligned software projects, software project fatigue (*e.g.*, delayed schedule due to misalignments), relationship fatigue, and, for individuals, the endless effect of multiple daily operational demands, different understandings of cause and effect, hierarchical fears, miscommunication or omission, and usually technical analysis design and build and test challenges.

It is this often-difficult context that calls for a Mediator, with specialist industry knowledge and demarcation and enhanced facilitation skills, that, via a safe without prejudice time out environment, can assist in reframing objectivity and clarifying perceptions or understandings, re-energizing relationships, and the exploratory pursuit (again) of a solution.

F. Why Adjudication?

There are subject matters that occur in software projects whose context is essentially technical, *e.g.*, was a complex software integration/systems configuration designed and implemented to the contracted performance standard?

Rather than a negotiation of interests and a consensus and compromise, they are suited to a qualified Adjudicator making a ruling or determination.

NZIAC designed in 2022 a plain language contractual Adjudication process[8] to deliver an effective and efficient model for application across a broad range of Disputes in trade sectors. It is a private, proportionate, effective, and

[8]) https://nziac.com/adjudication/adjudication-rules/.

efficient alternative Dispute Resolution process, based only on written submissions and documentary evidence. The parties can seek an expedited ruling that is binding in the interim, *i.e.*, in the future a party can arbitrate the matter and seek a new, final and binding determination.

However, it is NZIAC's experience with the use of Adjudication in physical constructions claims and or Disputes that most parties do not take the Dispute further (to Litigation or Arbitration) but abide by the determination of the Adjudicator. This perhaps reflects that commercial parties are not in the business of Dispute Resolution or Litigation and are content to move forward with their primary business after obtaining an independent determination on the merits of the Dispute, that is provisionally binding and enforceable, within 35 working days.

Adjudication is a mainstream dispute resolution mechanism in its own right for the final resolution of most disputes. Adjudication has received endorsement and support from the judiciary at the highest levels. The following comments from Lord Briggs and Lord Coulson in two recent cases in the United Kingdom are most apposite and reflect NZIAC's experience in New Zealand:

"[Adjudication] was designed to be, and more importantly has proved to be, a mainstream dispute resolution mechanism in its own right, producing a *de facto* final resolution of most disputes which are referred to an adjudicator… There is a chorus of observations from experienced TCC Judges and textbook writers to the effect that adjudication does, in most cases, achieve a final resolution of the underlying dispute which becomes final because it was not thereafter challenged."[9]

"I rather cavil at the suggestion that construction adjudication is somehow 'just a part of ADR'. In my view, that damns it with faint praise. In reality, it is the only system of compulsory dispute resolution of which I am aware which requires a decision by a specialist professional within 28 days, backed up by a specialist court enforcement scheme which (subject to jurisdiction and natural justice issues only) provides a judgment within weeks thereafter. It is not an alternative to anything: for most construction disputes, it is the only game in town."[10]

V. Case sample

The author undertook a remediation engagement (representing a customer) for a large government complex software project that concerned the replacement of existing software systems and business processes by a series of

---

[9]) *See, e.g., Bresco Electrical Services Ltd v Michael Lonsdale (Electrical) Ltd* 2020 UKSC 25, per Lord Briggs at 13 *et seq.*

[10]) *See, e.g., John Doyle Construction Ltd (In Liquidation) v Erith Contractors Ltd* [2021] EWCA Civ 1452, [2021] Bus LR 1837, [2021 WLR(D)516].

new modules implementation by a software vendor. It became bogged down in solution design and fit problems on a reoccurring basis despite the expectation they were acquired as well evolved standard software modules. The remediation process contributed to an ultimately successful reset and good outcome.

This is a description of the use and progression of the ADR conflict mitigation processes. These processes were executed in the context of a *Framework*, with detailed performance standards, that at the intervention phases below were subject to non-compliance and arguable breach of contract by a party.

A. First Intervention

Issue/Problem: Whole of solution fit (all module phases) + resourcing quality + schedule delivery confidence crisis

ADR process: (Initially) use of hybrid Mediation/facilitation being a safe environment to openly discuss and explore core causes of misalignment and failure centered around solution fit (all modular phases), resourcing quality, schedule delivery and confidence to continue. From this hybrid Mediation / facilitation, an agreed Negotiation framework (technical and commercial matters) was prepared by the author and then progressed through detailed sessions to an ultimate reset contract.

B. Second Intervention

Issue/Problem: Final major modules phase, resourcing quality and design issues

ADR process: Exhaustive renegotiation

C. Third Intervention

Issue/Problem: Final major modules phases – design redirection but again confidence in resource quality. Here in contemplation contract breach/Dispute/determinative process.

ADR process: Again, exhaustive re-Negotiation as determinative remedies would delay project delivery and change relationship exchanges.

As part of the re-Negotiation, the parties also agreed to vary the contract to include an element of the Contract Modules terms (*i.e.*, the mandatory risk obligation notification and recourse to Mediation).

VI. Conclusion

The Contract Modules contain processes designed to provide parties with a sequence of choice-based conflict mitigation or Dispute Resolution processes that assist in reviewing, unlocking and resetting too often misaligned software projects. Their core objectives are to:

- Best enable early identification of potential misalignment issues and emerging Disputes;
- Provide prompt, collaborative and least adversarial (but structured) resolution of such matters in a manner best for project; and
- Insofar as it is practicable, enable (if used early) software project resumption or progression.

Reluctance or failure to do so and engage in ADR in software projects contracts often see failed expenditure and effort and irreconcilable relationships. The author believes that the success rates of software project contracts can be improved when parties adopt and use the ADR processes set out herein that emphasize early and open identification of problems and conflict.

Chapter IV

Investment Arbitration

Alice Meissner/David Kirnbauer
The Labyrinth beyond Intra-EU Investment Protection:
The Uncertain and Inconclusive Future of intra-EU Investment Protection –
What Legal Remedies are Left to European Investors?

The Labyrinth beyond Intra-EU Investment Arbitration:

The Uncertain and Inconclusive Future of Intra-EU Investment Protection – What Legal Remedies Are Left for European Investors?

Alice Meissner/David Kirnbauer

I. Introduction

The end of intra-EU investment arbitration is inevitable. While the validity of a retrospective termination of an arbitration agreement as well as the abolishment of sunset clauses may remain disputable, the objective will of the EU Member States to retreat from any intra-EU investor-state arbitration agreement is undeniable. The EU Member States have not only terminated all intra-EU bilateral investment agreements ("BITs") with their Agreement for the termination of Bilateral Investment Treaties between the Member States of the European Union dated 29 May 2020 ("Termination Agreement"),[1]) they have also confirmed their exit from any investment arbitration agreement under the Energy Charter Treaty ("ECT") by signing an "*Inter-Se Declaration*"[2]) on 26 June 2024.

While there may be pending cases challenging the termination of sunset clauses or investors arguing the primacy of obligations under the ICSID Convention over EU law, a shift towards the acknowledgement of the end of intra-EU investment arbitration by arbitral tribunals has become obvious: For the first time, on 11 October 2024 two ICSID tribunals decided by majority to

[1]) Remaining EU Member States who have not signed the Termination Agreement have all subsequently terminated their intra-EU BITs bilaterally.

[2]) Declaration on the legal consequences of the judgment of the Court of Justice in *Komstroy* and common understanding on the non-applicability of Article 26 of the Energy Charter Treaty as a basis for intra-EU arbitration, 26 June 2024, https://energy.ec.europa.eu/document/download/740e62fc-a0d1-4a5b-9d00-01357802c307_en?filename=Inter%20se%20Declaration%20-%20all%20languages%20-%20260624.pdf (last visited 20 January 2025); Declaration of the representative of the government of Hungary on the legal consequences of the judgment of the Court of Justice in *Komstroy* and of the non-applicability of Article 26 of the Energy Charter Treaty as a basis for intra-EU arbitration proceedings, June 26, 2024, 228f2c9ba861fae2b70f183ee4b5ddc.pdf (last visited January 20, 2025).

uphold the "intra-EU objection". They decided that they do not have any jurisdiction over disputes between EU Member States and investors from other EU Member States under the ECT.[3])

So, *quo vadis*, what does that mean for damaged European investors having invested in another EU Member State going forward? What legal remedies are left for them to pursue? According to the European Commission ("EU Commission") in its *Communication from the Commission to the European Parliament and the Council* on "Protection of intra-EU investment" dated 19 July 2018, it states that "*EU law protects all EU cross-border investments throughout their lifecycle*". In particular, it highlights the important role of national courts acting explicitly as "EU courts" to guarantee the application of EU law and to disapply any national provisions which are contrary to effective provisions of EU law.[4])

This article analyzes the question of whether there are efficient legal remedies for European investors to protect their investments or to seek compensation from another EU Member State for its breaches of EU and international law.

II. Status Quo

A. *Achmea, Komstroy* and *PL Holdings* Confirming the Ending of Intra-EU Investment Arbitration

1. Intra-EU Bilateral Investment Treaties („intra-EU BITs")

At the time of the judgment of the Court of Justice of the European Union ("CJEU") in *Achmea B.V. v. Slovakia*[5]) ("*Achmea*"), the EU Commission had been requesting EU Member States to terminate their intra-EU BITs. Ireland and Italy had already terminated their intra-EU BITs in 2012 and 2013. For several years, the EU Commission had consistently been insisting on its view that intra-EU BITs are incompatible with EU law. The EU Commission follows

[3]) *Sapac v. Kingdom of Span*, ICSID Case No. ARB/19/23, Award (October 11, 2024); *European Solar Farms ("ESF") v. Kingdom of Spain*, ICSID Case No. ARB/18/45, Award (October 11, 2024).

[4]) EU Commission, Communication from the Commission to the European Parliament and the Council – Protection of intra-EU investment (July 19, 2018), https://eur-lex.europa.eu/legal-content/en/TXT/?uri=CELEX:52018DC0547 (last visited January 20, 2025).

[5]) Case C-284/16, *Slowakische Republik (Slovak Republic) v. Achmea BV*, ECLI:EU:C:2018:158 (March 6, 2018).

the "single market" opinion – according to consistent case law from the CJEU, such discrimination based on nationality is incompatible with EU law.[6])

The EU Commission's opinion was not perceived in the same manner by all EU Member States. Formal notice letters were sent to five EU Member States (Austria, the Netherlands, Romania, Slovakia and Sweden), launching the first slate of infringement procedures against those five EU Member States. At the same time, the EU Commission sought an administrative dialogue with the remaining 21 EU Member States who still had intra-EU BITs in place.[7]) The opinion of the EU Commission remained, however, controversial.

Achmea was submitted to the CJEU by the German Federal Court of Justice as a request for a preliminary ruling by the CJEU under Art. 267 of the Treaty of the Functioning of the European Union ("TFEU"). In this decision, the CJEU was confronted with the question of whether Arts. 267 and 344 TFEU preclude a provision in an international agreement concluded between EU Member States, for example under Art. 8 of the Dutch-Slovak BIT. Under such circumstances, an investor from one EU Member State may – in the event of a dispute concerning investments in the other EU Member State – bring proceedings against the latter EU Member State before an arbitral tribunal whose jurisdiction that latter EU Member State has undertaken to accept.[8])

Advocate General Wathelet (as a Member of the CJEU) submitted an opinion to the Grand Chamber of the CJEU that differed to the Court's decision in *Achmea*. He was of the opinion that there is no incompatibility between the investment arbitration clause of the Dutch-Slovak BIT and EU law and as a result, intra-EU investment disputes would not fall within the scope of the EU Treaties' *ratione materiae*.[9])

The Grand Chamber of the CJEU, however, did not follow the opinion of Advocate General Wathelet. It determined that arbitral tribunals were not able to submit their questions concerning the interpretation and application of EU law in a preliminary reference request under Art. 267 TFEU, as an investment tribunal was not considered "*a court or tribunal of a Member State*" under Art. 267 TFEU. Hence, without the possibility of submitting questions regarding the application and interpretation of EU law, intra-EU investment tribunals were not able to guarantee the full application of EU law. As the CJEU had exclusive jurisdiction concerning legal questions under EU law under Art. 344

[6]) *See* EU Commission, *Commission asks Member States to terminate their intra-EU bilateral investment treaties* (18 June 2015), https://ec.europa.eu/commission/presscorner/detail/en/ip_15_5198 (last visited January 20, 2025).

[7]) *Ibid.*

[8]) Case C-284/16, *Slowakische Republik (Slovak Republic) v. Achmea BV*, ECLI: EU:C:2018:158 (March 6, 2018), at para. 23.

[9]) *See* Opinion of Advocate General Wathelet, Case C-284/16, *Slowakische Republik v. Achmea BV*. Request for a preliminary ruling from the Bundesgerichtshof (September 19, 2017), at para. 55, eur-lex.europa.eu/legal-content/EN/TXT/PDF/?uri=CELEX:62016CC0284 (last visited January 20, 2025).

TFEU, Art. 8 of the Dutch-Slovak BIT was not able to guarantee the exclusive jurisdiction of the CJEU and was therefore incompatible with EU law.[10])

Following the CJEU's *Achmea* decision, the national courts of the EU Member States were, according to a communication from the EU Commission, obliged to ensure the annulment of all intra-EU arbitral awards and to deny the enforcement of such awards.[11])

In order to further solidify the EU's position regarding intra-EU BITs, the EU Member States signed the Termination Agreement.[12]) The Termination Agreement was based on declarations of the EU Member States from January 2019, where they declared to comply with the *Achmea* judgment and to terminate all intra-EU BITs.[13]) Austria, Finland, Ireland and Sweden were not signatories to the Termination Agreement. The termination clauses under the Termination Agreement and in termination agreements directly between EU Member States are considered final, offering no transition period or alternative means for investors to seek relief. The Termination Agreement under Section 2 also mandates the immediate termination of the sunset clauses, which were intended to ensure legal certainty for investors for a limited time post-termination. According to the Termination Agreement, these sunset clauses will no longer have any effect.[14]) Section 3 addresses arbitration proceedings initiated both before and after the *Achmea* judgment of 6 March 2018, as well as those concluded prior to this date.

Art. 5 of the Termination Agreement states that new arbitration proceedings – defined in Art. 1(6) of the Termination Agreement as any arbitration proceedings initiated on or after 6 March 2018 – cannot be initiated based on the arbitration clauses in the (terminated) intra-EU BITs. Regarding concluded arbitration proceedings, Art. 6 of the Termination Agreement stipulates that they shall remain completely unaffected by the Termination Agreement. Concluded arbitration proceedings are defined in Art. 1(4) of the Termination Agreement as those that ended with a settlement agreement or a

---

[10]) Case C-284/16, *Slowakische Republik (Slovak Republic) v. Achmea BV*, ECLI: EU:C:2018:158 (March 6, 2018), at paras. 49, 58.

[11]) *See* EU Commission, *supra* note 4, at 3.

[12]) Agreement for the Termination of Bilateral Investment Treaties between the Member States of the European Union (May 29, 2020), https://eur-lex.europa.eu/eli/agree_eums/2020/529/oj/eng (last visited January 20, 2025).

[13]) *See* Declaration of the representatives of the governments of the Member States on the legal consequences of the judgment of the Court of Justice in *Achmea* and on investment protection in the European Union (January 15, 2019), https://finance.ec.europa.eu/document/download/901c4f5e-9c4e-4559-92a1-dc946e174ac5_en?filename=190117-bilateral-investment-treaties_en.pdf (visited January 20, 2025), at 4.

[14]) *See August Reinisch & Johannes Tropper, The 2020 Termination Agreement of intra-EU BITs and its effect on investment arbitration in the EU: A public international law analysis of the Termination Agreement*, in *Klausegger/Klein/Kremslehner/Petsche/Pitkowitz/Welser/Zeiler* (eds.), Austrian Yearbook on International Arbitration 2022, at 304 *et seq.*

final award issued prior to 6 March 2018, provided that either (i) the award was duly executed before 6 March 2018 with no challenge or enforcement proceedings pending on that date, or (ii) the award was set aside or annulled before the Termination Agreement came into force.

However, arbitral awards from concluded proceedings that have not been enforced or settled and are still subject to enforcement proceedings are considered "pending" proceedings. In the case of pending arbitration proceedings, as defined in Art. 1(5) of the Termination Agreement, Section 3 of the Termination Agreement includes some transitional measures which result in less stringent treatment of such proceedings compared to new arbitration proceedings.

2. Article 26 Energy Charter Treaty

In its *Achmea* decision, the CJEU explicitly pointed out that the question of admissibility and validity of investment arbitration clauses is not only limited to those of intra-EU BITs, but will arise in connection with multilateral trade agreements to which EU Member States are parties, in particular it referred to Art. 26 ECT. The wording of Article 26 provides for the submission of a dispute to international arbitration or conciliation.

In its decision of *Komstroy v. Moldova*[15]) ("*Komstroy*"), the CJEU addressed the uncertainty noted in the *Achmea* decision – notably, that *Komstroy* concerned a dispute between a non-EU contracting party (Moldova) and a corporation domiciled in another non-EU contracting party (British Virgin Islands). Hence, the CJEU's approach may be somewhat surprising, as it discussed the core legal question in *obiter dictum*.[16]) Such *obiter dictum*, strictly speaking, does not constitute a binding precedent. It may, however, have a *de facto* binding effect assuming that the CJEU may decide such a case in the future.[17])

The arbitral proceedings of *Komstroy* were seated in Paris. Moldova initiated set-aside proceedings before the *cour d'appel de Paris* (the Paris Court of Appeal), which then referred to the CJEU for the interpretation of the term "investment" in a preliminary reference procedure under Art. 267 TFEU. The CJEU acknowledged the extra-EU constellation of the dispute, but noted that this did not preclude its jurisdiction.[18]) It then followed the reasoning as set out

[15]) Case C-741/19, *République de Moldavie* v *Komstroy LLC*, ECLI:EU:C:2021:655 (September 2, 2021).

[16]) *See, e.g., Alan Dashwood, Republic of Moldova v Komstroy LCC: Arbitration under Article 26 ECT Outlawed in Intra-EU Disputes by Obiter Dictum,* European Law Review 1/2022 (2022), at 127 *et seqq.*; *David Ingle & Jeffrey Sullivan* KC, *Arbitration under the Energy Charter Treaty: the Impact of EU Law,* in Lavranos/Castagna, International Arbitration and EU Law (2024), at para. 11.02.

[17]) *See Giulia Wolff, The Impact of the CJEU's Komstroy Decision on Investor-State Arbitration*, SchiedsVZ, Issue 5/23 (2023), at 281, 285.

[18]) Case C 741/19, *République de Moldavie v Komstroy LLC*, ECLI:EU:C:2021:655 (September 2, 2021), at para. 21 *et seq.*, 67.

in *Achmea,* noting that although arbitral tribunals constituted under Art. 26 ECT are required to interpret and even apply EU law, such arbitral tribunals do not qualify as "*a court of tribunal of a Member State*" under Art. 267 TFEU. They are therefore not eligible to submit questions to the CJEU. Further, awards rendered under Art. 26 ECT are not subject to review by a court of an EU Member State capable of ensuring compliance with EU law and guaranteeing that questions of EU law may be submitted to the CJEU for a preliminary ruling. Consequently, the CJEU determined that such ECT-based intra-EU investment arbitrations should be deemed invalid and Art. 26 ECT should be declared as incompatible with EU law.[19])

Following *Komstroy,* the first round of negotiations for a "modernization" of the ECT was initiated in July 2020. It did not bring an immediate result. To date, many EU Member States have either already withdrawn from the ECT or have announced they will do so.

To address any uncertainty regarding the invalidity of Art. 26 ECT, all EU Member States – with the exception of Hungary – executed a joint "*Inter-se Declaration*" on 26 June 2024 announcing "*(…) for greater certainty, that they share a common understanding on the interpretation and application of the Energy Charter Treaty, according to which Article 26 of that Treaty cannot and never could serve as a legal basis for intra-EU arbitration proceedings*".[20])

The Inter-se Declaration further declared that the sunset clause of the ECT under Art. 47(3) ECT shall not produce any legal effect between EU Member States. This applies both to withdrawals that have already taken place and to future withdrawals from the ECT.[21])

Hungary was the only EU Member State which did not sign the Inter-Se Declaration. Instead, it issued its own declaration which does not mention the sunset clause under Art. 47(3) ECT and further states that the withdrawal of the applicability of the arbitration clause of the ECT must materialize by amending the ECT through a treaty between all or certain contracting parties.[22])

On 3 December 2024, the statutory session of the 35th Energy Charter Conference held in Brussels ("Conference") finally announced an important milestone on the modernization of the ECT: It formally adopted a proposal for modernizing the ECT, including (i) Amendments to the ECT as set out in the Conference decision,[23]) (ii) Modifications and changes to Annexes to the

---

[19]) *Ibid.* at paras. 53 *et seqq.*

[20]) Inter-Se Declaration, *supra* note 2, at 7.

[21]) *See* Inter-Se Declaration, *supra* note 2, at 8.

[22]) *See* Declaration of the representative of the government of Hungary, *supra* note 2, at 2.

[23]) Decision of the Energy Charter Conference – Amendments to the Energy Charter Treaty (3 December 2024), https://www.energycharter.org/fileadmin/DocumentsMedia/CCDECS/2024/CCDEC202412_EN.pdf (last visited January 20, 2025).

ECT,[24]) (iii) Changes to Understandings, Declarations and Decisions with respect to the ECT[25]) and (iv) Provisions on the entry into force and provisional application of the adopted amendments to the ECT and approved changes to its Annexes, as set out in the Conference decisions.[26]) With the Amendments to the ECT the intra-EU investment disputes have explicitly been carved out by the insertion of a new sub-clause in Art. 24 which stipulates that "*for greater certainty, Articles 7, 26 (...) shall not apply among Contracting Parties that are members of the same [Regional Economic Integration Organization] in their mutual relations.*"[27])

3. Ad hoc Intra-EU Investment Arbitration Agreement

The third notable decision of the CJEU regarding intra-EU arbitration proceedings is *PL Holdings S.à.r.l v. Republic of Poland*, in which the CJEU was called upon for a preliminary ruling at the request of the Swedish Supreme Court with the following question: "*Whether Articles 267 and 344 TFEU must be interpreted as precluding national legislation which allows a Member State to conclude an ad hoc arbitration agreement with an investor from another Member State that makes it possible to continue arbitration proceedings initiated on the basis of an arbitration clause whose content is identical to that agreement, where that clause is contained in an international agreement concluded between those two Member States and is invalid on the ground that is contrary to those articles.*"[28])

The CJEU concluded that allowing EU Member States to replace invalid arbitration clauses with ad hoc agreements would undermine the autonomy of EU law and the principle of mutual trust between EU Member States. Consequently, in line with the reasoning of *Achmea*, the CJEU ruled that national legislation permitting such ad hoc agreements is precluded by Arts. 267 and 344 TFEU.[29])

---

24) Decision of the Energy Charter Conference – Modifications and Changes to Annexes to the Energy Charter Treaty (December 3, 2024), https://www.energycharter.org/fileadmin/DocumentsMedia/CCDECS/2024/CCDEC202413_EN.pdf (last visited January 20, 2025).

25) Decision of the Energy Charter Conference – Changes to Understandings, Declarations and Decisions (3 December 2024) https://www.energycharter.org/fileadmin/DocumentsMedia/CCDECS/2024/CCDEC202414_EN.pdf (last visited January 20, 2025).

26) Decision of the Energy Charter Conference – Entry into Force and Provisional Application of Amendments to the Energy Charter Treaty and Changes and Modifications to its Annexes (3 December 2024), https://www.energycharter.org/fileadmin/DocumentsMedia/CCDECS/2024/CCDEC202415_EN.pdf (last visited January 20, 2025).

27) Decision of the Energy Charter Conference, *supra* note 23, at 18.

28) Case C-109/20, *Republiken Polen v. PL Holdings Sarl*, ECLI:EU:C:2021:875 (October 26, 2021), at para. 37.

29) *Ibid.* at para. 65 *et seq.*

B. Latest Tribunal's Decisions on Upholding the Intra-EU Investment Objection

The views of arbitral tribunals regarding intra-EU investment arbitration are not quite as unambiguous as those of the EU and those of intra-EU investors. Their opinions strongly depend on whether those proceedings are concluded, pending or new as defined under the Termination Agreement (*see* section II.A.1 above). While concluded arbitration proceedings are not addressed by arbitral tribunals due to their lack of relevance (as the matter is determined by enforcement courts), they do deal with pending and new proceedings in accordance with the Termination Agreement. In pending arbitration proceedings, arbitral tribunals have frequently rejected the jurisdictional objections of EU Member States based on the argument that their jurisdiction is not based on EU law, but on international law.[30]) Regarding the handling of new arbitration proceedings, it depends on the timing of their initiation and their legal basis, which is why no general statement should be deduced.

Several arbitral tribunals have ruled that the *Achmea* judgment does not apply. They have dismissed intra-EU jurisdictional objections and argued that their jurisdiction is based on international law and cannot be thwarted by EU law.[31]) However, there are also a few outliers, the first and also most infamous decision being the *Green Power* award.[32]) In that case, the arbitral tribunal's reasoning to uphold the jurisdictional objection was that the seat of arbitration was in Sweden, and therefore in the EU. As a result, EU law was to be applied, and the primacy of EU law had to be considered.[33])

Initially the *Green Power* award was not seen as too concerning as this decision was considered a particular instance rather than a general precedent. However, this situation has evolved as two recent ICSID awards have also

[30]) *See, e.g., UP (formerly Le Chèque Déjeuner) and C.D Holding Internationale v. Hungary*, ICSID Case No. ARB/13/35, Award (October 9, 2018), at para. 253; *Foresight Luxembourg Solar 1 S. Á.R1. and others v. Kingdom of Spain*, SCC Case No. 2015/150, Final Award (November 14, 2018), at para. 218 *et seqq.*; *Eskosol S.p.A. in liquidazione v. Italian Republic*, ICSID Case No. ARB/15/50, Decision on Termination Request and Intra-EU Objection (May 7, 2019), at para. 110 *et seq.*

[31]) *See, e.g., Mathias Kruck et al. v. Kingdom of Spain*, ICSID Case No. ARB/15/23, Decision of the Respondent's Request for Reconsideration of the Tribunal's Decision dated April 19, 2021 (December 6, 2021), at para. 32 *et seqq.*; *Infracapital F1 S.a.r.l. et al. v. Kingdom of Spain*, ICSID Case No. ARB/16/18, Decision on Respondent's Request for Reconsideration regarding the Intra-EU Objection and the Merits (February 1, 2022), at para. 107; *Sevilla Beheer B.V. et al. v. Kingdom of Spain*, ICSID Case No. ARB/16/27, Decision on Jurisdiction, Liability and the Principles of Quantum (February 11, 2022), at para. 620.

[32]) *Green Power Partners K/S and SCE Solar Don Benito APS v. Kingdom of Spain*, SCC Case No. V 2016/135, Award (June 16, 2022).

[33]) *Ibid.* at para. 166.

rejected jurisdiction.[34]) These new decisions indicate a shift in the approach of ICSID tribunals, suggesting that the application of EU law in intra-EU disputes under the ECT might become more common.

The majority of two ICSID tribunals decided for the first time on 11 October 2024 to uphold the "intra-EU objection" in ECT-related cases. The disputes with yet-unpublished awards involve claims brought against Spain by *Sapac* and *European Solar Farms* based on the allegations that Spain had breached the ECT by reducing incentives owed to their investments in Spanish photovoltaic plants. The tribunals decided they do not have any jurisdiction over disputes between EU Member States and investors from other EU Member States under the ECT.[35])

The arbitrators decided by majority that Spain had not consented to arbitrate this dispute. Surprisingly, Spain did not argue the incompatibility of Art. 26 ECT with EU law, but contested the interpretation of Art. 1(3) ECT. The tribunals concluded that, based on Art. 1(3) ECT and the Treaty's object, purpose and supplementary means, the ECT's application is excluded among EU Member States where the competence in question lies with the EU.[36])

It may appear that the said recent ICSID awards from October 2024 represent a new norm and are not merely outliers following the *Green Power* award. However, such a shift towards upholding the intra-EU objection cannot be deemed as a strict view of tribunals. On 18 December 2024, the ICSID tribunal hearing the *Strabag SE et al. v. Republic of Germany*[37]) arbitration awarded Austrian investors damages based on the ECT to be reimbursed by Germany. In this case, claimants filed the case in 2019 requesting compensation for their investments in several offshore wind energy projects in the German North Sea and the development of related technology. It needs to be highlighted that the tribunal had already decided in its *Decision on the Respondent's Preliminary Objections pursuant to ICSID Arbitration Rule 41(5)* on 24 July 2020 – back then the Inter-Se Declaration regarding the non-application of Article 26 ECT had not yet been issued.[38])

[34]) *Sapac v. Kingdom of Span*, ICSID Case No. ARB/19/23, Award (October 11, 2024); *European Solar Farms ("ESF") v. Kingdom of Spain*, ICSID Case No. ARB/18/45, Award (October 11, 2024).

[35]) *See* Lisa Bohmer, *Breaking: ICSID tribunal majorities uphold intra-EU objection in duo of ECT arbitrations against Spain* (October 12, 2024), https://www.iareporter.com/articles/breaking-icsid-tribunal-majorities-uphold-intra-eu-objection-in-duo-of-ect-arbitrations-against-spain/ (last visited January 20, 2025).

[36]) *Ead.*

[37]) *Strabag, Erste Nordsee-Offshore Holding and Zweite Nordsee-Offshore Holding v. Germany*, ICSID Case No.ARB/19/29, *see* https://www.iareporter.com/articles/icsid-tribunal-issues-award-in-ect-offshore-wind-dispute-with-germany/ (last visited January 22, 2025).

[38]) *Ibid.*

The evolving landscape of international arbitration law suggests that future rulings will clarify whether upholding jurisdictional objections in intra-EU disputes will become standard practice or if these decisions are exceptions rather than the rule.

III. *Quo vadis* – What Legal Remedies are Left Going Forward?

A. Opinion of the EU Commission in the Communication Paper

The EU Commission expressed its opinion on the protection of intra-EU investment in its "Communication from the Commission to the European Parliament and the Council" dated 19 July 2018 ("Communication Paper"). The content of such Communication Paper "*focuses on the protection of investors against national measures and not against measures adopted by the EU institutions and bodies*".[39]) It emphasizes the fact that the EU is a single market and that EU law protects all EU cross-border investments throughout their lifecycle.

The EU Commission lays out examples of how the CJEU has ruled against EU Member States as guardian over the compliance of EU law, identifying national measures infringing the fundamental freedom rights of individuals, *i.e.,* the right to free movement of goods, freedom of capital, freedom of establishment and to provide services and free movement of persons. Examples are cases C-442/02-*Caixa Bank (France)* and C-493/09-*Commission v. Portugal.*[40])

The extent to whether damaged individuals have been appropriately reimbursed has not been addressed by the EU Commission in its Communication Paper. The fact remains that those said decisions of the CJEU do not impose any restitution obligations on the EU Member States but rather the burden of the EU Member State to cover the costs of the proceedings.

As stated by the EU Commission: "*(w)hile international investment law (for example bilateral investment treaties) focuses mainly on compensating investors after the violation has taken place, EU law enables the protection of cross-border investors in the EU through multiple ways and at different levels*".[41])

The examples addressed by the EU Commission address judgments of CJEU over infringement proceedings pursuant to Art. 258 TFEU. According to

---

[39]) EU Commission, *supra* note 4, at 4.

[40]) Case C-442/02, *CaixaBank France v Ministère de l'Économie, des Finances et de l'Industrie*, ECLI:EU:C:2004:586 (October 5, 2004); Case C-493/09, *European Commission v Portuguese Republic*, ECLI:EU:C:2011:635 (October 6, 2011).

[41]) EU Commission, *supra* note 4, at 17.

such provision, "*if the Commission considers that a Member State has failed to fulfil an obligation under the Treaties, it shall deliver a reasoned opinion on the matter after giving the State concerned the opportunity to submit its observations. If the State concerned does not comply with the opinion within the period laid down by the Commission, the latter may bring the matter before the Court of Justice of the European Union*". The infringement procedure may be divided into five different stages: (1) investigative, (2) commencement, (3) reasoned opinion, (4) referral and (5) enforcement.[42)]

Notably, the EU Commission retains absolute discretion over the decision of whether to commence infringement proceedings.[43)] So even though the EU Commission highlights relevant judgments of the CJEU, such procedure does not reflect any direct legal remedy for an intra-EU investor whose interests have been adversely affected.[44)] The EU Commission does not consider the infringement procedure as "*a means to provide redress for individuals*", but it is rather seen as an 'objective' mechanism to ensure the compliance with EU law by EU Member States.[45)]

As to any restitution rights of intra-EU investors, the EU Commission relies on the national courts to award damages for breaches against EU law (including for judicial wrongdoing).[46)] In the opinion of the EU Commission, the national courts acting as "EU courts" therefore plays an important part in the protection of EU investors. As discussed under section C.2 below, the case law established by the CJEU stipulates in principle that EU Member States may be held liable to pay damages to individuals for a breach of EU law ("*Francovich* Damages"[47)]), however the pre-conditions to succeed with such state liability claims are notably difficult to fulfill.

Lastly, the EU Commission concludes in its Commission Paper that even though "*EU law does not solve all problems investors may face in their activities. (...) in the single market, EU investors' rights are protected by EU law, which allows for the pursuit and development of economic activities in all Member States. Investors can enforce their rights before national administrations and courts, according to national procedural rules which are to ensure that these*

[42)] *See* Emilie Gonin & Ronan O'Reilly, *Intra-EU Investment Protection and the Rule of Law*, in Stanic/Baltag, The Future of Investment Treaty Arbitration in the EU: Intra-EU BITs, the Energy Charter Treaty, and the Multilateral Investment Court (2020), at 63, 82.

[43)] *Eid.* at 84.

[44)] *Eid.* at 83; *see* section III.D. for details of a Complaint with the EU Commission.

[45)] *Eid.* at 84.

[46)] The EU Commission refers to ex multis Joined Cases C-6/90 and C-9/90 *Francovich*, ECLI:EU:C:1991:428 (November 19, 1991) and Case C-224/01 *Köbler*, ECLI:EU:C:2003:513 (September 30, 2003) – *see* EU Commission, *supra* note 4, at 21.

[47)] Joined Cases C-6/90 and C-9/90 *Francovich*, ECLI:EU:C:1991:428 (November 19, 1991); Case C-224/01 *Köbler*, ECLI:EU:C:2003:513 (September 30, 2003).

rights are effectively protected. Member States have the responsibility and the power to enforce EU law in general and EU investors' rights, in particular (...)"[48])

B. Limited Legal Standing of Individuals with the CJEU

Natural persons and legal entities that are intra-EU investors have been granted very limited legal standing before the CJEU. The TFEU explicitly stipulates legal standing of natural and legal persons solely for the (1) action for annulment under Art. 263(4) TFEU and (2) action for failure to act under Art. 265 TFEU.

1. Action for Annulment under Art. 263 TFEU

According to Art. 263(4) TFEU the active legal standing of natural and legal persons is granted only if they aim to bring an action for annulment against an act issued by an EU institution, which is directly addressed to them or which is of direct and individual concern to them. This means that if a directive or a decision issued by the European Parliament, the European Council, the EU Commission or the European Central Bank ("ECB") directly affects an individual's legal position, they can challenge its legality before the General Court.

Since an intra-EU investor seeks relief against measures imposed by another EU Member State in the first place and not by the EU itself, such remedy may only be relevant under exceptional circumstances. It may be in the legal interest of the intra-EU investor to receive *ex nunc* relief from the CJEU, provided that they are successful in challenging an (i) EU regulation, should such regulation impose direct obligations or restrictions on individuals or companies, (ii) a decision of an EU institution, should such decision be addressed to specific individuals or companies, (iii) an EU directive in exceptional cases, as the directives are generally addressed to EU Member States, (iv) an EU Commission Communication if these communications produce new legal effects and directly affect individuals or (v) an EU Administrative Act, such as fines or sanctions imposed by an EU institution. Should an intra-EU investor have been damaged due to a measure imposed by another EU Member State, such action of annulment may only be relevant when either (i) such imposed measure is based on an EU act and the individual may claim sufficient legal interest to directly call upon the CJEU or (ii) such measure is connected to an EU act which may deem as a precondition to certain measures imposed by the EU Member State (for example, the ECB withdraws the banking license of a certain national bank).

---

[48]) EU Commission, *supra* note 4, at 26 *et seq.*

Such legal remedy, however, has existed in parallel to intra-EU investment arbitration. It is yet unclear whether such legal remedy will grow in importance in future. Notably, the action of annulment under Art. 263 TFEU aims at annulment and does not directly aim at restitution of any unlawful damaged individual. Such damages will need to be claimed with the initiation of a separate proceeding (*see* section III.C.2.).

2. Action for Failure to Act under Art. 265 TFEU

Further, individuals may file an action for failure to act under Art. 265 TFEU. This allows individuals besides EU Member States and EU institutions to challenge the inaction of EU institutions, bodies, offices, or agencies when they fail to take required action. Such remedy is deemed admissible only if the institution, body, office or agency concerned has first been called upon to act. If, within two months of being called upon to do so, the institution, body, office or agency concerned has not defined its position, the action may be brought within a further period of two months.

However, an individual has no right against the EU Commission to initiate infringement proceedings against an EU Member State. An individual may only submit a complaint with the European Commission regarding the breaches of EU law committed by an EU Member State (*see* section D below).

C. Remedies with National Courts

1. National Courts Entrusted as "EU Courts"

The current concept promoted by the EU Commission is largely built on "mutual trust" within the EU and among EU Member States. As quoted above under section A., the EU Commission empowers EU Member States to enforce EU law in general and EU investors' rights, in particular. According to the CJEU, national courts of EU Member States must apply and interpret national law consistently with EU law.[49]) The EU Commission refers in particular to the preliminary ruling procedure stipulated in Article 267 TFEU as a legal remedy when "*a question (of interpretation) is raised before a court or tribunal against whose decisions there is no judicial remedy under national law (…)*".[50]) However, it needs to be noted that an individual has not been granted the right to initiate the preliminary ruling procedure before a national court. The initiation of this procedure, however, is at the discretion of a national court, which makes the effectiveness of these measures strongly dependent on this discretionary power.[51])

[49]) *See* Case C-106/89, *Marleasing SA v. La Comercial Internacional de Alimentacion SA*. (November 13, 1990).

[50]) EU Commission, *supra* note 4, at 24.

[51]) *See Emilie Gonin & Ronan O'Reilly, supra* note 42, at 85 *et seq.*

From the perspective of core principles underlying investment arbitration, the referral of intra-EU investors back to the national courts of an EU Member State which was responsible for the breach of the investors' rights in the first place may be dissatisfying, if not paradoxical. Taking into account the reality of imbalanced standards of the rule of law existing among EU Member States (as acknowledged by independent bodies),[52]) damaged intra-EU investors may have difficulties trusting the national court system of that particular EU Member State to remedy its damage.

2. Damage Claims

a) Action for Damages Against an EU Member State (*Francovich* Damages)

According to case law of the CJEU as developed by the seminal judgment of the CJEU in *Francovich*, EU Member States may be held liable for damages to individuals for a breach of EU law.[53])

The following requirements must be met so that an individual can claim such damages: "*the rule of law infringed must be intended to confer rights on individuals; the breach must be sufficiently serious; and there must be a direct causal link between the breach of the obligation resting on the State and the damage sustained by the injured parties*".[54]) Regarding the effectiveness and the amount of compensation, there is little empirical data available. This makes it an area of great anticipation and interest. In addition to the requirements, the CJEU clarified that a state liability claim shall remain as a "last resort", requiring therefore the exhaustion of local remedies.[55]) Such local remedies must, however, be reasonable to pursue.[56])

b) State Liability Claims under National Law

The significant role of national courts in the protection of intra-EU investments is crucial to ensure that EU law is applied uniformly and effectively, providing a reliable judicial mechanism for investors to seek remedies. However, the true labyrinth reveals itself when looking at different national court systems of EU Member States, in an attempt to identify a uniform remedy

---

[52]) *See, e.g.,* OECD, Government at a Glance 2023, https://www.oecd.org/en/publications/government-at-a-glance-2023_3d5c5d31-en.html (last visited January 20, 2025).

[53]) Joined Cases C-6/90 and C-9/90, *Francovich and Bonifaci v. Italian Republic,* November 19, 1991, at paras. 28 *et seqq.*

[54]) Joined cases C-46/93 and C-48/93, *Brasserie du Pêcheur SA v. Bundesrepublik Deutschland,* ECLI:EU:C:1996:79 (5 March 1996), at para. 51.

[55]) *See* Case C-334/92, *Wagner Miret,* ECLI:EU:C:1993:945 (December 16, 1993), at paras. 20 *et seqq.*

[56]) *See* Case C-445/06, *Danske Slagterier v. Germany,* ECLI:EU:C:2009:178 (March 24, 2009), at paras. 58 *et seqq.*

for compensation claims for damaged intra-EU investors. While some EU Member States rely on existing state liability claims already embedded in the civil procedural or constitutional court system, other EU Member States have implemented explicit court competence clauses into their civil procedural rules, for example Latvia:

Section 24 of the Latvian Civil Procedure Law reads as follows:

"*(1) A district (city) court shall examine civil cases as a court of first instance. (...)*

(1^1) The Economic Court shall examine the following as the court of first instance: (...)

3) claims of investors of European Union Member States against the State of Latvia for the protection of investments (...)"[57])

In Austria, as another example, where there is no explicit norm in the civil procedure rules referring to "*claims of investors of European Union Member States*", the legal remedy available for compensation for damages directly caused by an organ or a legal entity attributable to the state in Austria is a public liability claim under Section 8 *et seqq.* of the Public Liability Act (Amtshaftungsgesetz – AHG). This procedure allows individuals to claim damages from the state for harm caused by unlawful and culpable actions of state organs. According to Section 9(1) AHG, the jurisdiction for deciding such claims lies with the local competent regional court. This means that the regional court in the district where the legal violation occurred is exclusively responsible for handling and deciding these public liability claims. This procedure provides a crucial legal basis for protecting the rights of investors and other injured parties in Austria.

The public liability claim needs to be distinguished from the state liability claim pursuant to Article 137 of the Federal Constitutional Law (Bundes-Verfassungsgesetz – B-VG).[58]) According to this Article, claims against the state and the municipalities may only be initiated if such claims are "*neither to be settled by ordinary legal proceedings nor by decision of an administrative authority*". The Austrian Constitutional Court is obliged to act pursuant to the principles developed by the CJEU under the so-called *Francovich* damages (*see* above section a). Hence, in the event that an unlawful act or omission under EU law is directly attributed to the national legislator, or in case of a violation of EU law by the highest courts has been alleged, the Austrian Constitutional Court (VfGH) is competent according to Art. 137 B-VG to decide such dispute.[59])

[57]) Latvian Civil Procedure Law, https://likumi.lv/ta/en/en/id/50500 (last visited January 21, 2025).

[58]) VfGH (Austrian Constitutional Court), June 20, 2007, A 20/06.

[59]) *Ibid.*

According to Art. 137 B-VG, the VfGH will only adjudicate a financial claim if it cannot be resolved through ordinary legal proceedings or by a decision of an administrative authority. Therefore, state liability can only be considered a "last resort". Furthermore, it is emphasized that only sufficiently qualified breaches of EU law have a liability-inducing effect.[60]) The claimant must also precisely demonstrate what specific damage is directly attributable to the manifestly inadequate implementation of EU law provisions and how these provisions confer rights upon individuals.[61]) From all these requirements, it is evident that the access barriers to such liability claims are immensely high.

D. Complaint with the EU Commission

Individuals and entities may lodge complaints with the EU Commission, which, upon finding an EU Member State in breach of its obligations, may initiate formal infringement proceedings pursuant to Art. 24(2) of the Procedural Regulation (Council Regulation (EU) 2015/1589).[62]) According to such clause, *"any interested party may submit a complaint to inform the Commission of any alleged unlawful aid or any alleged misuse of aid. To that effect, the interested party shall duly complete a form that has been set out in an implementing provision referred to in Article 33 and shall provide the mandatory information requested therein"*.

Hence, only interested parties may submit complaints to inform the EU Commission of any alleged unlawful aid or misuse of aid. This process involves a structured dialogue between the EU Commission and the EU Member State, aimed at rectifying the breach and ensuring compliance with EU law.[63])

Such complaint shall refer to any measure of an EU Member State which the intra-EU investor deems to be in violation of EU law. This includes legal acts, regulations as well as administrative actions. The EU Commission consistently emphasizes that attempts should first be made to resolve issues at the national level before the authorities and courts of the EU Member States. Furthermore, it is highlighted that this complaint mechanism is intended to address widespread systemic problems rather than individual situations that

---

[60]) *See, e.g.*, Joined cases C-46/93 and C-48/93, Brasserie du Pêcheur SA v. Bundesrepublik Deutschland, ECLI:EU:C:1996:79 (March 5, 1996), at para. 51.

[61]) VfGH (Austrian Constitutional Court), March 12, 2024, Decision: A 17/2023.

[62]) Council Regulation (EU) 2015/1589 dated July 13, 2015 laying down detailed rules for the application of Article 108 of the Treaty on the Functioning of the European Union (codification) ("Procedural Regulation").

[63]) *See* EU Commission, Report a breach of EU law by an EU country, https://commission.europa.eu/about/contact/problems-and-complaints/complaints-about-breaches-eu-law-member-states/report-breach-eu-law-eu-country_en (last visited January 20, 2025).

affect only single individuals. For such cases, the EU Commission asserts that there is already sufficient legal protection available at the national level.[64])

To submit a complaint, an electronic form must be completed detailing the key information regarding the alleged violation of EU law. This includes a description of the national measure that contravenes EU law and a justification of why this is the case, a list of the breached provisions of EU law, a description of the underlying facts, and the problem-solving attempts made at the national level. At this stage, concrete evidence does not need to be attached.[65]) After submitting the complaint, the complainant will receive an acknowledgement of receipt, in which it is again stated that if the EU Commission decides to take action following the submitted complaint, including initiating an infringement procedure, its primary objective is to ensure that EU Member States' laws and practices align with EU law and not to not resolve a specific and individual situation.

According to the EU Commission, a decision can be expected within one year from the submission of the complaint. However, the effectiveness of this remedy is limited for several reasons. These include the time frame in which a response is received, the fact that such a decision is non-binding for the individual, that less than 5% of complaints lead to concrete actions by the EU Commission and the lack of individual redress through this measure.[66])

E. ECtHR Complaint

Scholars have commented that the remedies of the European Court of Human Rights ("ECtHR") may be comparable to the relief granted under investment arbitration law.[67])

According to Art. 34 European Convention on Human Rights ("ECHR"), individuals may submit a complaint to the ECtHR if one of their rights under the ECHR or its protocols has been violated by one of the contracting parties. The admissibility requirements for such an application are laid down in Art. 35 ECHR. These include among others the exhaustion of all domestic remedies and the compliance with the time-limit under Art. 35(1) ECHR. Furthermore,

---

[64]) *Ibid.*

[65]) EU Commission, Submit a Complaint, https://ec.europa.eu/law/application-eu-law/report-breach/en/check-your-criteria (last visited January 20, 2025).

[66]) EU Commission, *supra* note 63.

[67]) *See Xavier Taton & Guillaume Croisant, Judicial Protection of Investors in the European Union: The Remedies Offered by Investment Arbitration, the European Convention on Human Rights and EU Law,* Indian Journal of Arbitration Law, Jodhpur 2018, Volume VII, Issue 2, at 61–145; *Yuka Fukunaga, Margin of Appreciation as an Indicator of Judicial Deference: Is It Applicable to Investment Arbitration?* in Schultz (ed), Journal of International Dispute Settlement, Oxford University Press 2019, Volume 10, Issue 1, at 69–87.

the application must not be anonymous and must not be the same as a matter that has already been examined by the ECtHR or has already been submitted to another procedure of international investigation or settlement and contains no relevant new information. The ECtHR shall declare any individual application inadmissible if it is incompatible with the ECHR or its protocols, manifestly ill-founded, an abuse of the right of individual application, or if the applicant has not suffered a significant disadvantage unless human rights considerations necessitate an examination on the merits.

According to the official website of the ECtHR, an individual that wants to submit an application to the ECtHR has to fill out and submit an application form.[68]) This application form includes general information regarding the applicant and its representative, a statement of facts, a statement of alleged violations of the ECHR or its protocols, an explanation regarding compliance with the admissibility criteria as well as (if applicable) information concerning other international proceedings.

In a recent decision, the German Federal Constitutional Court stated that an investor, upon the exhaustion of all domestic legal remedies, may submit an individual complaint to the ECtHR, particularly to address any potential violation of property rights under Art. 1 of Protocol No. 1 of the ECHR. The court recognized that investors are directed to a protection framework which, although not specifically designed for investment protection, offers adequate legal safeguards overall and is capable of effectively upholding the rights in question.[69])

It remains questionable how effective this complaint mechanism is for investors. The relevant provisions of the ECHR, whose violations are typically claimed in such complaints to the ECtHR, are Art. 1 of Protocol No. 1 of the ECHR and Art. 6 ECHR. According to case law of the ECtHR, beginning with *Stran Greek Refineries and Stratis Andreadis v. Greece*, an arbitral award can – if certain requirements are met – be seen as a possession for the purpose of Art. 1 of Protocol No. 1 of the ECHR.[70]) The refusal to enforce an award may thus interfere with the peaceful enjoyment of these possessions. However, such interference can be lawful if certain criteria are met. The interference has to meet a public purpose and be proportionate.[71])

Additionally, the refusal to enforce an intra-EU award could be qualified as a breach of the investor's constitutional right to a fair trial according to Art.

---

[68]) ECtHR, Applicants, https://www.echr.coe.int/apply-to-the-court (last visited January 20, 2025).

[69]) Bundesverfassungsgericht, July 23, 2024, 2 BvR 557/19, at para. 72.

[70]) ECtHR *Case of Strand Greek Refineries and Stratis Andreadis v. Greece*, Judgment (Merits and Just Satisfaction) (December 9, 1994), Application no. 13427/87, at para. 62.

[71]) *Andreotti, When Human Rights and Investment Protection Intertwined: The Role of the European Court of Human Rights in the Enforcement of Intra-EU BITs within the EU*, in *Lavranos/Mistelis* (eds), European Investment Law and Arbitration Review 2024, at 32.

6 ECHR. In *BTS Holding, A.S. v. Slovakia* for example the applicant company argued that the refusal to enforce a final and binding arbitration award in its favor was arbitrary, violated the principle of legal certainty and left them without an effective domestic remedy.[72]) The ECtHR referencing *Stran Greek Refineries and Stratis Andreadis v. Greece*, emphasized that the rule of law and the constitutional right to a fair trial under Art. 6 ECHR prohibit legislative interference with the administration of justice aimed at influencing outcomes. In this case, the ECtHR determined that the right to recover sums awarded by arbitral tribunals constitutes a 'civil right' under Art. 6 of the ECHR.[73])

Even if an investor succeeds in lodging a successful complaint with the ECtHR, the question arises as to what legal consequences the finding of a violation of the ECHR would entail. According to Art. 41 ECHR, the ECtHR shall afford just satisfaction to the injured party if there has been a violation of the ECHR or its protocols and if the domestic law of the relevant contracting party permits only partial compensation to be provided. However, it has to be noted that the difference between the amounts awarded by arbitral tribunals and those granted by the ECtHR is substantial. The highest sum that was awarded by the ECtHR amounts to EUR 1,866,104.634 in *OAO Neftyanaya Kompaniya Yukos v. Russia*.[74]) This amount is, of course, significantly lower than the sums awarded in various cases by investment arbitration tribunals.

Furthermore, there are additional hurdles for investors seeking to assert their rights before the ECtHR. According to Art. 25(1) ECHR, one of the prerequisites for lodging a complaint with the ECtHR is the exhaustion of all domestic remedies. This requirement is interpreted very broadly. This is particularly disadvantageous for investors because it completely negates the advantage they would have in arbitration proceedings, namely direct access to a dispute resolution forum that can issue a final and binding decision.[75]) It should also be noted that the number of complaints that are admitted and thoroughly examined by the ECtHR is very low. According to statistics published by the ECtHR for 2023, 67 % of complaints are directly dismissed as inadmissible.[76])

---

[72]) ECtHR *BTS Holding, A.S., v. Slovak*, Judgment (Merits) (June 30, 2022), Application no. 55617/17, at para. 74; Andreotti, *supra* note 71, at 34.

[73]) Andreotti, *supra* note 71, at 28 *et seq*.

[74]) ECtHR *OAO Neftyanaya Kompaniya Yukos v. Russia*, Judgment (Just Satisfaction) (July 31, 2014), Application no. 14902/04; Andreotti, *supra* note 71, at 36.

[75]) Laura Rees-Evans & Miglena Angelova, *Investors' Fundamental Rights Post-Achmea: Insights from the German Constitutional Court Decisions in Achmea* (January 7, 2025), https://arbitrationblog.kluwerarbitration.com/2025/01/07/investors-fundamental-rights-post-achmea-insights-from-the-german-constitutional-court-decisions-in-achmea/ (last visited January 20, 2025).

[76]) ECtHR, Analysis of statistics 2023, https://www.echr.coe.int/documents/d/echr/stats-analysis-2023-eng (last visited January 20, 2025).

F. Excursion: European Parliament Enquiry as Political Instrument

For the sake of completeness, it needs to be pointed out that besides the legal remedies noted above, it is possible for an intra-EU investor to draw attention to violations of EU law conducted by another EU Member State by addressing these issues at a political level.

From the point of view of an intra-EU investor with the urge to seek immediate relief from unlawful measures and obtain compensation or restitution for consequential losses, the limited remedies as stated above bear significant risks to be timely and costly. Since the representatives of the European Parliament are subject to the outcome of elections, lobbying attempts may be taken into consideration by intra-EU investors.

In this regard, Rule 144 of the Rules of Procedure of the European Parliament allows any member of the European Parliament to submit a written enquiry addressed either to the President of the EU Council, the EU Council, the EU Commission, or the Vice-President of the EU Commission/High Representative of the Union for Foreign Affairs and Security Policy.

According to the Rules of Procedure of the European Parliament, the EU institutions are obliged to answer such official enquiries addressed to it by a representative of the European Parliament. According to Rule 144(3) of the Rules of Procedure, these questions shall be answered by such institutions within six weeks.[77)]

However, the obstacles include the political barrier of addressing an intra-EU breach with a member of the European Parliament who may be willing to make this request on its behalf. In theory, this may lead to considerations of the EU Commission for an initiation of infringement proceedings against that particular EU Member State.

IV. Summary and Outlook

The continued fading out of intra-EU investment arbitration proceedings is undeniable. For the first time ICSID tribunals – and therefore tribunals administered in a non-EU Member State – have also upheld the intra-EU objection in an ECT case.

The question of whether intra-EU investors may draw on legal remedies with the same effectiveness as investment arbitration must be answered with a resounding "no". According to the findings set out in this article, the window of access to justice has indeed narrowed for intra-EU investors. While the EU

[77)] Rules of Procedure of the European Parliament for the 10th parliamentary term (July 2024), https://www.europarl.europa.eu/doceo/document/RULES-10-2024-07-16-RULE-144_EN.html (last visited January 20, 2025).

Commission elaborates in detail the substantive EU law applicable, which in theory is to provide a solid ground for intra-EU investment protection, it has not (yet) extended the legal standing of intra-EU investors to guarantee their access to a fair trial. The core advantage of investment arbitration was the effectiveness of the proceedings and the neutrality of the forum.

EU Member States do not have any aligned transparent procedural rules to provide intra-EU investors the means for an effective local remedy before national courts. They have yet to harmonize their national procedural rules to adopt a more transparent system of legal remedies for breaches of national and EU law directly available to intra-EU investors. In light of the lengthy contesting procedures at different instances of national courts, intra-EU investors may perceive that they have been forced to enter the sphere of political discussions, either with a supporting member of the European Parliament or by other means of lobbying.[78])

Hence, the abolition of intra-EU investment arbitration has, as of today, not been replaced with comparable legal remedies directly accessible to intra-EU investors as individuals.

The EU legislature should, therefore, consider granting individuals an extended legal standing before the CJEU to challenge the measures of an EU Member State and at the same time to be able to obtain a judgment on damages. The CJEU could be considered as a neutral dispute resolution forum in contrary to those local courts of such particular EU Member State which has been perceived as responsible for the damage caused to an intra-EU investor.

[78]) *See* also *Alice Meissner*, Chapter 31: *Investment Arbitration, Political Risk and the European Union*, in Sottilotta/Campisi/Leitner/Meissner (eds.), Handbook of Political Risk, Routledge 2025, at 451–468.

Chapter V
Recent Publications

Alfred Siwy
Recent Publications

Recent Publications

Alfred Siwy

Dietmar Czernich, *Non-Signatories im österreichischen Schiedsrecht*

published in:
SchiedsVZ 162 (2024)

The article examines several important topics related to extension of arbitration agreements to non-signatories under Austrian arbitration law. It discusses the general principles and conditions under which third parties can be bound by arbitration agreements and the implications of corporate succession and assignment of claims on arbitration agreements. It also addresses the matter in connection with guarantees and sureties, the impact of corporate restructuring, and form requirements. The article also compares Austrian arbitration law's approach with the French "group of companies" doctrine.

Eric Decker, *Wirtschaftssanktionen im Schiedsverfahren*

published in:
SchiedsVZ 229 (2024)

The article analyzes categories of economic sanctions – financial, trade, communication, and developmental – and their implications for arbitration, highlighting conflicts between sanctions regimes and judicial systems, including compliance with the European Convention on Human Rights. It reviews critical case studies, such as sanctions against Russia. The author further explores the impact of sanctions on arbitration agreements, party relationships, and tribunal decisions, particularly regarding enforceability under public policy constraints. The article concludes with a reflection on sanctions' broader role in crisis management and their potential to disrupt arbitration's core principles.

Jörn Erbguth, *Blockchain-basierte Arbitration*

published in
Die Mediation 2024 H 2, 76

The publication by Jörn Erbguth delves into blockchain-based arbitration, a novel approach that utilizes decentralized technologies like smart contracts and platforms such as Kleros for dispute resolution. It explores the mechanics of blockchain arbitration, including the role of anonymous jurors, incentive systems rooted in game theory, and the integration of these systems with traditional legal frameworks. The article highlights both the advantages, such as efficiency and cost reduction, and the limitations, including legal uncertainties, technical barriers, and challenges in adapting the system for complex or high-stakes disputes. It also discusses potential applications in blockchain-specific contexts, such as verifying identities and resolving cryptocurrency-related disputes, while reflecting on the broader implications for arbitration and dispute resolution in innovative environments.

Katia Fach, The Technological Competence of Arbitrators

published by:
Springer Cham (2023)

This monograph delves into the growing importance of technological competence in arbitration. It examines what this competence entails, why it matters, who needs it, how it is regulated, and how arbitrators can achieve it. While most legal sources do not explicitly mandate technological competence, it is increasingly tied to the duty of efficient case management, particularly as arbitration involves tools like remote hearings and cybersecurity measures.

Philipp Fölsing, *Schiedsgerichte am Ende ihrer Geduld: Widerstand gegen den Anti-Arbitration Torpedo*

published in:
RIW 2024,473

The article by Philipp Fölsing examines the increasing resistance of international arbitration tribunals to so-called “anti-arbitration torpedoes”. It provides an overview of the EU’s opposition to intra-EU arbitrations, citing the incompatibility of such proceedings with EU law as interpreted in landmark cases like *Achmea* and *Komstroy*. The article discusses the legal tactics employed by EU Member States to challenge arbitration proceedings and awards, including judicial interventions and policy declarations. It also evaluates the reform efforts of the ECT to address climate policy goals and the contentious role of arbitration in disputes over renewable energy subsidies and fossil fuel phase-outs. Lastly, the article explores potential countermeasures available to arbitration tribunals, such as provisional measures and procedural innovations, to mitigate the impact of external interventions on their jurisdiction and integrity.

Ulrike Frauenberger-Pfeiler, *Zu den Mindestanforderungen an obligatorische Mediationsklauseln*

published in
ecolex 2024/214

The article examines the Austrian Supreme Court's recent decisions on mandatory mediation clauses and their implications for contractual dispute resolution. It discusses the minimum requirements for such clauses and explores the Vienna International Arbitration Centre (VIAC) Mediation Rules for their potential to enhance the functionality of mandatory mediation clauses.

Philipp Kehl & Sebastian Wunschka, *The Energy Charger Treaty at Tipping Point – Modernization Efforts, Withdrawal Plans and their Legal Consequences*

published in
ZEuS 2024, 59

The article explores the current state and future trajectory of the Energy Charter Treaty (ECT) amidst modernization efforts and withdrawal plans by key member states, including the European Union and its member states. It examines the challenges posed by conflicting agendas, such as the push for sustainable energy goals aligned with the Paris Agreement versus the treaty's continued protection of fossil fuel investments. The article delves into the legal ramifications of withdrawal plans, including the operation of the treaty's "sunset clause" and its implications for ongoing and future energy investments. It also discusses the potential for implementing a modernized ECT among remaining parties, the interplay with intra-EU arbitration objections, and the broader impact on international energy law and investment arbitration.

Christian W. Konrad, *"BITs in Pieces"? Intra-EU-Investitionsschutzabkommen nach der Entscheidung in Green Power*

published in:
ecolex 2024/78

The article analyzes the implications of the European Court of Justice (ECJ) decision in Green Power, marking a significant shift in intra-EU investment arbitration. It discusses the ECJ's stance on the incompatibility of intra-EU bilateral investment treaties with EU law, tracing the judicial progression from Achmea to Komstroy and their impact on the Energy Charter Treaty (ECT). The article examines the Green Power tribunal's decision to reject jurisdiction, emphasizing the role of EU law as lex superior and highlighting the legal uncertainties this creates for international arbitration. The article also explores challenges in enforcing intra-EU awards.

Ursula Kriebaum, *International Investment Law*

published in:
S. McInerney-Lankford, R. McCorquodale (eds.), The Roles of International Law in Development, Oxford University Press (2023)

Today, international investment law balances foreign investment protection with sustainable development goals. Integration of sustainability measures such as environmental priorities into the treaties together with tribunals' interpretation of these frameworks are discussed. Emphasis is put on the challenge of balancing state regulatory autonomy with investor rights.

Ursula Kriebaum, *Interpretation of Investment Treaties over Time*

published in:
https://ssrn.com/abstract=4442977 or http://dx.doi.org/10.2139/ssrn.4442977

This article explores how the temporal element impacts treaty interpretation, focusing on evolving treaty terms, state practices, and case law. Using the Vienna Convention on the Law of Treaties as a framework, it examines debates between static and evolutionary interpretations, particularly regarding environmental concerns and sustainable development.

Ursula Kriebaum & Kilian Wagner, *Interpretation of Exceptions*

published in:
Katia Fach Gómez & Catharine Titi (eds.), The Award in International Investment arbitration (Oxford University Press, 2024), 219

This contribution examines exception clauses in international investment agreements, which allow states to regulate for public policy while respecting treaty obligations. It explores their role, challenges in interpretation, and overlap with the "right to regulate," highlighting their significance in balancing economic and public interests.

Ursula Kriebaum, *Interstate Dispute Settlement in the EU/UK Withdrawal Agreement*

published in:
Thomas Jaeger, Matthias Lehmann, Alexander Somek & Michael Waibel (eds.), Consolidating Brexit, The future of EU/UK cooperation (2023), 133

An important issue in Brexit negotiations was dispute resolution and the role of the Court of Justice of the EU (CJEU). The UK aimed to minimize the CJEU's influence, while the EU sought a settlement mechanism ensuring legal autonomy and effective implementation of the Withdrawal Agreement. This contribution examines three key areas: first, the applicability of the EU law and institutional powers during the transition period from 31 January to 31 December 2020, second, the CJEU's jurisdiction post-transition, and third, the dispute settlement process before an Arbitration Panel introduced by the Withdrawal Agreement as well as the role of the CJEU in an arbitration before that panel.

Ursula Kriebaum, *Judicial Expropriation (Agora on the "Certain Iranian Assets" Judgment)*

published in:
ICSID Review – Foreign Investment Law Journal (2024), 1

The article inspects the ICJ's decision in *Certain Iranian Assets*, a case in which U.S. asset seizures were deemed violations of the Treaty of Amity due to unreasonable measures and lack of compensation. The court clarified that judicial actions only amount to expropriation if linked to illegality, applying a proportionality test to assess regulatory powers versus property rights.

Ursula Kriebaum, *Parallel Proceedings – Investment Arbitration and the European Court of Human Rights*

published in:
Stephan Wittich & Jane A. Hofbauer (eds.), Austrian Review of International and European Law Online 27 (June 2024), 91

This contribution examines the overlap between international human rights law and international economic law, focusing on cases where investors can pursue claims under both frameworks. It discusses the challenges posed by multiple proceedings arising from the same set of facts, identifying scenarios where duplication occurs and analyzing the legal and practical problems this creates. The article reviews domestic and international measures designed to mitigate such issues, with a particular focus on the case law of the European

Court of Human Rights and investment arbitral tribunals. Finally, it evaluates the effectiveness of mechanisms employed by these bodies to address the complexities of parallel or consecutive proceedings.

Ursula Kriebaum, *The Uneasy Co-Existence of EU-Law and International Investment Law*

published in:
Diritto Del Commercio Internazionale, Anno XXXVIII Fasc. 1 – 2024, 11

The coexistence of EU Law and international investment law is complex, with overlapping jurisdictions and differing interpretations. This article examines the challenges at the intersection of these legal frameworks and their implications for investors and EU member states. It analyzes recent jurisprudence, particularly how treaties involving third states impact the relationship, and the diverging rulings of EU courts and investment tribunals. The article advocates for a balanced approach, emphasizing the need for respecting the rule of law and the integrity of both legal systems.

Nicolaj Kuplewatzky, *Upstream Review of intra-EU ICSID Arbitration and its Inherent Consequences*

published in:
ZEuS 2024, 349

The author presents an analysis of the legal and procedural challenges posed by intra-EU investment arbitration under the ICSID Convention, focusing on the German Federal Court of Justice's groundbreaking decisions. They examine the court's interpretation of Section 1032(2) of the German Civil Procedure Code as a mechanism for "upstream review," allowing national courts to preclude arbitration proceedings incompatible with EU law. Key topics include the tension between the ICSID Convention's self-contained system and the EU's judicial framework, the role of EU law's primacy in disapplying incompatible international agreements, and the implications of these decisions for mutual trust among EU Member States.

Florian Laher & Julian Spadinger, *Zur Abgrenzung von Schiedsgutachtenabrede und Schiedsvereinbarung*

published in
ÖJA (2024) 03

The publication analyzes the distinction between expert determination (*Schiedsgutachterverfahren*) and arbitration proceedings (*Schiedsverfahren)* within the framework of Austrian law. It examines the conceptual and practical boundaries of these alternative dispute resolution mechanisms, focusing on the scope of authority granted to third parties in each method, also taking relevant jurisprudence into account.

Jake Lowther, *International Arbitration: Navigating a Clash of Cultures and Conflicts of Interest*

published in:
SchiedsVZ 26 (2024)

This contribution examines recent developments in respect to the legitimacy of international arbitration, with a particular focus on notions of integrity and conflicts of interest. It covers the IBA Guidelines and their role in identifying and mitigating potential conflicts. The social and professional aspects of the arbitration community, particularly their influence on perceived impartiality, are discussed, along with practical tools for junior practitioners to prevent conflicts of interest and uphold ethical standards.

Martin Meisel, Martin Reichard, Anna Valeria Backé, Christian Breitler, Natalie Starowicz & Ulrike Köhler, *Recent Austrian Practice in the Field of European Union Law*

published in:
ZÖR 2024, 549

In this contribution, the authors explore a broad spectrum of recent developments in European Union law. In relation to investment arbitration, they mention the discussion on the latest developments in relation to the Energy Charter Treaty, namely its modernisation and *inter se* Agreement and Declaration.

August Reinisch & Johannes Tropper, *Introductory Note: From Coping with Enlarged Intra-EU Objections to the Interpretative Intricacies of Exceptions Clauses in International Investment Agreements – ICSID Arbitration in 2021*

published in:
The Global Community Yearbook of International Law and Jurisprudence 2022 (2023), 588

The 2021 jurisprudence of ICSID tribunals and ad hoc committees explored key jurisdictional issues, including the definitions of "investment" and "investor" under Article 25 of the ICSID Convention, the use of MFN provisions to establish jurisdiction, intra-EU objections, illegality-based jurisdictional challenges, and claims of abuse of process. Procedural developments focused on the dismissal of meritless claims and the allocation of security for costs. Substantive matters addressed included expropriation, fair and equitable treatment, minimum standards of treatment, and denial of justice. Notably, two tribunals examined the application of general exception clauses, while some cases denied damages despite treaty violations. Additionally, annulment committees reviewed the narrow grounds for overturning awards under the ICSID Convention.

August Reinisch, *Settlement of disputes involving international organizations*

published in:
Collected Courses of The Hague Academy of International Law – Recueil des Cours (2024), 83

This extensive publication delves into how disputes involving international organizations are resolved, focusing on conflicts between states, members, non-members, and private parties. It analyzes mechanisms such as the WTO, ITLOS, regional arbitration, and administrative tribunals, alongside negotiation, mediation, and fact-finding. The limited role of national courts due to jurisdictional immunity is also discussed. Key issues like access to justice, procedural fairness, and effective dispute resolution are explored, with policy recommendations offered.

August Reinisch & Kilian Wagner, *State Immunity in investment arbitration*

published in:
Andreas Kulick & Michael Waibel (eds.), Commentary on General International Law in International Investment Law (Oxford University Press, 2024), 489

The contribution deals with state immunity in investment arbitration, focusing on its role during the enforcement of arbitral awards. It contains an analysis of the development of customary international law principles on state immunity, their use in investment tribunals for issues such as attribution and enforcement, and the distinctions between sovereign and commercial acts.

Bajar Scharaw, *Looking at Environmental Protection through the Lens of International Investment Law: Trends and Developments in the Investment Treaty-Making and Investment Arbitration*

published in
SchiedsVZ 202 (2024)

The publication explores the relationship between international investment law and environmental protection, focusing on how investment treaty-making and arbitration practices have evolved to address environmental concerns. It examines the inclusion of environmental rights and obligations in investment agreements, the application of international environmental principles, and the challenges of balancing investor protections with state measures to safeguard the environment and public health. The publication also analyzes recent developments in bilateral and multilateral investment treaties.

Annika Streicher, *Zur primärrechtlichen Zulässigkeit umsatzsteuerlicher Schiedsverfahren*

published in
AVR 2024, 83

The article deals with the potential introduction and legal compatibility of arbitration mechanisms for resolving value-added tax (VAT) disputes within the framework of European Union law. It addresses issues of cross-border VAT conflicts arising from diverging interpretations of rules by different jurisdictions, both within the EU and in mixed settings involving third countries. The article examines the legal challenges such mechanisms face, particularly in relation to the autonomy of EU law and the exclusive jurisdiction of the European Court of Justice (ECJ). It discusses the compatibility of VAT arbitration with EU primary law, referencing the requirements for preserving the ECJ's interpretative monopoly. Finally, the article considers international VAT agreements and their implications for dispute resolution, drawing on past cases and EU Commission proposals.

Hellwig Torggler, Friederike Schäfer, Venus Valentina Wong, Florian Mohs & Lukas Wedl (eds.), Schiedsgerichtsbarkeit Deutschland – Österreich – Schweiz

published by:
Nomos; Verlag Österreich; Schulthess

The third edition of Schiedsgerichtsbarkeit Deutschland – Österreich – Schweiz serves as a comprehensive handbook on arbitration for

German-speaking jurisdictions, focusing on Germany, Austria, and Switzerland. It provides a practical and comparative legal approach, covering the full lifecycle of arbitration agreements, enforcement, and procedural aspects.

Lukas Wedl, *Neues zur Schiedsfähigkeit von gesellschaftsrechtlichen Beschlussmangelstreitigkeiten*

published in
RdW (2024), 457, Heft 7

The article discusses the evolving legal framework for the arbitrability of corporate resolution disputes, with a focus on Austrian law and the implications of a recent landmark decision of the Austrian Supreme Court. Key topics include the requirements for arbitrating disputes related to corporate decisions, the need for arbitration clauses to ensure the participation and rights of all shareholders, and the impact of these clauses on the binding effect of arbitral awards. The article also examines the constitutional guarantees of fair proceedings under Article 6 ECHR and their role in shaping the minimum procedural standards for arbitration agreements.

Eva-Marie Wettstein & Carla Müller, *13. Tagung des Krickenbecker Kreises zum Internationalen Investitionsrecht*

published in
SchiedsVZ 50 (2024)

The authors examine several pressing topics in international investment law discussed during the *13. Tagung des Krickenbecker Kreises zum Internationalen Investitionsrecht* meeting. These include the role of investment protections in the context of Russia's aggression against Ukraine, addressing legal challenges related to territorial disputes, expropriation, and BIT violations. Another focus is the intersection of international investment law and climate change. Next, the fragmentation of the Energy Charter Treaty amidst EU modernization efforts and its implications for energy sector investments is examined. The next topic was application for a declaration of the inadmissibility of investment arbitration pursuant to Section 1032 (2) of German Civil Procedure Code. Finally, some issues surrounding state representation in ICSID arbitration were addressed.

Index

The figures refer to page(s).